Big Data, Code and the Discrete City

Big Data, Code and the Discrete City explores how digital technologies are gradually changing the way in which the public space is designed by architects, managed by policymakers and experienced by individuals. Smart city technologies are superseding the traditional human experience that has characterised the making of the public space until today. This book examines how computers see the public space and the effect of algorithms, artificial intelligences and automated processes on the human experience in public spaces.

Divided into three parts, the first part of this book examines the notion of discreteness in its origins and applications to computer sciences. The second section presents a dual perspective: it explores the ways in which public spaces are constructed by the computer-driven logic and then translated into control mechanisms, design strategies and software-aided design. This perspective also describes the way in which individuals perceive this new public space, through its digital logic, and discrete mechanisms (from Wi-Fi coverage to self-tracking). Finally, in the third part, this book scrutinises the discrete logic with which computers operate, and how this is permeating into aspects of city life.

This book is valuable for anyone interested in urban studies and digital technologies, and more specifically in big data, urban informatics and public space.

Silvio Carta is an ARB RIBA architect and Head of Art and Design, and Chair of the Design Research Group at the University of Hertfordshire. Previously, he taught at Delft University of Technology School of Architecture, University of Rotterdam and University of Cagliari (Italy). His studies have focused on digital design, digital manufacturing, urban informatics, data visualisation and computational optimisation of the design process. Silvio has published 100+ articles, infographics and reviews in journals and magazines in the field of design, urban studies and architecture, and exhibited his digital projects worldwide. He is editor-at-large of Seoul-based *C3-Korea* magazine, editor of *Architecture Media Politics and Society* (AMPS), and the curator of the international lecture series AUDITORIUM 2015–16: The Architecture of Information, Data, People and Public Space (Leuven, Belgium).

Routledge Studies in Urbanism and the City

For more information about this series, please visit www.routledge.com/
Routledge-Studies-in-Urbanism-and-the-City/book-series/RSUC

Big Data, Code and the Discrete City

Shaping Public Realms

Silvio Carta

Routledge
Taylor & Francis Group

LONDON AND NEW YORK

First published 2020 by Routledge

2 Park Square, Milton Park, Abingdon, Oxon, OX14 4RN
605 Third Avenue, New York, NY 10017

Routledge is an imprint of the Taylor & Francis Group, an informa business

First issued in paperback 2020

British Library Cataloguing-in-Publication Data
A catalogue record for this book is available from the British Library

Library of Congress Cataloging-in-Publication Data
A catalog record for this book has been requested

ISBN: 978-1-138-54309-6 (hbk)
ISBN: 978-0-367-72746-8 (pbk)

Typeset in Times New Roman
by Apex CoVantage, LLC

For Emma and Oliver

Contents

Figures

Tables

Boxes

Acknowledgements

This book originated as a collection of various pieces of research, journal articles, conference papers, annotations at margin of my books, conversations with colleagues, positive and negative comments from anonymous reviewers and a great interest for coding and computing in all its forms, from TV series fictions, to the algorithmic editors I use in my practice and simple scripts I use to simplify my daily routine.

This book would not have been possible without the support of many colleagues and friends. Firstly, I would like to thank Faye Leerink for believing in this project since the early stages and Ruth Anderson for guiding me though the entire editorial process. The peer blind reviewers provided me with very helpful feedback and suggestions that informed the development of the entire book. I thank Steven Adams at the University of Hertfordshire for the continuous support and collegiate attitude towards my work and the School of Creative Arts for the generous financial support and for granting me a mini-sabbatical to finish the latest stages of this book.

All chapters have been discussed with colleagues who provided me with guidance, support and positive feedback. In particular, I thank Michael Ostwald, Mario Carpo, Michael Biggs, Davide Pisu, Eray Çaylı, Anna Stanton and Angelos Psilopoulos for their comments on Chapter 1, Rob Kitchin, Grace Lees-Maffei, Alana Jelinek and Barbara Brownie for their comments on Chapter 2, Alessio Malizia, Paul Cureton, Marcus Foth and Philippe Morel for their comments on Chapter 3, Graham Cairns for his suggestions on Chapter 4, Austin Smyth, Tom Avermaete and Alessandro Aurigi for their help with Chapter 5, Olga Sezneva, Claire Jamieson and Ian Owen for Chapter 6, and Megan Knight for her suggestions on the introduction.

A word of appreciation goes to Paul Cureton and Ian Wyn Owen whose frequent chats over a cup of tea or instant messages helped me to navigate through the frustrations, tiredness and excitement that characterised these past three years.

I would also acknowledge the support that companies, practitioners and individuals gave me in sourcing information and data for this research. In particular, Luc Wilson at KPF, Joel Simon, John Frazer, Rory Hyde, Philippe Morel, Wolfgang Beyer, Wolfram Media, ESRI, scratchapixel, TurnKey Linux, salesforce,

WAYMO, Streetscore, ScanLab Projects, Paul and Tara at NUMINA, Autodesk, Sidewalk Labs, MVRDV and Gehry Partners.

Lastly, I would like to thank my wife for the constant support and encouragement in the writing of this work, and to be immensely patient in my very early morning disappearances on Saturdays and Sundays, bank holidays and any other possible free time, where I spent most of the time at university libraries working on this book. My gratitude goes also to my children Emma and Oliver whose constant comments (both verbally while trying to edit chapters and in writing with bright colours on my printed notes and diagrams) have proven very helpful and inspiring.

Without all the people mentioned here (and those who I accidently forgot), this book would not have been possible.

Introduction

Computers everywhere

Over the last thirty years, our public life has changed radically. Computers have a significant responsibility for this, as they are increasingly involved in any human activity. We find computers everywhere: from satellites in the thermosphere that exchange information between remote points of the planet, to microchips embedded in our clothing that continuously monitor us, telling how active we are. Increasingly, computers are connected to each other and to a plethora of code-enabled objects (smart objects). Software, as diffused and globally interconnected entities, controls computers and objects and, by extension, also influences people and space. In the following chapters, I analyse and discuss this scenario in an attempt to describe the cities and urban spaces in which we are living. This book scrutinises how computers operate in the urban environment, showing both the machine's and the human's perspective on cities. This work started from the need to understand what computers see when they scan the tangible world through cameras, microphones and sensors. The reality they detect is a reality in its own right, as it is part of our phenomenological experience of the world. To discard their version of the world as incomplete, partial and intangible, and therefore less important than the one we experience through human senses, would be reductive. For humans to ignore the computers' view of reality would be sensible if computers were not increasingly involved in any action we take and any modification of the built environment. Since the advent of the Internet of Things and ubiquitous computing, the omnipresence of machines and, by extension, of their algorithmic logic, significantly influences the nature of our lives and its social and behavioural facets.

The new environment

The work presented in this book hinges on the overarching idea that there exists a new form of environment, here called *new environment*, which transcends the physical, as well as the epistemological boundaries of objects, people and the digital world. The new environment here presented is an indivisible combination of three main elements: the built environment, individuals and software. This tripartite agency is proposed as an assemblage (Marcus and Saka 2006) by which we can understand the continuous interactions among our world's physical and digital dimensions. The three actors operate in a dynamic manner that can be considered un-structured, for they continuously adapt themselves to the current configuration of the environment, mutually influencing each other. In this perspective, the new environment can be considered as an emergence, rather than the result, imposed by software on the other two actants.

The built environment, individuals and software are considered in an equal hierarchical level, whereby none of them controls the others. They rather influence each other, continuously modifying the configuration of the environment with their actions. The new environment is considered as an alternative to those cognitive approaches whereby the physical is observed in opposition to the digital, and the software is considered separately from individuals.

As a whole, the three actors are underpinned by an information layer that is characterised by a purely discrete logic. Information is what relates the three elements together. Individuals and spaces are connected by information, which is then translated into labour, entertainment, education and all the other facets of social life. Software is the infrastructure through which information can circulate and be exchanged through spaces and people. Software, as the mechanism by which computers operate, is discrete (digital) in its nature. As such, it applies discreteness to every element in the environment, representing the world and the built environment in a discrete manner, and operating with people following digital principles, namely neglecting any form of continuous dimension.

The existence of the new environment is underpinned by a number of recent technological achievements and societal changes. To date, technology has evolved up to a point where it is possible to have knowledge of virtually everything, everywhere at any time, providing computational power that "moves with the person, regardless of environment" (Kitchin 2014a). Information technology is already (and will increasingly be) everywhere, through the combined action of software and its growing geographical reach. This idea of Everyware (software + everywhere) (Greenfield 2006) provides the infrastructural framework for the connections between computers and individuals to occur on a global scale and almost in real time. Like never before, people can access information and connect to each other transcending the boundaries of space and time. This new ability has modified the way people interact and behave in cities, whereby mobile devices have increasingly become an essential part of urban individual and collective experience.

Ubiquitous computing

In order to geographically and topologically contextualise the new environment, the first notion to be examined is the one of computers everywhere. Underpinning the idea of ubiquitous computing is the assumption that the reach of computers, namely their computational power, could potentially arrive everywhere. This would include the physical dimension of the world (think of radio signals), as well as its digital extent (an example being the Internet of Things). This idea is clearly articulated through the notions of pervasive computing (Kang and Cuff

2005), the ubiquitous Internet (Shepard 2011) and big data (Kitchin 2014b). The three topics are interconnected and interdependent. Computers can reach every part of the world, so being pervasive as far as they are connected to each other through a global network (the Internet). The continuous connections and growing accumulation of information can only happen as the result of the increasing computing capacity of computers through large datasets. Pervasive computing, ubiquitous Internet and big data have become fundamental parts of the same system, whereby the more data computers can process, the more they will gather and produce, and the more powerful computers are, the more extended is the reach of their interconnections (Internet). These three elements feed each other in a spiral of self-optimisation and growth.

Big data

The volume of data produced every day in the world is growing exponentially. The invisible layer of today's datascape that makes the new environment possible is increasingly a sophisticated combination of involuntarily and voluntarily generated data. Within the context of this work, data and big data are considered from two perspectives at the same time. On the one hand, there are data voluntarily and unconsciously generated by individuals during the usual daily activities in their lives; this includes social media feeds, GPS coordinates, and passively generated anonymous mobile phone data (Chen et al. 2016). On the other hand, there are data automatically generated by machines with the purpose of monitoring human activities and the environment, like sensors, automated surveillance and scan data (Kitchin 2014a:89). Albeit of a different nature, the two sets are occasionally combined in some of the design processes examined in the book. For example, the tests included in Chapter 5 (the liminal space) illustrate a hybrid model where ordnance survey geospatial data are factored with open source available behavioural data.

In an attempt at illustrating a reliable picture of today's datascape, within the context of this work, big data are here considered under the lens of a vertical model, where information is gathered by attributes (topic, keywords, place, action, etc.), as opposed to a horizontal model based on ordered lists (Lemire 2009). This categorisation follows the Inverted Indexing (from content to location) as opposed to a Forward Index (from documents to content) (Zobel, Moffat, and Ramamohanarao 1998).

A discrete logic

The technological achievements in computing and networking briefly mentioned so far are characterised by the mathematical and philosophical dichotomy of continuum-discrete.

The discrete logic, namely a logic based on the digital notion of non-continuum, granularity and either-or defines that approach whereby reality is considered (represented, perceived, designed) by means of discrete values (e.g. by integers).

The digital/physical public space is regulated by algorithms that, by their nature, consider the built environment, the commons and people as individual entities, following a binary logic (yes/no, 1/0, etc.). In order to "understand" the built environment, computers need to make it discrete, turning it into a set of numeric values, units, pixels, voxels, etc. Following this logic, every phenomenon (whether spontaneously occurring in nature or man-made) can be viewed as computation (Wolfram 2002), and the urban and public space are increasingly characterised by fragmentation (Aurigi 2005). A discrete logic of existence is embedded in an information-theoretical conception of the world (Chu 2013:190). Although the distinction between discrete and continuum is here presented clearly, a more detailed account of the mutual relationships of the two notions will show that systems that are utterly characterised by one system or the other have not been observed to date. Within each continuum system, a discrete logic can be found and vice versa. The clear-cut distinction used here is instrumental to the study of how computers work while examining the built environment.

The discrete city

The discrete city is what emerges as an outturn of the new environment. This term describes our contemporary urban condition, whereby software is directly or indirectly ramified into every aspect of the public life. Software characterises urban spaces directly, through management and control of the various infrastructures and telecommunications, through the plethora of sensing devices installed everywhere, including CCTV cameras, sensors, logging devices and the like, and by means of GPS signals, tracking devices, Wi-Fi and 3G/4G networks. Software is present indirectly as the fabric of the Internet of Things, connecting everyday objects to servers and databases. The discrete city is a place where individuals have an active role in the making of their environment, sharing this with the physical place (buildings, streets, squares and the like) and the omnipresent software. As mentioned, none of these three actors prevails over the others; they all contribute to the continuous making of the environment. The discrete city is structured by the digital logic, represented and understood through 1s and 0s and everything that is ineffable, ethereal and abstract is routinely converted into digital formats in order to be represented and become something to be shared with the other actants.

Designing urban spaces through discreteness

If data are becoming the driving force of the design and control of space, the definition of the urban designer is changing accordingly. In opposition to the previous models, where policymakers, architects and urban planners decided on the physical space where people live, today a new dispersed configuration is offered. Data are created by individuals within environments designed and managed by corporations. Digital environments are partially controlled by a still ill-defined set of global governmental rules and agreements. Data are often owned, and partially made available, by data brokers who profit from their use. Programmers and coders make data meaningful and useful by algorithms, that are often open source and written by other individuals. This new configuration results in a scenario where it will be increasingly difficult to define a sole actor in the creation of the public space. If corporations and governments provide and administer, respectively, a broad loose framework for data to be shared, the real driver of the public realm becomes whoever generates the prime material to be exchanged. Individuals produce data that enable the public space to happen in its current form and thereby gain the ability to shape it while living in it. With an increasingly integrated role within the design process, designers are gradually losing their unique decision power on space-making. Rather, they can provide part of the environment in which individuals will act, producing data and configuring space as they use it (Kitchin and Dodge 2011).

Kitchin and Dodge (2011) started to provide an account of the implications that this data revolution (Kitchin 2014a) is having on the physical environment, where "space emerges as a process of ontogenesis" (Kitchin and Dodge 2014:68). Space "engenders . . . a spatiality that can never be static, but emerges, varying over time, and across people and context" (Kitchin and Dodge 2014:69). In order to describe the implications that the extensive use of code is having on space, they introduced the notion of transduction as: "the constant making anew of domain in reiterative and transformative practices" (Kitchin and Dodge 2014:263). Space is described through a dynamic definition, where its physical configuration is not only continuously redefined over time, but, more importantly, is inextricably related to the people who actively produce it, while using it in a continuous progress.

The attempts to explore the extent to which software and ubiquitous computing are impacting on the physicality of the public space have already started with some avant-garde projects and experiments. Digital practitioners and theorists have been exploring the potentialities of big data in the design process. For example, Offenhuber and Ratti (2014) provided a large spectrum of projects using big data as the main driver at the urban and regional scale, unveiling new patterns for the use of urban space (Real Time Rome 2006), revealing urban dynamics (NYTE 2007), and the existence of new regional delineations (Borderline 2010) which differ from the institutional ones. Although his projects are not data driven and do not provide any scientific account, Keiichi Matsuda's work provided a strong visualisation of the impact of data in our everyday life. Projects like Domestic Robocop (2010) and Hyper-Reality (2016) convincingly illustrate a possible future scenario, wherein the digital and physical aspects of space are synthesised. Matsuda's projects are very successful in offering a visual representation of how public life is changing due to the ubiquity of the increasing computing power of software and networked systems.

Redefining space

The action of the ubiquitous software is redefining the notion of space in all its facets. The main characteristic analysed in this book is the fact that space in the networked city is in a state of continuous evolution and dynamic modification.

Within the context of this book, the urban space as qualified by the new environment is characterised by a discrete logic and the presence of a continuously evolving shape. The urban space is discrete, as algorithm-based digital processes determine the configuration and appearance of the physical space and the objects in the built environment. Configurations are the outturn of the systematic use of the digital logic, where the notion of discreteness is embedded in the very basic nature of the dichotomy 1–0.

The urban space is characterised by amorphousness and a continuous evolution. As such, its shape is not static, but dependent on the live stream of data factored in the process. The shape that can be observed is not the final one, but a snapshot of the progression of their evolution. The shape of the public realm has not a determined form *per se*; it can rather be described and visualised by a certain phase, which is a part of its continuous evolution. Elaborating on the notion of transduction Kitchin and Dodge (2014) explained that: "space is always in the process of becoming, . . . in the process of taking place. . . . Space is a practice, a doing, an event, a becoming – a material and social reality forever (re)created in the moment" (Kitchin and Dodge 2014:68). Urban space seems not to have a definitive configuration at the end of the design process. On the contrary, its shape is related to the data that are factored into its creation, and varies accordingly. Since data are often continuously updated, the final shape evolves along with the becoming of space itself, underpinned by the unpredictability of human actions. In this respect, one may note that the shape is not changing, but evolving. This is determined by the fact that the final configuration depends on the trail of operations performed by the algorithms used. The modifications of shape are subsequent to each other in an evolutionary sequence.

Model and granularity

If it is true that urban space is changing its nature from fluid, analogue and continuous to granular, digital and discrete, it should also be noted that the majority of the design processes employed to design and modify the built environment still rely on a different paradigm based on standardisation. The notion of the model (where nature can be represented by its samples) is being flanked by the quantitative approach to design, proposed by the digital design that represents the "inherent discreteness of nature" (Carpo 2014). If algorithms are increasingly used to control and define the public realm following a digital and discrete axiom, the paradigm of the standardisation of public space is to be reconsidered, in light of the notion of discrete public space as an alternative.

The extensive employment of the model, as a generalised axiom in the design processes, clashes with the growing use of big data-based digital techniques. Approximation, standardisation and normalisation are being superseded by accuracy, individuality and idiosyncrasy. By definition, the notion of a model cannot comprehend the individuality that characterises big data processes. Mayer-Schönberger and Cukier (2013) expanded on the concept of sampling that, within the context of big data, is superseded by the possibility of obtaining "all" possible data (Mayer-Schönberger and Cukier 2013:26). Big data can be used to increase significantly the degree of detail of each observation, where N = all (with N as all cases used in an observation).

Mathematical, social and spatial models hinge on the assumption that "people" can be considered as a general category, where every individual has similar needs, desires and behaviour. As such, people are the main users of the built environment and they are still considered as a catch-all category in architectural and urban design. The idea of considering people in general categories based on their relationship with the city is in high contrast with the actual idiosyncrasies that distinguish people in the networked city. Today buildings are still being designed using macro-groups such as tenants, retailers, shoppers, *flâneurs*, passers-by, residents, etc. Through a closer view of how individuals contribute to the public life of the city from the digital perspective, we can infer that each individual is characterised by her own qualities, which differ from those of any other individual. Ubiquitous software and big data allow us to acquire and comprehend this new necessary granularity that transform the category of people into a complex system of individuals.

A new role for individuals

One of the most interesting findings in this study of the new environment is the impact that computers and their logic have on people. If big data and ubiquitous software allow the transformation from people to individuals, the latter have a growing responsibility in the contribution of the public life. The growing extension of ubiquitous computing and overall Internet availability created a clear separation between a pre-networked society and the current one, where individuals can potentially be always connected to each other and to common platforms and resources. Mario Carpo described this shift in the notion of agency as "the networked environment [which] has evolved from monodirectional information technologies ('one-to-many') to a fully symmetrical, bidirectional informational network" (Carpo 2011:113). As the result of this continuous availability of connections in real time, vectors have changed from individual to public to individual to individuals. The second point of the vector constitutes a significant shift in the making of the public realm. By being continuously engaged in public platforms (social media, forums, chats, online comments and the like), individuals are now empowered with new tools to communicate their presence, opinions and ideas. In the networked society, individuals continuously and ubiquitously express themselves, continuously affecting the configuration of the public realm with their actions.

Public realms

The increasing presence of computers working in global networks and the processing of exponentially growing large datasets is not only dramatically changing how public space is produced every day, but also the way in which individuals perceive it. The processing of datasets to describe, monitor and manage people's lives in public spaces is increasingly being automated, rationalised and optimised by machines. The more the design processes are automated, the more the public sphere assumes a cryptic configuration, where the mechanisms underpinning the design and management of the public are at the same time increasingly invisible and ubiquitous.

Availability of large datasets, pervasive computing and the ubiquitous Internet are having a radical impact on the way we experience space, the public space and the environment around us. The traditional perception of physical space through senses is augmented by what we learn from machines and their digital representation of reality. This is made of data and information systematically gathered by networked devices, and automatically processed by artificial intelligences. Through the deployment of complex interrelated systems of algorithm-driven networks, computers are creating a parallel public space governed by the rules of data. Seen through the machines' eyes, the public realm is gradually losing its seamless, ambiguous and dynamic nature to become discrete, scripted and characterised by a binary logic.

As technologies applied to design and monitoring people's behaviour in public space are evolving at a significant fast pace, there is a need for new insights on the theme of data and urban space; not only to have a better understanding of the current situation from several perspectives (technological, social and cultural), but also to have practical hints on how to design the current and future public realm. This work focuses in particular on the physical elements that characterise the new digital public space, where individuals are at its core. This book provides a detailed account of the direct relationship between the discreteness that big data and ubiquitous software provide in the design process and the tangible characteristics that result in the urban and public space.

Although this work analyses a series of epitomising case studies, where the physical qualities of big data projects emerge, the real extent of the digital shift is yet to be seen in its entirety. The fast-paced shifts that big data allow (and impose) differ significantly from the order of decades that traditionally characterises contemporary cities. Public space is changing, and our cities with it. The theories, methods and projects analysed in this book provide a detailed picture of the seeding of this rapid and continuous change.

How would the public realm be if the fluidity, seamlessness and continuity of analogue systems and processes were definitely superseded by a digital infrastructure that pervades all aspects of human life? Is the space in the new environment different? Would individuals and their single and common behaviour change as a consequence of it? Finally, to what extent would the role of architecture and architects be different under this hypothesis?

While it is too soon to be in a position to fully appreciate what the effects of the digital revolution and the information age will be on any field of knowledge and human practice, this work should be read as a preliminary attempt at a spatial and physical account of the new big data space that is pervading the public sphere within the context of an environment where digital and physical are inseparably entangled, where individuals have a digital life that is not different from their physical experience, where the built environment has a digital extent that exceeds the physicality of its boundaries and, finally, where a ubiquitous software directly or indirectly permeates all aspects of our lives.

Articulation of the book

This book is organised in three parts and six chapters. The first section provides an account of key topics and concepts that are the foundation of this work. In particular, the mutual relationships between the ideas of continuum and discrete in mathematics, philosophy and computer sciences that underpin the discrete logic applied by computers onto the environment are explored in Chapter 1, together with the notion of discretisation and cognate notions and theories, including fractals, mereology and cellular automata.

Chapter 1 The Idea of Discretisation examines the notion of discretisation from different points of view, including the idea of discrete and set theory in mathematics, geometry and philosophy. The evolution of this dichotomy is then analysed in the subject of computer sciences, through the concepts of granularity (Zadeh 1997), quantum computing (Knill 2010) and cellular automata (Wolfram 1986). This chapter details the evolution of the ideas of continuum and discrete from 400 BC and the debate between atomists and synechists to the studies on quanta of energy and matter. These are followed by an account of applications of such theories into shape forming (fractals), shape analysis (shape grammar), composition (pixels and voxels) and their implications for the formation of space. The chapter concludes with a summary of this evolution through history and theories, across different disciplinary fields. A final scheme of the evolution of the logic of the discrete spatial framework is included where the passage from atoms to quanta, from finite space to grids, from objects as discrete elements to space as organised cells in mutual relationship and the production of space based on these principles is described.

Chapter 2 Discrete Public Space analyses the application of the notions of discretisation and ubiquitous computing in space in general, and the urban environment in particular. It focuses on how the urban environment is being gradually reconfigured by machines and algorithms, following a digital logic. This chapter provides the theoretical premises to discuss the contrast between the analogue physical experience of space that characterises the human approach to public space and the digital approach imposed on it by computers. I discuss a number of fundamental notions and technologies to explain to what extent the nature of the built environment is changing and increasingly becoming a hybrid new entity where digital and physical qualities are fused together. Chapter 2 illustrates how a new degree of complexity results in a new understanding of space and time and, in it, I discuss the mechanisms that underpin the ubiquitous presence of digital intelligent agents. I review and analyse all these new dynamics to explore the extent to which the digital logic percolates in all aspects of the urban life, and how people and software together become a new form of agency in the making of the new built environment. These include: an updated notion of time (Batty 2012) and space (Kitchin and Dodge 2011); an account of the digital infrastructure that enables the discrete logic to permeate the city (Graham and Marvin 2002a); the notion of pervasive computing (Cuff 2003); ambient intelligence (McCullough 2013); the idea of the stack and the cloud (Bratton 2016); the notion of remediation (Graham and Marvin 2002a); the spatiality of software and the relationship between physical space and software reach; and the idea of assemblage (Marcus and Saka 2006). The chapter concludes with a reflection on the ideas of Non-lieux (Bauman 2000; Augé 2008) and generic spaces in light of this new notion of a hybrid built environment and under the lens of the pervasive discrete logic.

The second part describes the urban environment as seen by computers through scripts and algorithms following a rigid digital and discrete logic. The contemporary city is examined and analysed through two distinct lenses: on the one hand, the production and management of urban spaces as operated by computers, decision makers and designers who adhere to the digital logic; and, on the other, the perception that individuals have of the public realm. The aim of this dual view is to highlight the co-existing facets of the contemporary city: the design and the use; the production and the consumption; the conscious and unconscious view on the built environment; and the active and passive use of the urban space in a context chiefly characterised by the presence of data in the public realm.

In particular, Chapter 3 Production of the Discrete City analyses the technologies and techniques that underpin the making of the urban environment, focusing on the design aspects and the management tools. The actors involved in the process of designing and running the urban spaces and infrastructures are architects, urban and city planners, decision makers, public and governmental bodies and private stakeholders. This chapter focuses in particular on three tiers of actions or conditions. Firstly, the control of space and human activities in the public space. Examples are the operators of CCTV, security cameras and GPS trackers. The city that these actors see through the computer's lens is characterised by stops, boundaries, points, lines, tracks and areas of coverage among different devices. In this chapter, a number of algorithmic processes are dissected and analysed at the core of their functions, with the help of scripts and the back-end of some of these processes. The idea is to illustrate and comment on how computers run programmes and, therefore, what they are able to see.

Finally, this chapter focuses on the production of the urban environment from the designers' perspective. Architects and planners increasingly employ parametric software and Building Information Modelling (BIM) systems not only to assess the feasibility and impact of new projects and urban modifications, but also to design and construct buildings and public spaces. In particular, the impact that BIMs are having in the way buildings are designed and built is growing and will be visible in the next decades. In fact, BIMs are characterised by a rigid logic based on exchange of information among the different actors involved in the design process and across different platforms (engineering, contractors and construction companies, suppliers, building regulation approval, community involvement and final users). The way information is shared and distributed is constrained to the software logic, which has an impact on the final shape of buildings and spatial distribution of public spaces in and around buildings.

Such aspects are here analysed in depth and illustrated by a series of case studies that help to visualise the relationships between the discrete logics used in the processes and the resulting shape of the public realm.

Chapter 4 Perception of the Discrete City focuses on the discrete city as perceived by the individuals in the urban environment. People move in the built environment following a system of discrete references, guided by GPS map indications on Smartphones, and then describing lines, touching definite points that are translated from a digital map to the physical environment. Each individual's perception of the city is filtered by digital devices such as satnavs, mobile phones and tracking devices (e.g. Fitbit). This means that the urban scenario is perceived as a combination of digital inputs available to the individual at a particular moment in a specific place, and grey areas characterised by the absence of Wi-Fi or GPS signal or digital details. Cities are increasingly characterised by the presence or absence of specific information, and the notion of place is increasingly related to the data availability in the area. This concept results in a radical new way by which an individual sees and understands the urban environment. This chapter investigates the mechanisms that underpin the digital experience of individuals in the physical city, where the two perceptions, the physical and the digital, are combined and where the latter augments the former.

The third part of this book synthesises the premises of the first section and the case studies and applied notions of the second part in order to provide a detailed account of the spatial characteristics of the public realms as the result of the new environment and ubiquitous software.

Building on the findings presented in Chapters 3 and 4, Chapter 5 The Spatial characteristics of the new environment provides a detailed account of the public space resulting from big data and related technologies. This chapter focuses on the physical characteristics of the public space as produced by big data systems and perceived through digital tools. It explores the extent to which the discrete logics used by computers translate into spatial characteristics in the urban environment. In this chapter, I describe the extension of objects between their physical and digital limits, discussing their properties, including their permeable boundaries and the separation of their body from the actual space they occupy. Chapter 5 includes a number of case studies that illustrate the dynamic nature of space as the consequence of the presence of software. This includes, for example, those liminal spaces that emerge when the resolution used to define objects or actions in the city is changed by the scripts that analyse and compute them. This chapter concludes with a description of the spatiality that characterises those architectural forms generated by big data and ubiquitous software. Finally, Chapter 5 includes an account of the spatial characteristics of the new environment that, where space is not fixed, it is never only physical or digital but is everywhere, ubiquitous and pervasive. Space is dependent on the resolution computed by software, and finally, space is discrete, describable only through a series of finite elements related to each other.

Table 0.1 List of terms used in this book

Main term	Cognate terms used and comments
Computer	Machine, software
Code	Software, script, algorithm
New environment	Hybrid environment, physical/digital environment, discrete environment, environment
Big data	Large datasets, datasets, data
Software	Used as singular term, it is occasionally used as plural to indicate computer programmes.

Chapter 6 Built Environment, Big Data and the New Public Life illustrates how the new technologies and big data-driven systems are permeating throughout individuals' private and public spheres, bringing significant changes. The analysis is based on the impact of the physical environment on individuals which, through an extensive use of digital technologies and big data, is changing their behaviour in space. While Chapter 5 provides a detailed description of the spatial qualities of the new public space, this part examines the public life of individuals and how they respond to the discrete reality put forward by computers. This chapter discusses aspects of the new environment, including the idea of the occurrence of public life from the bottom up, and correlated issues like surveillance and digital discrimination to determine the social aspects of the public realm.

Overall, the Discrete City offers a multifaceted view of the contemporary urban environment and public space dominated by big data and pervasive computing. The computer's lens, the designers' perspective and the individual's point of view are combined into a holistic description whereby the public space acquires a new set of characteristics adhering to the digital, granular and discrete logic of computers.

A note on terminology

Within this book, we used a few terms and their cognates interchangeably, yet their use may need some explanation. Within this book, I use the term data and big data interchangeably, for the major part of the data discussed are large datasets. A list is provided in Table 0.1. Unless otherwise specified, the main term is used for its main semantic.

References

Augé, Marc. 2008. *Non-places: An Introduction to Supermodernity*. Translated by John Howe. London and New York: Verso.
Aurigi, Alessandro. 2005. *Making the Digital City: The Early Shaping of Urban Internet Space*. Harldershot: Ashgate Publishing, Ltd.
Batty, Michael. 2012. *Smart Cities, Big Data*. London: Sage.
Bauman, Zygmunt. 2000. *Liquid Modernity*. Cambridge: Polity Press.

Bolter, Jay David, and Richard Grusin. 2000. *Remediation: Understanding New Media*. Cambridge, MA: MIT Press.

Borderline. 2010. "MIT Senseable City Lab." Accessed March 2, 2018. http://senseable. mit.edu/network/network&society2.html.

Bratton, Benjamin H. 2016. *The Stack: On Software and Sovereignty*. Cambridge, MA: MIT Press.

Carpo, Mario. 2011. *Alphabet and the Algorithm (Writing Architecture)*. Cambridge, MA: MIT Press.

Carpo, Mario. 2014. "Breaking the Curve: Big Data and Design." *ArtForum International* 52 (6): 168–73.

Chen, Cynthia, Jingtao Ma, Yusak Susilo, Yu Liu, and Menglin Wang. 2016. "The Promises of Big Data and Small Data for Travel Behavior (Aka Human Mobility) Analysis." *Transportation Research Part C: Emerging Technologies* 68: 285–99.

Chu, Karl. 2013. "Evolutionary Information." In *Architecture in Formation: On the Nature of Information in Digital Architecture*, edited by Pablo Lorenzo-Eiroa and Aaron Sprecher. London: Routledge.

Cuff, Dana. 2003. "Immanent Domain: Pervasive Computing and the Public Realm." *Journal of Architectural Education* 57 (1): 43–49.

Graham, Steve, and Simon Marvin. 2002a. *Splintering Urbanism: Networked Infrastructures, Technological Mobilities and the Urban Condition*. London: Routledge.

Graham, Steve, and Simon Marvin. 2002b. *Telecommunications and the City: Electronic Spaces, Urban Places*. London: Routledge.

Greenfield, Adam. 2006. *Everyware: The Dawning Age of Ubiquitous Computing*. Berkeley, CA: New Riders.

Kang, Jerry, and Dana Cuff. 2005. "Pervasive Computing: Embedding the Public Sphere." *Washington and Lee Law Review* 62 (1): 93–146, Winter.

Kitchin, Rob. 2014a. *The Data Revolution: Big Data, Open Data, Data Infrastructures and their Consequences*. London: Sage.

Kitchin, Rob. 2014b. "The Real-time City? Big Data and Smart Urbanism." *Geo Journal* 79 (1): 1–14.

Kitchin, Rob, and Martin Dodge. 2011. *Code/Space: Software and Everyday Life*. Cambridge, MA: MIT Press.

Knill, Emanuel. 2010. "Physics: Quantum Computing." *Nature* 463 (7280): 441.

Lemire, Daniel. 2009. "Changing Your Perspective: Horizontal, Vertical and Hybrid Data Models." http://lemire.me/blog/2009/09/04/changing-your-perspective-horizontal-vertical-and-hybrid-data-models/.

Marcus, George E., and Erkan Saka. 2006. "Assemblage." *Theory, Culture & Society* 23 (2–3): 101–06.

Mayer-Schönberger, Viktor, and Kenneth Cukier. 2013. *Big Data: A Revolution that will Transform How We Live, Work, and Think*. London: Houghton Mifflin Harcourt.

McCullough, Malcolm. 2013. *Ambient Commons: Attention in the Age of Embodied Information*. Cambridge, MA: MIT Press.

NYTE. 2007. "MIT Senseable City Lab." Last accessed March 2, 2018. http://senseable. mit.edu/nyte/.

Offenhuber, Dietmar, and Carlo Ratti. 2014. *Decoding the City: Urbanism in the Age of Big Data*. Basel: Birkhäuser.

Real Time Rome. 2006. "MIT Senseable City Lab." Last accessed March 2, 2018. http://senseable.mit.edu/realtimerome/.

Shepard, Mark. 2011. *Sentient City: Ubiquitous Computing, Architecture, and the Future of Urban Space*. Cambridge, MA: MIT Press.

Wolfram, Stephen. 1986. *Theory and Applications of Cellular Automata: Including Selected Papers 1983–1986*. Cambridge, MA: World Scientific.

Wolfram, Stephen. 2002. *A New Kind of Science*, Vol. 5. Champaign, IL: Wolfram Media.

Zadeh, Lotfi A. 1997. "Toward a Theory of Fuzzy Information Granulation and Its Centrality in Human Reasoning and Fuzzy Logic." *Fuzzy Sets and Systems* 90 (2): 111–27.

Zobel, Justin, Alistair Moffat, and Kotagiri Ramamohanarao. 1998. "Inverted Files Versus Signature Files for Text Indexing." *ACM Transactions on Database Systems (TODS)* 23 (4): 453–90.

Part I
Continuity and discreteness

1 The idea of discretisation

Introduction

This chapter is a reflection on the granular nature of discreteness, resulting from the use of extensive computational power (for example in the case of big data) in digital processes, as a logical evolution of the most recent computer-based advancements.

The numerous studies on the notion of post-Cartesian mathematics have been beneficial for the development of the idea that any system (from social to mathematical) can be seen as a discrete entity, characterised by the aggregation of its elements. These discrete systems are characterised by the modularity (and equipollence) of their parts. Every element is considered as important as every other, with no differentiation in the role, weight or impact on the overall system. Following a statistical approach, every element counts for the same as every other within the overall totality of the system. If N represents a generic element, in all discrete systems we can observe that $N_1 = N_2 = N_3 \ldots = N_n$ where n is the (possibly infinite) number of discrete elements that constitutes the system.

The substantial difference that the use of big data brings to this discussion is the fact that, in scenarios where large datasets are involved, elements in a system are unique, and, therefore, different from each other. The system is always describable as the summation of its parts, but, contrary to the approaches based on the notion of model, the final description of the system is a richer, variable and multifaceted entity that embodies every possible idiosyncrasy that characterises each individual element. By the same token, in a big data discrete system we have: $N_1 \neq N_2 \neq N_3 \ldots \neq N_n$, for every N is unique.

This chapter describes the rise of discrete logic in general, and its gradual evolution as a consequence of the growing use of approaches based on the growing computational power and capacity of today's computers. These changes are used to observe the way in which the public realm is changing (in Chapter 2) when public space is considered to be the aggregate form resulting from the uniqueness of individuals, in opposition to the statistical concept of the model.

The atomists and the synechists

Around 400 BC, Democritus and his mentor Leucippus elaborated the first known atomic theory, whereby they conceptualised the entire world as being made of indivisible elements that freely run within a limitless space. Atoms are indestructible and constitute the "elementary grain of reality" (Rovelli 2018:8). As the smallest possible fraction of any object in the world, atoms are characterised by a finite number and finite size. Democritus's theory can be considered a solid starting point for the idea that the world (and – by extension – the universe) is not a continuous entity but characterised by granularity (Bailey 1929; Pyle 1995). Democritus's view of the world can be seen as the starting point for the tension between the idea of continuity and discreteness that still persists today. Prior to Democritus, when the idea of indivisible finite elements was not available to humankind, the world and all phenomena were conceptualised as the sequence of various events that fluidly connected to each other, perhaps related by extra- or intra-terrestrial forces that bound them all. Aristotle offers a good example of this, where in the Categories (Ackrill 1961) he provided a definition for the notions of continuous and discrete elements. These are quantitative attributes that characterise objects. For those objects where a point of contact with other objects, namely a beginning and an end, is identifiable are continuous (Bell 2005:21). For example, a line where two points at the extremes are easily findable is continuous, so the line can be joined up with other lines. By the same token, surfaces have edges (lines) as contact elements, and bodies where points of contact can be found. Aristotle includes in this category time and space too, whereby the present is in constant contact with the past and the future and space, where objects can have common boundaries with which they can be joined up. Where contact points are impossible to find, those objects are characterised by a discrete quantity. For example, this can be seen in numbers or language where a number is considered as an individual entity with no possibility of joining other numbers. Even considering numbers in a sequence, we need to regard them as separate entities by their nature.

The atomistic view of the world proposed by Democritus and Leucippus and the existence of continua, of which Aristotle was one of many promotors, share a common interest in the notion of divisibility and the infinite. For the atomist, any object in the world is divisible into smaller elements a finite number of times until the smallest and most irreducible elements: the atoms. This view implies the idea of a plurality included within each object. For the advocates of the continua, objects are divisible ad infinitum and without limit. This view elevates the idea of unity over the one of plurality. However, the distinction between elements which are infinitely or finitely divisible adds another layer of complexity to the debate over the two positions. The Zeno's paradoxes provide an illustrative example here. In particular, in the Achilles and the tortoise puzzle where, according to Zeno's rigorous logic in dividing the distance between the two an infinite number of times, Achilles will never be able to reach the tortoise, as he would require an infinite time to do so. Rovelli (2018:14) explains this paradox by discussing the example of the length of a piece of string. If we imagine cutting a piece of string in two halves, then again, each piece into another two halves and so on ad infinitum, we will obtain an infinite number of pieces of finite length. Their sum will be equal to a finite length of string, namely the original length before the experiment. An infinite number of strings will result in a string of finite length and, by the same token, an infinite number of time divisions will be equal to a finite time. This is easily representable through the notion of convergent series, whereby the sum of an infinite number of values converges to 1.[1]

$$\sum_{n=0}^{\infty} x^n \rightarrow \frac{x}{1-x} \; if \; 0 < x < 1$$

The contrast between the two interpretations of the world endures until now and many mathematicians, thinkers and philosophers have contributed for centuries to a more sophisticated understanding of the two camps. In particular, a number of positions are helpful in the discussion of the theoretical framework presented in this chapter. In the fifteenth century, Nicolaus Cusanus (*Idiota de mente/The Layman on Mind* 1450) proposed an in-between position whereby it is possible to divide a continuum into two levels: the ideal sense that progresses to infinity and the actual sense where a finite number of divisions concludes in a large number of atoms (Bell 2013). Boyer (1956:91) associates the notion of actual infinite to Cusanus with the quadrature of the circle, whereby a circle is approximated into a mathematical series of polygons that approximate to the curvature of the circle. This experiment is explained in more detail in the following section. Almost two centuries later, Gottfried Wilhelm (von) Leibniz explored the notion of continua and their divisibility in his work *The Labyrinth of the Continuum* (2001). For Leibniz, there are entities that are neither single elements, nor the aggregation of several ones. Starting from the axiom that each real entity is either a single one or an aggregation of many, he noticed that there are a number of cases where continua cannot exist. The line, for example, can be considered as the repetition of several dimensionless points, and already Aristotle demonstrated that points cannot produce a continuous entity (Bell 2013). This led Leibniz to formulate that continua do not belong to the realm of real entities and that they are, by their nature, ideal. Continua are now outside of the initial axiom, and do not have to obey the principle of being either a simple entity or an aggregation of them. By doing this, Leibniz was able to discern ideal entities, like lines or space and time, from the real entities like matter that are purely discrete, i.e. made by monads, single substances with no ulterior parts and therefore indivisible (Leibniz 1989), or a multiplicity of them (or compound in Leibniz's terms).

At the other end of the scale, we can find the synechists: those who consider the world as truly a continuum. Peirce used the term synechism, using the ancient Greek term synechismos, syneches (continuous) to refer to that interpretation of the world that

> exists as a continuous whole of all of its parts, with no part being fully separate, determined or determinate, and continues to increase in complexity and connectedness through semiosis and the operation of an irreducible and ubiquitous power of relational generality to mediate and unify substrates.
>
> (Esposito 2007)

The limit of series in topological space

Within the context of this study, the notion of liminal spatiality stems from the idea of approximation and the limit of geometries (Cornu 1991; Edwards 2012). This notion was first identified by classical Greek mathematicians as the outcome of the application of the method of exhaustion. In Euclid Book XII,[2] proposition 2, there is a clear account of the extent to which this method can be used to demonstrate the approximation by polygons. A demonstration of the emergence of the liminal space as the difference between the area of the circle and the inscribed polygon can be found in Casselman (2003), where Figure 1.1 is also provided.[3]

McFarlane (2004) provides an extensive description of the development of the concept of exhaustion in relation to the ideas of limit and the potential infinite. He traces back these notions to Aristotle, Eudoxus and Archimedes, providing a powerful method to approximate the area of a circle (intended as infinite), by calculating the areas of the polygons inside the circle using triangulation.

> The area of the circle can thus be found with any desired precision by selecting a sufficiently large value of n and calculating the areas of the two polygons. This method, however, does not provide a precise value for the area of the circle. To arrive at a precise formula for the actual area of the circle, one would need to take n equal to infinity. But this would require one to add up an infinite number of triangles, which is impossible.[4]

(McFarlane 2004)

Another way to visualise the emergence of liminality is through a simple code, where the computational power of a computer can be used to automate the process of increasing the number of sides in a polygon in the approximation of a circle.

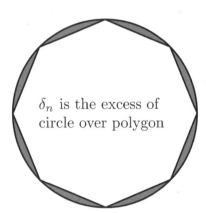

δ_n is the excess of
circle over polygon

Figure 1.1 The surface between the circle and the polygon represents the exceeding space
between the two

Source: http://www.math.ubc.ca/~cass/courses/m446-03/exhaustion.pdf, page 5

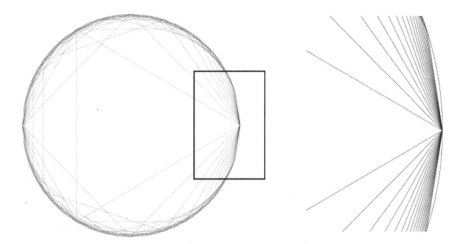

Figure 1.2 Code-generated incremental approximation of polygons to the curve (entire generation on the left-hand side, and a close up of the approximation on the right)

Figure 1.2 has been obtained using Python for Rhino, where a loop ran a number of iterations, generating a series of polygons with an incremental number of sides, from 4 to 50. The more sides the polygon has, the closer to a circle it is, and the difference between the two is less evident. The system created allows the number of sides in the polygon to be increased at will, whereby the polygon can theoretically become incrementally closer to the circle ad infinitum, but never coincides with it.

The space generated at each iteration between the polygon and the circle underpins, here, the idea of liminal spatiality. The more sides the polygon has used in the process, the smaller is the area between the circle and the polygon. By the same token, the more resolution the polygon has (namely, the more information used to define it), the smaller and more accurate the liminal space will be.

Quantifying the world

The work on calculus and infinitesimals by Isaac Newton, Leibniz, Bernard Bolzano (1781–1848) and Augustin-Louis Cauchy (1789–1857) has been fundamental in paving the way for the understanding of mathematics and physics we have today. A big part in this process has been played by the idea of arithmetisation of the world. Mathematicians like Cantor, Dedekind and Kronecker shared the idea that all world phenomena can be reduced to numbers and that mathematics can be considered a science with a clearly defined domain of objects (Petri and Schappacher 2007:368). This reduction of every phenomena to numbers is underpinned by the reduction of irrational numbers to rational and to natural ones (Petri and Schappacher 2007:368). The German mathematician Karl Weierstrass

(1815–97) developed this idea even further by considering numbers at the centre of any analytical work, replacing the idea of the continuous with the discrete (Bell 2013). Similarly to Weierstrass, Georg Cantor (1845–1918) continued the study of numbers as main discerning elements of phenomena, by reducing the relevance of geometry from the mathematical analysis; thus, numbers are considered elements per se, with no pre-existing relation with each other or order-based relationships (Bell 2013). The world is not constituted solely by numbers, but they can be rightfully employed to study it, represent it and understand it.

Quanta

One of the most significant breakthroughs in physics of the twentieth century has been the introduction of quantum mechanics. This revolutionary theory represented a watershed in the way of seeing the world, whereby we can have a before and after quanta. In quantum theory, those quantities that were thought to have continuous values in classical physics assume a discrete value. Within quantum theory, amongst the many characteristics that qualify objects like wave particle duality, uncertainty or the relational structure, the idea of granularity is particularly relevant to our discussion. If we reconsider Zeon's story of Achilles and the tortoise in the light of quantum theory, we observe that the distance between the two at any given time is made up of a series of finite possible values. Before quanta, we could have said that there is an infinite possible number of values between Achilles and the tortoise. Let us assume that the distance at the time of the observation is around one metre. In classical physics, we could argue that there are an infinite number of possible values within this metre (0.5m, 0.005m, 0.00000005m, etc.). In quantum theory, the Plank's constant h provides us with the elementary scale of the different values in the system, expressed in terms of granularity (Rovelli 2018:112). We learn then that, in quantum physics, there is a finite amount of information we can have regarding the state of the phenomenon observed. In the Planck – Einstein relation $E = hf$, the energy that characterises a phonon (E) is equal to the Plank's constant (h) multiplied by the frequency of the electromagnetic wave associated with it (f). The distance between Achilles and the tortoise contains an infinite number of classical states, but only a finite number of quantum states (Rovelli 2018:112). The exact moment in history when the quantum view (related to the atomism of energy) was born can be indicated as the 14th of December 1900, when Max Planck announced his results on black-body radiation during a lecture at the Physical Society of Berlin (Haken and Wolf 2012:2). In particular, he explained that the energy of harmonic oscillators can only be described through a series of discrete values. This contradicted the other classical physics approaches whereby energy was considered to have continuous values.

> It is necessary to interpret U_n [the vibrational energy] not as a continuous, infinitely divisible quantity, but as a discrete quantity composed of an integral number of finite equal parts.
>
> (Planck 1901:3)

Mereology

A first coordinate in the development of an understanding of discrete reality can be found in the notion of mereology, where the relationships between parts and parthood are explored. Varzi (2016) provides an account of the development of this theory throughout history, from the Presocratic and Roman philosophers to the twentieth century. He describes that, although traces of the concept of mereology can be found in the work of several thinkers throughout history, a clear definition was given by Stanisław Leśniewski in his *Foundations of the General Theory of Sets* (1916) and *Foundations of Mathematics* (1927–1931). Leśniewski developed the mutual relationships of objects and classes of objects, introducing important terminology, including the notion of "element", "overlapping" and "being exterior to" (Simons 2015). Moreover, Varzi (1993) explored the relationship between mereology intended as a "theory of parthood" (Varzi 1996) and topology as a "theory of wholeness" (Varzi 1996), whereby he proposed four possible strategies: topology is to be added to a mereological basis, topology is used to define mereological notions, topology is a domain-specific chapter of mereology and, finally, mereo-topological primitives can be conceived together (1996:13).

These studies established an important milestone in the understanding of phenomena through the relationships of parts and the whole. If the notion of mereology is important to establish the existence of elements in a system, the nature of individual parts is further elaborated in Set Theory. Kanamori (1996) examined how Georg Cantor's work on Set Theory has been seminal for a significant shift in mathematics, whence the continuum is regarded as a collection of objects (1996:3). Space (intended here as generic containing volume) began to be seen as a series of finite elements, with real numbers being possibly related to geometrical entities like points and lines (1996:3). Penrose (2014) provides an account of theories where geometry is characterised by discrete elements (2014:958). Particularly relevant to this article are Sorkin (1991) and Rideout and Sorkin (1999). Sorkin describes the causal set as "possible discrete substratum for spacetime" (1991:150), and the structure for spacetime as discrete. In their account of discrete topologies, Seebach and Steen (1970) explain that every point in a discrete typology is an isolated point, and, "since each point is a neighbourhood of itself, each discrete space is locally compact"[5] (1970:41).

Cellular automata

Stephen Wolfram's work on cellular automata (1986) is seminal for understanding the extent to which machines are reconsidering everyday phenomena in discrete terms. Moreover, Wolfram's processing of rules in cellular automata is here considered the pivotal point in the development of discretisation from a purely mathematical and geometrical notion (cf. Kanamori 1996) to their application to the digital environment. In fact, processes that are based on Machine Learning algorithms require the discretisation of complex problems and phenomena into a series of separate attributes that can be more easily computed (Dougherty et al.

1995; Sotirisand and Kanellopoulos 2007). Wolfram showed how this "simple mathematical model" can be used to determine evolutions (of phenomena, statistics, models, etc.) by using fixed values in discrete time steps, in relation to the value of the neighbouring elements (1983:601). In Wolfram's terms, this is called the "Principle of Computational Equivalence" (1983:716), and it provides a "uniform framework in which to discuss different (natural) processes" (1983:716).

Wolfram offered a model to consider particle dynamics by discrete values and finite variations that operate within a grid-like space (Wolfram 1984). Through cellular automata, he describes a system where simple rules govern the behaviour of neighbouring cells in creating patterns. Depending on the rule used, both

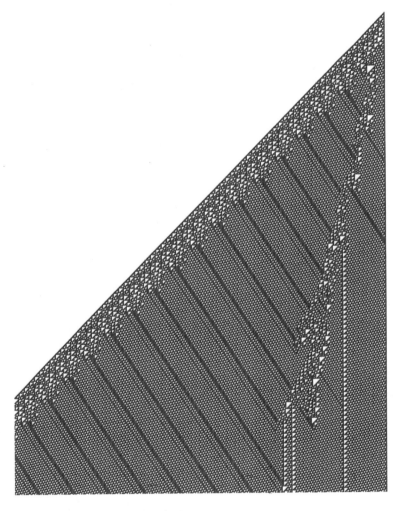

Figure 1.3 Wolfram's Rule 110 (portion)

Source: Image from Wolfram (2003:33)

regular and irregular patterns can occur, as well as "remarkable" combinations of them (1983:31), as in the rule that Wolfram named no. 110. Wolfram's work on knowledge-based systems (with Mathematica and then Wolfram Language)[6] illustrates one of the concrete applications of the digital logic used to solve complex problems.

Although Wolfram's notion of cellular automaton is still considered controversial (Giles 2002), it is helpful in explaining how discretisation as a computational system can be applied to a variety of subjects, from social science (Hegselmann 1998) to urban models (Couclelis 1997).

The discretisation underpinned by any process of digitalisation, in the form of finite numbers, bits, definite values and packets of information ultimately supersedes continuity as the main logic for understanding the world's phenomena.

When the volume of data underpinning digitalisation and discretisation processes is increased significantly, and beyond the capacity of normal computers and systems, the sight on the world that computers offer to us changes in nature. In the big data scenario, the precision, availability, ubiquity and depth of detail that characterise every single datum makes it possible for observations to appreciate the single individual along with her/his own idiosyncrasies and peculiarities. This is significantly different from the digital scenario where individuals are considered as part of a sample.

If new tools are developed to disentangle the complexity of the world, computational logics can be increasingly applied to a variety of fields, from medicine to public security. In this upsurge, big data can be considered a watershed, for they mark the difference between a before and after the appreciation of world phenomena in a dramatically different manner. The shift from considering data as an asset for storing information and preserving knowledge, to the awareness that an "information explosion", which is changing the understanding of reality as we know it, is currently occurring can be traced back in several scholarly contributions, chiefly starting from the 1980s. Press (2013) provides a concise account of the seminal studies on big data, from Micheal Lesk's description of "How much information is there in the world?" (1997), where one can see one of the first compelling quantitative descriptions of the spiralling global increase in data, to Bounie and Gille (2012), where the global amount of new information produced in the world is estimated to have gone from 5.6 to 14.7 million Terabytes in five years (from 2003 to 2008). The sheer number of new data produced every day since the turn of the century, combined with the growing computational and storing capacity of networks, has had a significant impact on the nature of data usage and on the way in which digital systems operate.

Shape grammar

If geometry includes discrete elements, are shapes to be regarded as continuous or discrete objects? The opposite nature of numbers and shapes can be illustrated through the work of Lionel March, George Stiny and James Gips (Stiny and Gips 1978; Stiny and March 1981) about design machines and shape grammar. For them, in any intelligent system the mediation between reception (input) and reaction (output) to phenomena is mediated by language, which follows the rules of shape grammar (March 2000). In particular, March pointed out the "computational dilemma" (2000) between numbers and shapes that computers face, distinguishing between the notion of multitude (to which arithmetic, numbers and digits are related) and magnitude (which refers to geometry and shapes). The digitalisation is, explained March, the "arithmetisation of Euclid's geometry" (2000:25). March established two opposite (yet related) camps: on the one side, the idea of the continuum, embodied by the category of geometry, which is "pure thought, and it does not exist in the corporeal world" (2000:27), and the side of the "particulate digits, (which) are the unreconcilable antagonist of shape" (2000:25).

Fractals

Another application of the idea of analysing space discretely is through the observation of repetitive patterns that evolve and involve in themselves. This approach is better defined through fractal geometry. After initial experiments and discoveries by Karl Weierstrass and David Hilbert on complex geometries and their replicability (Turner 2009), fundamental advancements in the study of fractals are attributed to Benoît Mandelbröt and his fundamental work *The Fractal Geometry of Nature* (1977). In contrast to what Euclid categorised as amorphous and shapeless, Mandelbröt studied those irregular phenomena (reliefs and coastlines, lightning, dust, snowflakes, etc.) to give them a consistent geometrical description. He coded the complexity and irregularity of the patterns produced by nature through the theory of fractals. This "family of geometrical shapes" involves chance and statistics amongst the main characteristics underpinning their regularities and irregularities (Mandelbröt 1977:3).

Fractals can be considered as ulterior elements in the tension between the continuous and the discrete. They are continuously evolving (or involving), have ad infinitum possibilities, yet their spatial development proceeds by steps, not analogously. When Mandelbröt was observing and measuring the index of roughness of natural elements, from lakes and mountains to the surface of cauliflowers, he exposed the recursive complexity of the same shape expanding in space through itself. Space is occupied by the object (for instance a bolt of lightning) repetitively whereby the same shape branches out from the source point. The generative shape does not progress in a continuous manner, it rather replicates itself in steps, using its own shape as a module.

What fractals seem to suggest is the increasing relevance of discretisation as the level of complexity increases in an observed phenomenon. In his *Fractals Everywhere*, Michael Barnsley (2014) introduced in 1988 the Chaos Game: an algorithm that generates a shape starting from a simple set of generative rules.[7] Starting with a random point inside a regular polygon (with any number of edges), the algorithm generates a second point located at a fraction (r) of the distance between the first point and another point chosen randomly among the polygon vertices. By repeating this operation a number of times, the algorithm generates

Figure 1.4 Computer-generated Mandelbröt set

Source: https://en.wikipedia.org/wiki/File:Mandel_zoom_00_mandelbrot_set.jpg

a regular, repetitive pattern that is dependent on the number of edges of the poly-gon (n), the fraction (r) and the points picked at random. The algorithm is math-ematically describable through the following sets of linear mappings: (iterated function system or IFS):

$$A_i(p) = J(p - p_i) + (P_i), 1 \leq i \leq n$$

where p is a point defined by (x, y) and $p_i(x_i, y_i)$ is a randomly given point on the same plane of p associated with A_i. The multiplier J is $0 < J < 1$ (Mata-Toledo and Willis 1997:3; Jeffrey 1992:25).

The maps of patterns in the shape generation appear to develop around an attractor point related to an iterated function system (IFS). Points generation is not dependent on a specific point (e.g. a centre), but on a fractal attractor. This type of development is typical of Chaos Theory, whereby the determination of the exact position of a specific point is related to a number of variables in a chaotic system. Any small change in the variables results in a different configuration, where the entire system changes its relationship with the attractor. Perhaps one of the most iconic visualisations of the IFS function is the Barnsley's Fern, whereby

n = 3, r = 1/2

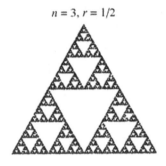

n = 5, r = 1/3

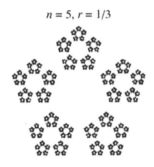

n = 5, r = 3/8

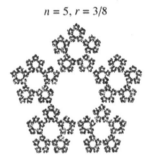

n = 6, r = 1/3

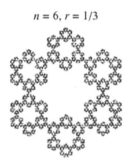

Figure 1.5 Iterations of the Chaos Theory algorithm

Source: http://mathworld.wolfram.com/ChaosGame.html

the algorithm is used to generate a Black Spleenwort fern (Barnsley 2014:101). The code below shows a simple way to compute a Barnsley's Fern using a random function to select the initial points.

Box 1.1   Example of the code to generate a Barnsley fern in Python

```
import random
from PIL import Image


class BarnsleyFern(object):
def __init__(self, img_width, img_height, paint_color=(0, 0, 0),
bg_color=(255, 255, 255)):
```

```
self.img_width, self.img_height = img_width, img_height
self.paint_color = paint_color
self.x, self.y = 0, 0
self.age = 0

self.fern = Image.new('RGB', (img_width, img_height), bg_color)
self.pix = self.fern.load()
self.pix[self.scale(0, 0)] = paint_color

def scale(self, x, y):
h = (x + 2.182)*(self.img_width - 1)/4.8378
k = (9.9983 - y)*(self.img_height - 1)/9.9983
return h, k

def transform(self, x, y):
rand = random.uniform(0, 100)
if rand < 1:
return 0, 0.16*y
elif 1 <= rand < 86:
return 0.85*x + 0.04*y, -0.04*x + 0.85*y + 1.6
elif 86 <= rand < 93:
return 0.2*x - 0.26*y, 0.23*x + 0.22*y + 1.6
else:
return -0.15*x + 0.28*y, 0.26*x + 0.24*y + 0.44

def iterate(self, iterations):
for _ in range(iterations):
self.x, self.y = self.transform(self.x, self.y)
self.pix[self.scale(self.x, self.y)] = self.paint_color
self.age += iterations

fern = BarnsleyFern(500, 500)
fern.iterate(1000000)
fern.fern.show()
```

Source: https://rosettacode.org/wiki/Barnsley_fern

Pixel and voxels

Pixels continue the graphic implementation of the idea of discrete representation and generation of space. Pixels, or picture elements, are discrete areas that constitute images in a raster graphic (Lyon 2006). Pixels are considered the smallest unit, and therefore indivisible, in a raster data grid. In order to generate a digital

Figure 1.6 Barnsley's Fern generated with a simple Python script

image, a dot matrix data structure is created where a virtual camera (a digital camera, a sensor, etc.) captures the amount of light in a certain area of the real world and translates it into a series of points with different colour and light values. These points (pixels) are then inserted in the dot matrix previously generated. The points are organised in an ordered array of grid cells that are referenced through a system of rows and columns numerically organised.

In order to generate a digital image, a machine needs to compute the amount of light that corresponds to each pixel in the grid. This works through a simulation of the light energy transported by photons in any given case. The simulation approximates through an algorithmic model the amount of light per pixel, discretising the real light of the real scene into a matrix-based digital version. One of the methods for doing this is rasterisation (Hughes et al. 2014:387).

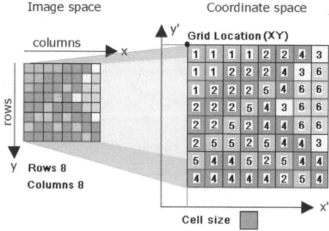

List of cell values

[1111224311222436122254662225436622524466255254435445254444444254]

Figure 1.7 Allocation of cells

Source: https://geog214-7.wikispaces.com/Raster+data+structure

Figure 1.8 The same image is represented in a 16 × 16 pixels grid (1 and 2) and in a 120 × 120 pixels grid (3)

In this technique, any visible object in the scene is captured by a camera and projected into a view plane. This latter contains a grid that subdivides the captured objects into an ordered number of points that are referenced in a data matrix. For each point, the quantity of light, brightness, colours and location are gathered and transferred into the matrix. To optimise this process, some techniques employ meshes, whereby each surface in the view plan is subdivided into simpler polygons, most likely triangles. In the following pseudocode from Hughes et al. (2014:392) we can observe how the rasterisation works at the implemented algorithm level.

Once the view plan has a grid of subdivided cells that represent the triangulated surfaces extrapolated from the scene, the algorithm scans the cells following the conventional left to right and top to bottom sequence (Hughes et al. 2014:392). Following this scanning order, information about each triangle is gathered and stored into a Cartesian coordinate system where positional values are sorted into (x, y).

```
1  for each pixel position (x,y):
2      closest[x, y] = ∞
3
4  for each triangle T:
5      for each pixel position (x,y):
6          let R be the ray through (x,y) from the eye
7          let P be the intersection of R and T
8          if P exists:
9              sum = 0
10             for each direction:
11                 sum += ...
12                 if the distance to P is less than closest[x, y]:
13                     pixel[x, y] = sum
14                     closest[x, y] = |P − O|
```

Figure 1.9 Example of rasterisation algorithm

Source: Hughes et al (2013)

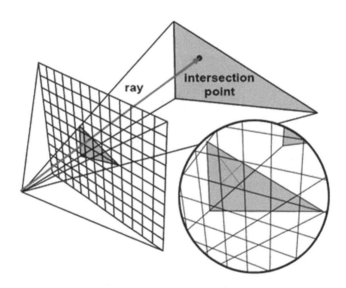

Figure 1.10 Allocation of cells in the generation of a digital image

Source: www.scratchapixel.com/lessons/3d-basic-rendering/rasterization-practical-implementation

At line 12, it is noticeable how the algorithm starts to generate the approximation of the point locations into the discrete representation of the original scene.

By observing Figure 1.10, we can see how the light and colour values for each cell in the view plan grid correspond to an RGB (Red Green Blue) value which digital screens can easily render. To each pixel, a chromatic (RGB) number value is uniquely assigned. The richness and the nuances of the original scene are converted into a numerical description that offers a discrete value ranging from 0 to 256 for each colour. Any possible quantity of energy carried out by the photons captured by the camera is reduced to a value arranged into a standard (255, 0, 0) or hexadecimal (#FF0000) notation (for an 8-bit system) (Poynton 2012).

Whilst pixels are designed to represent objects and scenes through a flat screen, their three-dimensional evolution in a digital environment is constituted by voxels (volume/pixels). A voxel is a "quantum unit of volume [that] has a numeric value (or values) associated with it that represents some measurable properties or independent variables of a real object or phenomenon. The voxel is the 3D conceptual counterpart of the 2D pixel" (Kaufman, Cohen, and Yagel 1993).

The data contained in a voxel is considered homogeneous in the description of certain geometry, whereby "the region of constant value that surrounds each sample is known as a voxel with each voxel being a rectangular cuboid having six faces, twelve edges, and eight corners" (Kaufman 1999:2). The conversion of objects into a voxel-based system is known as voxelisation. This consists of the translation of continuous geometries into irreducible quanta of volumes that best represent the continuous properties of the real object (Kaufman 1999:4). The voxelisation generates a database, which stores data in the format f (x, y, z) of a volumetric discretisation (voxel) of a continuous object (Kaufman 1999:4). Voxels do not contain data about their absolute position in space, but relative to other voxels. This is related to the notion of voxel adjacency. Within a contained 3D digital space, where the overall volume is subdivided into 3D pixels displaced into a 3D Cartesian system (x, y, z), a voxel is the single and irreducible cubic unit. As cubes, adjacent voxels can share at minimum either a vertex, an edge or

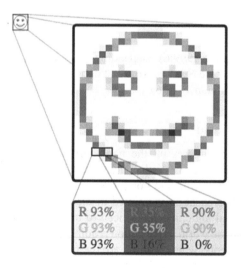

Figure 1.11 Assignment of chromatic values of pixels

Source: https://en.wikipedia.org/wiki/Raster_graphics#/media/File:Rgb-raster-image.svg

Figure 1.12 An example of urban environment built through voxels with MagicaVoxel

Source: https://ephtracy.github.io/#ss-carousel_ss urban

an entire face (Kaufman 1999:6). Depending on their reciprocal position, voxels can be N-adjacent, where N is the value that defines the relation of adjacency with N = 6, 18 or 26 (Kaufman 1999:6).

Discretising the world

The mathematical progresses on the nature of discreteness and digitalisation which occurred during the twentieth century paved the way for digital computing to find a fertile terrain in which to flourish.

The notion of discretisation is imbued in the very nature of digital thinking. Within computational logic, machines need to translate everything into digits in order to understand the world. Digitisation requires the transformation of any reality into binary elements, where 0 and 1 are the main constituents. In this regard, the works of Shannon (1997) and Servin (2012) on theories of communication and telecommunication, respectively, have been seminal in providing a working model for data and information to be translated into binary digits in order to be transmitted across different systems and provide accurate and reliable communications. There is no fluidity between two digits, or in-between values. Continuum systems are translated into discrete ones by machines in order to make sense of phenomena like fluid turbulence (Turcotte 2004) and snowflakes (Coxe and Reiter 2003). Negroponte (1995) distinguished between the macroscopic level, where things are perceived in a continuous manner, and microscopic scale, where "things we interact with *(electrons in a wire or photons in our eyes)* are discrete" (1995:15).

In general terms, this tendency goes under the name of datification. Igual and Seguí (2017) describe the phenomenon as "the process of rendering into data aspects of the world that have never been quantified before" (2017:1). Within this category, both tangible (noise level in a room, or number of visitor accesses in a museum) and esoteric (e.g. moodmaps in different urban areas) elements, as well as quantitative and qualitative aspects of everyday life, from number of minutes spent commuting, working or exercising, to happiness or level of stress, are gradually falling. Harari (2016) provides an account of the notion of dataism, where "the universe consists of data flows, and the value of any phenomenon or entity is determined by its contribution to data processing" (2016:367).

The idea of digitalisation of the world entails that entities are considered in a discrete manner with no analogue conditions. This claim is particularly true with regard to the increase of computational power that has characterised the history of computers since the 1970s. In order to expand their capacity, machines need to perform increasingly more complex elaborations, processing a staggering amount of data taken from the world.[8] The more machines can (and need to) compute, the more data, facts, notion, ideas and knowledge of the world are digitalised. By their nature, computers tend to read the world in digits and bits, reflecting what Negroponte called the DNA of information (1995). In the first instance, computers replicated the analogueness of the world by means of digits. However, the further advancements in computing and data processing that characterised the turn of the century have allowed machines to halt the translation of (continuous) reality into its discrete computer version, generating instead a new image of the real that is utterly discrete in its own nature. The idea of continuous reality is no longer emulated by processors to be rendered in a digital environment. Gradually, computers are generating a new reality, which is utterly machine-driven, hence discrete.

Granular computing

To date, one of the most advanced applications of the idea of granularity-inferred logic is the notion of granular computing (GrC). Complex problems can be divided into granules of information where: "informally, granulation of an object A results in a collection of granules of A, with a granule being a clump of objects (or points) which are drawn together by indistinguishability, similarity, proximity or functionality" (Zadeh 1998:112). Granulation requires a process of analysis and synthesis whereby a phenomenon (or a problem) characterised by incomplete or corrupt information (Yao 2000) is divided into a myriad of small parts (granules) that are then recombined following processes of association, functionality, efficiency, etc. following a problem-solving approach. Granularity greatly exploits the potentiality of big data by tackling problems where there is not enough information to process with other methods. This is what Zadeh calls "soft computing", the guiding principle of which is: "(to) exploit the tolerance for imprecision, uncertainty and partial truth to achieve tractability, robustness, low solution cost and better rapport with reality" (Zadeh 1997).

Big data

Although several definitions of big data have been produced (e.g. Ward and Barker 2013; Gandomi and Murtaza 2015), in the context of this book the following is considered:

> Big data can be defined as data sets that exceed the boundaries and sizes of normal processing capabilities, thus forcing a non-traditional approach to analyzing these data sets.
>
> (Nordicity 2014:6)

More specifically, big data can have a significant impact on architecture, with growing technologies like tracking, sensing, mapping, etc. Although the use of big data in architecture can be helpful in a speculative sense, in inferring information from surveying a particular case study (building, urban area or behaviour in public space) in great detail, the focus of this study is chiefly on the results of the use of big data in the final shape and spatial characteristics.

The use of data is here presented in two substantially different ways: one that characterises a manageable amount of data, and one that requires alternative solutions to handle significantly more complex systems, where data are considered "big" in their volume, variety, velocity and veracity.[9]

The passage from "manageable data" to big data is characterised by two aspects: (a) the increment of computational capacity and (b) the transition from sampling to determination.

(a) The passage from the use of data to large sets of data has been gradual and never clearly planned. The way the computational capacity has increased over the last decades (and is still growing today) results in a gradual and continuous increase of information involved in every computational process. The definition of big data is an expanding one. Manovich (2011) holds that the term is used when supercomputers are necessary to process the amount of data. Snijders et al. (2012) describe them as "a data set so large and complex that they become awkward to work with using standard statistical software". Al Nuaimi et al. hold that big data are: a "large set of data that is very unstructured and disorganized", and "a form of data that exceeds the processing capabilities of traditional database infrastructure or engines" (Al Nuaimi et al. 2015). Batty proposes a very simple definition: "any data that cannot fit into an Excel Spreadsheet" (Batty 2013:274). In the general acceptance of the term, when data sets become so large that standard computers or software are unable to process them, the data become big. Boyd and Crawford (2012) observed that big data are more about the computational capacity (to search, aggregate and cross-reference) and less about the size of data sets per se.

(b) The second distinctive aspect of big data is the capacity to work with the unknown. Castells (2009) explained that one of the main characteristics of the information age is to cope with the uncertainties of a fast-changing economical, institutional and technological environment (Castells 2009:163). One of the main differences between the use of data and big data is described by Hilbert (2013) and lies in the idea that, while every decision is regulated by a certain degree of "uncertain probabilistic gamble based on some kind of prior information" (Hilbert 2013:3), in the big data environment, the base for prior information is significantly increased, reducing the level of uncertainty. In big data, the high volume of information provides very detailed "models and estimates that inform all sort of decision" (Hilbert 2013:3). This point is expanded by Mayer-Schönberger and Cukier (2013:26), where the concept of sampling is superseded by the fact of being able to obtain "all" possible data. With the concept of N = all (with N as all cases used in an observation) Mayer-Schönberger and Cukier hold that it is possible to use big data to significantly increase the degree of detail of each observation.

Discretisation in seven logical steps

This chapter has described the evolution from the initial debates about continua and atoms of matter from the ancient Greek philosophers and mathematicians to the more recent developments and their application to the realm of computing and methods. It is important to reiterate that, with respect to the two possible visions of the world discussed here, there is no one that supersedes the other in absolute terms. The discussion is very much still on at the present time, and Pierce's synechists approach is as valid and applicable to reality as is Planck and Einstein's one. The aim of this section was to bring these two possible approaches to the fore, and to highlight some of the main figures and theories in the development of these two lines of thought.

The idea that the world can be divided into elements that are reducible to a limit-entity (the atom), that is considered as smallest possible, is the first step in this debate. This raises questions about the relationships between each of these infinitesimal elements. The relationships existing among atoms can be considered in two directions. On the one hand, we can study what happens between atoms and what configurations they assume in space. On the other hand, we can focus on the relationships between each atom and the whole. This is exactly what Stanisław Leśniewski and colleagues have been studying through the notion of mereology and Set Theory (Cantor). Through this, we can learn how elements in a system are mutually organised and ordered. But to do this, we need to accept the assumption that the world is constituted by a number of objects whose divisibility is finite. By embracing the atomic view of the world, the discrete notion gradually acquired relevance in the scientific realm. Although Leibniz, Newton, Cantor et al. significantly contributed to the further development of this view, it is with quantum mechanics that the atomic theory eventually takes a radical shift. What were atoms for Democritus and Leucippus become a determined quantity of energy whose expression is related to the frequency of the waves produced by their motion. Through the theory of quanta, we understand that the world can be regarded through the atomic framework, whereby finite elements compose everything we see and experience.

In order to understand how we can use this information to make sense of how cities are analysed and designed today in the following chapters, we need to consider a spatial perspective on this discussion.

In spatial terms, the Greek atomists transformed what was considered a continuous, ungraspable and diffused set of substances into a combination of distinguishable elements that can be possibly quantified and qualified. As mentioned above, Plank and colleagues developed this further into a more sophisticated view which helped to give more in-depth knowledge of these individual elements. In particular, we learned that the space between atoms, quanta or any other elements in a given observation can be considered finite and can be calculated with great accuracy. If the space in-between elements is finite, then the movement of objects in space should logically happen in hops, albeit at a microscale.

By introducing a clear and measurable spatial system by which objects and their position can be described, René Descartes provided a key part of this discrete framework. Seen through Cartesian space, objects move within a grid of values, whereby geometries can be univocally described through numeric forms. By the same token, numerical information can be extracted from any geometry at any time. The Cantor – Dedekind axiom is a clear example of this logic, whereby there is a one-to-one correspondence between any point of a line and the realm of the real numbers (Weisstein 2002). If a line or any other geometry can be defined through real numbers, we can infer the impossibility of having inter-states, where a point has intermediate values. Under the Cantor – Dedekind axiom, any given point is either in one position (expressed through a number) or in another. We can see the digital logic in place here: a point is described by one value and not another. Points in a line are described following a discrete logic, where their position considered within a function changes through either/or logic, whereby the point is represented by one value or another.

Table 1.1 Evolution of the logic of the discrete spatial framework

Logic step	Key actor/work
1 World in atoms	Democritus and Leucippus
2 From atoms to quanta	Planck, Einstein et al.
3 Space is finite	Cantor, Set Theory
4 Space as a grid	Descartes
5 Objects as discrete	Cantor – Dedekind axiom
6 Spaces as organised units (cells)	Cellular Automata, von Neumann, Wolfram
7 Production of space through units/ cells/blocks	pixels/voxels/fractals

If objects are discrete (or discrete-able), so is the space surrounding and containing all objects. Space can then be expressed through a finite number of numeric values, where each value can be intended as a fixed quantity of change. Each irreducible quantity of space can be imagined as a cell. Cellular automata, and the work of Stephen Wolfram (1986) in particular, is helpful in illustrating this principle. Within a cellular automation environment, a regular grid of cells has a finite number of possible states (on/off, or I/0). Each cell has a number of neighbourhood cells and their configuration evolves through a number of discrete steps with a time (t) increment, normally using a set of mathematical rules (Weisstein 2002). This system clearly illustrates a spatial configuration where entities are treated as cells that can move or modify themselves following discrete jumps into a rigid given spatial grid.

Within such spatial framework and logic, we can easily understand the mechanisms that underpin the organisation of space into pixels and voxels. If the space of the world is structured in a three-dimensional grid that extends everywhere, the objects moving in it need to do so in progressive hops characterised by discrete values. Through numbers, any object in the world, any phenomenon and any possible change of state for them can be described accurately. In working with fractals, for example, we realise the mechanism of producing an object that replicates itself in space through logic and organised discrete steps. Space, in this instance, is understood and modified cell by cell in a natural progression.

Under this perspective, it is possible to describe the world in a quantistic manner, where space is intended as a large grid of a finite number of values and in which objects operate following a discrete logic.

Notes

1 A detailed description can be found at: http://web.mat.bham.ac.uk/R.W.Kaye/seqser/exseries.html and http://mathworld.wolfram.com/ConvergentSeries.html. Last accessed 4 November 2018.
2 http://aleph0.clarku.edu/~djoyce/elements/bookXII/propXII2.html. Last accessed 10 June 2017.
3 www.math.ubc.ca/~cass/courses/m446-03/exhaustion.pdf. Last accessed 10 June 2017.
4 Article accessible online at: https://integralscience.wordpress.com/1999/03/23/nicholas-of-cusa-and-the-infinite/ Last accessed 8 May 2017.
5 Quote rephrased by the author.
6 This can be found at: www.wolfram.com/?source=nav. Last accessed 8 May 2017.
7 A detailed description is available at: http://mathworld.wolfram.com/ChaosGame.html. Last accessed 28 July 2018.
8 In 2010, Google CEO Eric Schmidt claimed that "Every two days now we create as much information as we did from the dawn of civilization up until 2003" (Siegler 2010).
9 IBM, The Four V's of Big Data www.ibmbigdatahub.com/infographic/four-vs-big-data. Last accessed 19 May 2017.

References

Ackrill, J. L. 1961. *Aristotle Categories and De Interpretatione* (Clarendon Aristotle Series). Oxford: Clarendon Press.

Al Nuaimi, Eiman, et al. 2015. "Applications of Big Data to Smart Cities." *Journal of Internet Services and Applications* 6 (1): 25.

Bailey, Cyril. 1929. *The Greek Atomists and Epicurus: A Study.* Oxford: Clarendon Press.

Barnsley, Michael F. 2014. *Fractals Everywhere.* Cambridge, MA: Academic Press.

Batty, Michael. 2013. "Big Data, Smart Cities and City Planning." *Dialogues in Human Geography* 3 (3): 274–279.

Bell, John L. 2005. *The Continuous and the Infinitesimal in Mathematics and Philosophy.* Milan: Polimetrica.

Bell, John L. 2013. "Continuity and Infinitesimals." In *Stanford Encyclopedia of Philosophy*, edited by Edward N. Zalta. Stanford: Stanford University.

Bounie, David, and Laurent Gille. 2012. "International Production and Dissemination of Information: Results, Methodological Issues, and Statistical Perspectives." *Methodological Issues, and Statistical Perspectives* (February 1, 2012).

Boyd, Danah, and Kate Crawford. 2012. "Critical Questions for Big Data: Provocations for a Cultural, Technological, and Scholarly Phenomenon." *Information, Communication & Society* 15 (5): 662–679.

Casselman, B. 2003. *The Method of Exhaustion.* Department of Mathematics at the University of British Columbia.

Castells, Manuel, et al. 2009. *Mobile Communication and Society: A Global Perspective.* MIT Press.

Cornu, B. 1991. "Limit." In *Advanced Mathematical Thinking*, edited by D. Tall, 153–166. Springer Science & Business Media.

Couclelis, Helen. 1997. "From Cellular Automata to Urban Models: New Principles for Model Development and Implementation." *Environment and Planning B: Planning and Design* 24 (2): 165–174.

Coxe, Angela M., and Clifford A. Reiter. 2003. "Fuzzy Hexagonal Automata and Snowflakes." *Computers & Graphics* 27 (3): 447–454.

Dougherty, James, Ron Kohavi, and Mehran Sahami. 1995. "Supervised and Unsupervised Discretization of Continuous Features." *Machine Learning Proceedings* 1995, 194–202. Morgan Kaufmann.

Edwards, C. J. 2012. *The Historical Development of the Calculus.* Springer Science & Business Media.

Esposito, Joseph L. 2007. "Synechism: The Keystone of Peirce's Metaphysics." In *Digital Encyclopedia of Charles S. Peirce.* London, Canada: University of Western Ontario.

Foley, James D., Dan Van, Van Dam, Andries, Feiner, Steven K., Hughes, John F. 2013. *Computer Graphics: Principles and Practice.* Boston: Addison-Wesley Professional.

Gandomi, Amir, and Murtaza Haider. 2015. "Beyond the Hype: Big Data Concepts, Methods, and Analytics." *International Journal of Information Management* 35 (2): 137–144.

Giles, Jim. 2002. "Stephen Wolfram: What Kind of Science Is This?" *Nature* 417 (6886): 216–218.

Haken, Hermann, and Hans C. Wolf. 2012. *Atomic and Quantum Physics: An Introduction to the Fundamentals of Experiment and Theory.* Stuttgart: Springer.

Harari, Yuval Noah. 2016. *Homo Deus: A Brief History of Tomorrow.* Random House.

Hegselmann, Rainer, and Andreas Flache. 1998. "Understanding Complex Social Dynamics: A Plea for Cellular Automata Based Modelling." *Journal of Artificial Societies and Social Simulation* 1 (3): 1.

Hilbert, Martin. 2013. "Big Data for Development: From Information-to Knowledge Societies." Available at SSRN 2205145.

Hughes, John F., Andries Van Dam, James D. Foley, Morgan McGuire, Steven K. Feiner, David F. Sklar, and Kurt Akeley. 2014. *Computer Graphics: Principles and Practice.* Boston, MA: Pearson Education.

Igual, Laura, and Santi Seguí. 2017. "Introduction to Data Science." Introduction to Data Science. Springer, Cham. 1–4.

Jeffrey, H. Joel. 1992. "Chaos Game Visualization of Sequences." *Computers & Graphics* 16 (1): 25–33.

Kanamori, Akihiro. 1996. "The Mathematical Development of Set Theory from Cantor to Cohen." *Bulletin of Symbolic Logic* 2 (1): 1–71.

Kaufman, Arie E. 1999. "Introduction to Volume Graphics." *SIGGRAPH.* Conference Proceedings. New York.

Kaufman, Arie E., Daniel Cohen, and Roni Yagel. 1993. "Volume Graphics." *Computer* 26 (7): 51–64.

Kotsiantis, Sotiris, and Dimitris Kanellopoulos. 2006. "Discretization Techniques: A Recent Survey." *GESTS International Transactions on Computer Science and Engineering* 32 (1): 47–58.

Leibniz, Gottfried Wilhelm. 1989. "The Monadology." In *Philosophical Papers and Letters*, 643–53. Dordrecht, NL: Springer.

Leibniz, Gottfried Wilhelm. 2001. *The Labyrinth of the Continuum.* New Haven: Yale University Press.

Lesk, M. 1997. How Much Information Is There in the World? Retrieved from http://www.lesk.com/mlesk/ksg97/ksg.html

Lyon, Richard F. 2006. "A Brief History of 'Pixel'." In *Digital Photography II*, edited by Nitin Sampat, Jeffrey M. DiCarlo, and Russel A. Martin. SPIE Proceedings Vol. 6069. San Jose, CA.

March, Lionel. 2000. "From Digital and Beyond." In *Truth, Radicality and Beyond in Contemporary Architecture*, edited by A. Papadakēs, Vol. 5. Andreas Papadakis Pub.

Mandelbrot, Benoit B. 1983. *The Fractal Geometry of Nature*, Vol. 173. New York: WH Freeman.

Manovich, Lev. 2011. "Trending: The Promises and the Challenges of Big Social Data." *Debates in the Digital Humanities* 2: 460–475.

Mayer-Schönberger, Viktor, and Kenneth Cukier. 2013. Big Data: A Revolution That Will Transform How We Live, Work, and Think Houghton Mifflin Harcourt.

Mata-Toledo, Ramón A., and Matthew A. Willis. 1997. "Visualization of Random Sequences Using the Chaos Game Algorithm." *Journal of Systems and Software* 39 (1): 3–6.

McFarlane, T. J. 2004. "Nicholas of Cusa and the Infinite." Accessed June 6, 2018. www.integralscience.org.

Nicholas, Negroponte. 1995. *Being Digital.* Alfred Knopf Inc.

Nordicity. Big Data for Public Good: A Primer (Mar 2014). Retrieved from https://www.icecommittee.org/reports/ice-event-reports/big-data-for-public-good-a-primer/

Petri, Birgit, and Norbert Schappacher. 2007. "On Arithmetization." In *The Shaping of Arithmetic After CF Gauss's Disquisitiones Arithmeticae*, 343–74. Berlin: Springer.

Planck, Max. 1901. "On the Law of Distribution of Energy in the Normal Spectrum." *Annalen der physik* 4 (553): 1.

Poynton, Charles. 2012. *Digital Video and HD: Algorithms and Interfaces.* San Francisco, CA: Elsevier.

Pyle, Andrew. 1995. *Atomism and Its Critics Problem Areas Associated with the Development of the Atomic Theory of Matter from Democritus to Newton.* London: Thoemmes Press.

Rideout, David P., and Rafael D. Sorkin. 1999. "Classical Sequential Growth Dynamics for Causal Sets." *Physical Review D* 61 (2): 024002.

Rovelli, Carlo. 2018. *Reality Is Not What It Seems: The Journey to Quantum Gravity*. London: Penguin.

Seebach, J. Arthur, and Lynn Arthur Steen. 1970. *Counterexamples in Topology*. New York: Springer.

Servin, Claude. 2012. *Telecommunications: Transmission and Network Architecture*. Springer Science & Business Media.

Shannon, Claude E. 1997. "The Mathematical Theory of Communication. 1963." 306–317.

Simons, Peter. (2015). "Stanisław Leśniewski." In *The Stanford Encyclopedia of Philosophy* (Winter 2015 Edition), edited by Edward N. Zalta. https://plato.stanford.edu/archives/win2015/entries/lesniewski/

Snijders, Chris, Uwe Matzat, and Ulf-Dietrich Reips. 2012. ""Big Data": Big Gaps of Knowledge in the Field of Internet Science." *International Journal of Internet Science* 7 (1): 1–5.

Sorkin, Rafael D. 1990. "Spacetime and Causal Sets." *Relativity and Gravitation: Classical and Quantum* 50–173.

Stiny, George, and James Gips. 1978. *Algorithmic Aesthetics: Computer Models for Criticism and Design in the Arts*. Univ of California Press.

Stiny, George, and Lionel March. 1981. "Design Machines." *Environment and Planning B: Planning and Design* 8 (3): 245–255.

Turcotte, Donald L. 2004. "The Relationship of Fractals in Geophysics to "The New Science"." *Chaos, Solitons & Fractals* 19 (2): 255–258.

Turner, Martin J. 2009. "The Origins of Fractals." Retrieved from https://plus.maths.org/issue6/turner1/2pdf/index.html/op.pdf

Varzi, Achille C. 1993. *On the Boundary Between Mereology and Topology*. Istituto per la Ricerca Scientifica e Tecnologica.

Varzi, Achille C. 1996. "Parts, Wholes, and Part-Whole Relations: the Prospects of Mereotopology." *Data & Knowledge Engineering* 20 (3): 259–286.

Varzi, Achille. "Mereology." *The Stanford Encyclopedia of Philosophy* (Spring 2019 Edition), edited by Edward N. Zalta. https://plato.stanford.edu/archives/spr2019/entries/mereology/

Ward, Jonathan Stuart, and Adam Barker. 2013. "Undefined by Data: A Survey of Big Data Definitions." arXiv preprint arXiv:1309.5821.

Weisstein, Eric W. 2002. "Cantor-Dedekind Axiom." *From MathWorld-A Wolfram Web Resource*. http://mathworld.wolfram.com/Cantor-DedekindAxiom.html.

Wolfram, Stephen. 1984. "Computation Theory of Cellular Automata." *Communications in Mathematical Physics* 96 (1): 15–57.

Wolfram, Stephen. 1986. *Theory and Applications of Cellular Automata: Including Selected Papers 1983–1986*. World Scientific.

Wolfram, Stephen. 2003. *A New Kind of Science*. Champaign, IL: Wolfram Media.

Yao, Y. Y. 2000. "Granular Computing: Basic Issues and Possible Solutions." In *Proceedings of the 5th Joint Conference on Information Sciences*, Vol. 1.

Zadeh, Lotfi A. 1998. "Roles of Soft Computing and Fuzzy Logic in the Conception, Design and Deployment of Information/Intelligent Systems." In *Computational Intelligence: Soft Computing and Fuzzy-Neuro Integration with Applications*, 1–9. Berlin, Heidelberg: Springer.

2 Discrete public space

A new degree of complexity

Michael Batty provides a recursive definition of what a complex system is: "a system that is composed of complex systems" (Batty 2007:2). Batty explains that complex systems can never be accurately defined. Part of this is due to the fact that, when applying a high degree of accuracy in calculating the complexity of cities, we incur an almost unmanageable number of values and parameters to control simultaneously that result in a very large number of possible outcomes. This idea is represented by the formula

$$C = \sum_{k=1}^{n} (n!/ k!(n-k)!)$$

where C indicates the degree of variety in the system with (n) number of components relating to a number of possible states (Batty 2007:8). Batty applies this to the case of London, where with almost five million buildings, the number of possible combinations of urban forms/configurations is significantly large, and many orders of magnitude greater than the 10^{69} atoms in the universe" (Batty 2007:9), that is larger than: 1 000 000 000 000 000 000 000 000 000 000 000 000 000 000 000 000 000 000 000 000 000. The level of complexity which characterises urban environments today is underpinned by this "combinatorial explosion" (Batty 2007:9). The only way to deal with such complexity is through the increasing computation power of machines. Due to the elevated complexity of some urban systems, the process of calculating variable and possible configurations in their systems becomes so sophisticated that the individuals designing and controlling those processes need to apply a certain degree of trust in the system they create. In Chapter 3, we see how a mathematical-based algorithm is designed in the first instance to address certain problems or tasks. The algorithm is then implemented into a scripted series of instructions (a programme) for a machine to compute. We can control the set of rules that the machine will run, predicting the results within a range of acceptable values. However, quite often the operation that we ask the computer to process results in so complex a set of outcomes that we necessarily need to skip parts of the procedure, losing control of the process as a whole, while grasping only certain selected parts. In other words, we input all the instruction and data into the machine and we expect certain results to be outputted as result. We rely so much in this method that we attribute a certain level of trust to the machine in finding the results we are after. Mario Carpo defines this approach by suggesting that "computers can now predict things that science cannot explain" (Carpo 2017:94). This prediction works through a process of modelling. The programme employs a range of simplified instructions, shortcuts and mathematical operations to reduce the computation work. This means utilising less memory resources, shorter computation time and optimised results. Most of these models establish a system of cause and effect relationships within the environment in which they operate, comparing and interpolating data. They generate abstract representations and simulations of the environment, recursively selecting the relevant data to process, and repeat the loops until the correct value is found. These models are in a way simpler than the complexity of the environment they occupy yet they capture all the relevant parameters for the task assigned. Such programmes can function properly (monitor, take control, predict certain states of the environment, etc.) because they operate in the simplified reality that they created as a representation (Johnson 2016:19). While instructing programmes to run the complex operations for us, we trust the results, yet with the awareness that the models on which they are based can be fallacious. "Models don't have to be true in any objective sense, as long as they are useful" (Johnson 2016:19). We temporarily suspend our scientific rigorous view while the programme is running through its models, to reactivate it in the objection of the results.

Urban environments are now what Kaufmann defined as System Class IV (Kaufmann 1993). Whereby systems of Class I, II and III are characterised by static configurations based on nodes and interactions, Class IV are complex adaptive systems (De Roo and Hillier 2016:135). Digital cities are today a strong example of Class IV systems. These systems present dual qualities: they are robust (in the resilience and persistence of the built environment) and flexible (in adopting new technologies and embracing them throughout) at the same time (De Roo and Hillier 2016:135). Although they have significantly increased the degree of their complexity, digital cities are extremely adaptable. Not only do they embrace any technological changes both from the top-down (at the governmental level for example) and bottom-up (e.g. through the individuals who buy into new technologies), but also they self-organise in order to maintain a certain level of balance (De Roo and Hillier 2016:135). Cities as a whole change with their environment. As the environment evolves into a hybrid form of physical and digital, cities mutate with it in a process of co-evolution (De Roo and Hillier 2016:135). This form of adaptive evolution is depicted by the passage of cities from being purely driven by work, function and optimisation (cities a machines) to cities as adaptable entities that, by embracing the new complexities, evolve around and within their own environment (cities as organisms) (Batty 2012a:9).

A powerful method to work with this complexity is the one based on the use of Cellular Automata (CA) and agent-based modelling system (ABS) elaborated by Batty (2007). As described in Chapter 1, Cellular Automata is based on the idea that a system can be considered a series of discrete cells where the interactions amongst neighbouring cells become fundamental. Batty represents the physical and spatial structure of the environment through cells and the individuals moving around the city as agents (Batty 2007:6). Like buildings, compounds or parks, the cells are considered fixed in their location, so their proximity and the elements that neighbour them are a fundamental part of the environment. Individuals are considered as the moving cells in the system that are free to go in any part of the environment (Batty 2007:7), producing the dynamics and the indeterminacy that characterises the city from the bottom-up.

The fact that Batty and other planners and scholars have been using sophisticated algorithms and systems like cellular automata or fractals (Batty 2013:247) to analyse the complexity of urban environments, simulate their growth and study patterns of behaviour is testimony to the convergence of the discrete logic in mathematics and computer sciences and the new complexity of the built environment. The more cities become complex, the more the digital logic percolates into the system. This argument is partially recursive, for one of the factors of the increase of the complexity is the creeping of digital technologies into every aspect of the environment. We know that cities are more complex today because we have more accurate tools to measure their complexity. Since we discover more complexity, we need to develop and employ new and more sophisticated tools that enable us to deal with such complexity. The more we deploy new tools (agents) in the environment, the more we contribute to the development of the Internet of Things, and the fusion of the physical with the digital dimension of reality.

An updated notion of time

One of the big changes that the discrete and digital logic brought to the study and design of cities is an updated understanding of time. The timescale of urban design and development is not comparable to the near real-time changes that characterise the combination of the digital and the physical environments. On the one hand, we have traditional urban design processes, whereby not only does the design happen in the future, considering the impact of a proposal for its existing, context, future developments and improvements of a certain area and a sort of vision (again, placed somewhere in a future time), but also the entire process includes a number of necessary steps to ensure that the implementation of these goals is successful. This includes several prototypes and tests that guarantee the quality of the proposal, a series of consultations (with experts, local communities and stakeholders in general) and different levels of approvals by public and statutory bodies. The traditional planning and urban design process has a timescale of ten to fifty years, with some developments that range from one to five years in general terms. Within these activities, small changes, adjustments or routines are not included (Batty 2012b:193). The new digital and discrete environment embeds short-term changes, small adaptations and routines as an integral part. The new environment embraces continuous adaptations and small adjustments for several reasons. The first is that the accuracy and the granularity in sensing the city is greater than ever before. Cities are able to be sensible to the smallest alternation of trends and routines, and are equipped with enough technology to react quickly to them. The second reason is the nature of the machine-driven approach to the environment. Machines have objectives and are empowered to operate all the necessary changes to the system in order to achieve their goals. Quick fixes and timely adjustments are characteristics of the proactive that machines have. Because of their iterative nature, before doing any small change to the environment, they run an extensive number of simulations evaluating the different possible outcomes. The final action is determined by the outcome that is closer to the goal set at the beginning of the process. Machines and, by extension, the Internet of Things need to operate small changes, consider routines and intervene to continuously improve the parameters of the environment in which they are working.

The third reason is the speed of processing that characterises computers. Machines are notoriously fast (and increasingly faster) in computing repetitive and long calculations that can be difficult and challenging for the human brain. Whereas people find almost natural the activity of strategically planning, considering a number of factors, variable and possible outcomes at the same time to coalesce into one final solution, computers are able to do none of this. Following their computational logic, machines simply follow a script, whereby a pre-set range of values (and possible scenarios) are routinely tested until the outcome is the closest to the desired (Johnson 2016:164). Simplifying, whereas the human brain carefully looks for a solution (often taking the necessary time), computers work through continuous approximation of the outcomes until their pre-set criteria are satisfied.

In the discrete city, time is denser, for it is appreciated in all its infinitesimal variations that are unnatural to the human brain (and traditional planning) but reflect the very basic functions of computers, where repetition, speed and continue incremental adaptations supersede carefully thought and future-facing planning.

The production of space

This section reflects on the extent to which the nature of space is changing in the discrete city. Before the percolation of the digital logic through the built environment, architectural space in cities was created by buildings with their physical characteristics: arcades, setbacks or protrusions, urban elements like squares, streets, avenues or alleys, in conjunction with the topography and other territorial elements (mountains, rivers, coastlines, etc.). The spatial dimension of the built environment emerged as the combination of the physical characteristics of the urban (tangible) elements, with their position, size, orientation, proportion and mutual distance. This space was the direct consequence of human choice: in the work of architects and planners, and use: where people use these spaces over time adapting them according to their needs and preferences. This space was chiefly the production of human activities over time.

The new invisible layer of information brought by ubiquitous computing generates a new background which continuously evolves. Everything else in the urban environment, this background of communication, information movement and continuous processing, was considered in the first instance as the consequence of human activities and under people's utter control (Thrift and French 2002:309). However, as the result of the increasing number of studies on the mechanisms that underpin the functioning of this information background, we are now aware that part of this space is produced automatically (Thrift and French 2002). By increasing the number of automated processing functions that computers operate to replace human labour in onerous, complex and repetitive tasks, software is today designed to modify the environment in an active fashion. There are three main positions that help to examine how computers produce space without the direct human intervention.

The first is provided by Rob Kitchin and Martin Dodge (2011) with their work on the *transduction of space*. This is presented as the latest evolutionary step in the understanding of space. Within several possible interpretations, including an implicit backdrop with specific characteristics where events take place, an absolute ontology, and space as relational entity (Kitchin and Dodge 2011:66–67), the becoming of space seems to emerge. In fact, the previous considerations of space are based on the assumption that space is already produced when it can be studied. The analysis of its characteristics during its making was not contemplated. Rather, space is in continuous production (Doel 1999) and is "always in the process of becoming [and] taking place" (Kitchin and Dodge 2011:68). In here, space emerges as a result of individuals' actions (2011:68) and it is presented as a dynamic production that: "engenders . . . a spatiality that can never be static, but emerges, varying over time, and across people and context" (Kitchin and Dodge 2011:69). In the attempt of defining this active production of space, they introduced the notion of transduction as: "the constant making anew of domain in reiterative and transformative practices" (Kitchin and Dodge 2011:16). The term transduction has a Latin origin and is the combination of the prefix *trans* (across) and verb *ducere* (to lead) meaning leading/bringing (something) across/beyond (something else). This term suggests then that space is continuously led across or along human activities as their actions in the environment unfold.

The second is the idea of code/space. For Kitchin and Dodge, code/space is the description of the state that occurs when "software and the spatiality of every life become mutually constituted, that is, produced through one another" (Kitchin and Dodge 2011:16). From this perspective, space is the product of the code, and the primary task of the latter is to generate a particular spatiality (Kitchin and Dodge 2011:16). These two elements are so connected to each other that: "the space cannot function without the information and there is no uncoded, manual alternative" (Crang and Graham 2007:794). Software (or code in Kitchin and Dodge's terms) generates space, yet this relation is highly dependent on the context in which they operate, on the human activities taking place and the nature of the relations among all the agencies involved (Kitchin and Dodge 2011:18). It is relevant to note that the software has a determinist nature, for it is based on a system of organised instructions designed to determine a certain goal or result. A simple programme designed to run inside a computer might function in purely determinist terms, whereby a series of inputs corresponds to a series of computed outputs (e.g. input = sum 3 + 5 would always give the output = 8). However, when computers need to operate in the built environment, they necessarily need to include a large number of variables, including human interactions. These computers run significantly more sophisticated programmes that allow for a certain degree of indeterminacy and causality. This results in the fact that the same input will not necessarily correspond to the same output, since the variables play a significant role in the system. "Code/space unfolds in multifarious and imperfect ways, embodied through the performance and often the unpredictable interactions of the people within the space (between people and between people and code")" (Kitchin and Dodge 2011:18).

The third point concerns the automatic production of space that Nigel Thrift elaborated in terms of the impact of technology on the practice of space-making through the idea of *technological unconscious* (Thrift 2004): a "means of sustaining presence which we cannot access but which clearly has effects, a technical substrate of unconscious meaning and activity" (Thrift and French 2002:312). Drawing from Clough (2000), Thrift relates the growing need of high performance that characterises urban infrastructures today to the reliable repetitiveness, considered in positive terms as an achievement (Thrift 2004:177). An accurate knowledge of sequence in processes, routines, organisation and repetition allows for a trusted unconscious, whereby people will devolve laborious and time-consuming tasks to machines. The essence of the technological unconscious is defined as the: "bending of bodies-with-environments to a specific set of addresses without the benefit of any cognitive inputs, a prepersonal substrate of guaranteed correlations, assured encounters, and therefore unconsidered anticipations" (Thrift 2004:177). Moreover, software transforms space from un-coded to machine-readable, and "work to maintain that transformation through an ongoing set of contingent and relational processes" (Kitchin and Dodge 2011:72). Whilst the growing complexity of urban activities requires an organised and reliable automation where people suspend their consciousness of the process in trust of technology, such technologies, in the form of software, operate in a continuous state of change. As the relationship between code and the produced space is in a continuous evolution, the ways in which they mutually operate "alters as one passes through coded assemblages" (Kitchin and Dodge 2011:74). We can therefore infer that software actively and autonomously modifies the context in which they operate, namely the built environment, by the nature of the code/space relationship.

Summarising, space is produced in its becoming, as the result of the unfolding of human activities and their relationships with the environment. Secondly, space is intimately fused with code (software) and ubiquitous computing in general terms. Thirdly, software works, by its nature, by automation of processes, iteration and repetitive tests until the final goal of the script is reached. If software is embedded in all aspects of the everyday life, it inevitably produces space without direct human control, and it does so seamlessly and continuously as human activities unroll. Thrift and French suggest that the automation of space production might be considered as an epochal event (Thrift and French 2002:329). By embracing the active role of code and software in the making of the built environment, we should consider the idea that they are operating a "fundamental reorganisation of the environment, a vast system of distributed cognition through which the environment increasingly thinks for itself, an extra layer of thinking" (Thrift and French 2002:329). In this scenario, the environment would no longer be the result of the interaction between human activities and the world. It would rather become part of a new form of entity, whereby humans and software (read machines) contribute to the continuous making and adaptation of the environment. Further elaborating this concept, as the presence and influence of software are ubiquitous, they are, by this extent, the environment itself. If software is the environment and it autonomously produces a type of space which is in continuous development, humans share this production with the software/environment itself. In this new definition, the spatiality of the discrete world is the result of the combination of human and software activities which are constantly produced in its making.

Digital infrastructures

With the advance of digital technologies, the majority of urban infrastructures have been significantly influenced by new technological systems. If not changing completely their nature from analogue to digital, the majority of them have started incorporating monitoring and controlling devices based on digital systems. For years, the physical and the digital dimensions of the built environment have been considered in a sort of conflictive relationship, whereby the digital one was gradually superseding or substituting the physical infrastructure in a scenario where the physical city was doomed to be dematerialised in a possible future (Graham and Marvin 2002b:243). However, with the progresses made by digital technologies and the spread of digital systems in cities around the world, we soon learned that the two are to be considered complementary to each other (Graham and Marvin 2002b:256). Their relationship is complex and characterised by a number of variables and factors in continuous change, so the two dimensions have an evolving co-existence. The city has been described today as an amalgam of urban places and electronic spaces (Graham and Marvin 2002b:379), whereby the urban life of our cities is shaped by the interaction between the physical presence of objects (and people) and the interaction in electronic spaces. Any physical presence in the urban environment appears to have a counterpart in the digital realm so much that this relation seems to define contemporary urbanism (Graham and Marvin 2002b:379).

However, urbanism in the digital city is also characterised by a certain degree of fragmentation. This is experienced by people in the urban context as the consequence of the way the various infrastructures are deployed and ramified in the environment. This approach has been defined as Splintering Urbanism by Steven Graham and Simon Marvin: "Splintering Urbanism . . . reveals how new technologies and increasingly privatised systems of infrastructure provision – telecommunications, highways, urban streets, energy and water – are supporting the splintering of metropolitan areas across the world" (Graham and Marvin 2002a:iii).

One of the examples is the Wi-Fi network that establishes invisible boundaries within the reach of its signals. These areas represent watersheds whereby people are either inside the coverage with access to information through the Internet, or outside, where they may be considered isolated from the Internet of Things. This can happen at the scale of the public space, in a square, a coffee shop or a train station, or at a more intimate scale, for instance between devices used by the same person, like mobile phone and laptop or even keyboard and desktop (Mackenzie 2010:6) At times, Wi-Fi networks can become unreliable, uneven and patchy (Mackenzie 2010:3). This tendency to experience irregular access to information through Wi-Fi Internet connection is defined by Mackenzie as Wirelessness as something that: "designates an experience trending towards entanglements with things, objects, gadgets, infrastructures, and services, and imbued with indistinct sensations and practices of network-associated change" (Mackenzie 2010:6).

Pervasive computing

If machines are virtually everywhere, and their reach extends across the world, we can describe this through the notion of ubiquitous computing or pervasive computing (Cuff 2003) or "everyware" (Greenfield 2010). There are a number of significant aspects that this phenomenon brings to the built environment that are discussed in this section.

The first aspect is that the dichotomy of virtual and physical loses its raison d'être, for the digital realm is no longer simply overlapped or over-imposed onto the physical world (like in the case of a virtual reality scenario) but the two dimensions are inextricably fused together. This means that the digital world brings its qualities with it. Aspects like interactiveness, real-time updates, the presence of agents that collect information and autonomously react to it are just some examples (Kang and Cuff 2005:94–95). The new built environment (an indistinguishable combination of physical and digital) is enabled with sensing capabilities, responsiveness and the ability to geo-locate any object or person in any part of the world with great accuracy. This property would be a direct application of the Internet's unique addressing system like URLs for online contents and the TCP IP protocol for messages. This new environment is therefore enacted, which corresponds to some sort of new version of the physical environment updated as a "potential source of coordinated, interdependent actions and reactions" (Cuff 2003:43). Dana Cuff describes this as *cyborg*: a spatial embodied computing system, in opposition to the cyberspace (considered as simply digital environment) where all elements are dematerialised (Cuff 2003:44). As reality is somehow augmented, and the potentialities at people's disposal are increased, in this new environment humans utilise agencies of themselves. In doing so, people experience a new empowerment of their ability to interact with the environment: "not only do the walls have ears, but networks of eyes, brains, and data banks to use for purposeful actions" (Cuff 2003:44). If the urban environment can empower us in carrying on our most mundane activities (walking, commuting, shopping, driving, etc.), the relationship is somewhat mutual. People can interact with the built environment by enhancing it, participating in its making and contributing to the data collection and monitoring carried out by the agents. "We can be complicit with the sidewalks, rejected or embraced by a park, bombarded in the street with advertisements" (Cuff 2003:45).

Conditions for the Internet of Things to become pervasive are that the Internet is ubiquitous, embedded and animated (Kang and Cuff 2005:94). While using the term "ubiquitous" the reference is not on the omni-presence of the physical devices in the built environment. It is rather about their potential reach on the one hand and about the access to information that can virtually happen from everywhere through them on the other hand. In the first instance, consider the limitation of a single technology, for example a street camera, with grey areas outside of the camera reach, poor light conditions and visibility problems, possible failures, maintenance, etc. However, if the street camera is combined with satellite images, LiDar (Light Detection and Ranging) technology, sensors, microphones, beacons and all these are constantly exchanging information with cloud and Internet-based trackers that monitor, log and store any activity in space and time and the overall results are then systematically considered with a large database, the ubiquity becomes almost inevitable. The same system can be somewhat used in the opposite direction, whereby an individual can access this wealth of information through one of the devices above listed. In other words, anybody from any part of the world could potentially access any type of information about anything (in the past and present), provided that he/she has an Internet connection. This is obviously an optimistic forecast, as currently Internet access is not really ubiquitous and many factors influence its success, including blind spots not covered by the 3G/4G or Wi-Fi networks, isolated areas, such as areas enclosed in concrete or metal that prevent signals from being received, or reasons related to the way telecommunication companies operate within the global context, whereby access to data through mobile devices is subject to fees that vary according to country or simply some services are not offered in some parts of the world. Nevertheless, the Internet can be considered ubiquitous even today as the infrastructure allows for this and the scale and extent of its reach is truly global.

The Internet can be embedded into practically anything: in cars, building components like walls, facades, or even in wearable items (watches, key fobs, hats, clothing, etc.). More extremely, it can be embedded in food, or even in human bodies. The Internet is no longer contained in the environment, it has become an integral part of it (Kang and Cuff 2005:97). Weiser and Brown (1996) describe the evolution of the relationship user – computer in four steps. From the era of mainframe computers, where several expert individuals used the same computer, as the complexity of it required a combination of different expertise, we pass to the advent of the Personal Computer (PC), where one individual (not necessarily technology-savvy) owned and used one computer. The third step is represented by the widespread use of the Internet, where that information that was previously stored in individual machines, it is all of a sudden shared and distributed through several computers over the Internet. The last evolutionary step is the ubiquitous computing era, where we

> have lots of computers sharing each of us. Some of these computers will be the hundreds we may access in the course of a few minutes of Internet browsing. Others will be imbedded in walls, chairs, clothing, light switches, cars – in everything.
>
> (Weiser and Brown 1996:2)

The last aspect that qualifies the pervasive computing in the cyburg is the quality of being animated. This means that those elements with computational power are equipped and designed in such a way that they are able to interpret their surrounding and react to it, by responding to external inputs. They can detect any variation of values in a context they are able to measure and monitor and intervene when a specific condition has been met. In this regard, what Kang and Cuff have imagined and suggested in 2005 was "networks of miniaturized, wirelessly interconnected, sensing, processing, and actuating computing elements kneaded into the physical world" (Kang and Cuff 2005:99).

A significant consequence of the spreading of ubiquitous computing technologies is that not only data, but the processing is becoming an integral part of the built environment (Crang and Graham 2007). "Everyware is information processing embedded in the objects and surfaces of everyday life" (Greenfield 2010:18). Through computers' processing, machines acquire an active part in the making of the environment and the influence on people's behaviour in it (Greenfield 2010:26). This represents a significant leap forward with regards to a passive approach whereby computers are limited to responding to the user's inquiries or simply log pre-set data from their context. Crang and Graham (2007) suggest four ways in which the environment becomes animated (i.e. responsive) through hidden computing systems routinely working in the background of every human and urban activity. One is the enacting space described by Dana Cuff in her narrative of the cyburg, whereby the environment is equipped with such technology that enables it to the context-aware and react to it accordingly. The second one is Kitchin and Dodge's transduction space, where the spatial dimension of the environment is produced while it is being used. This concept is further elaborated in Chapter 5. The third way is Julian Bleecker's blogjet space: the space produced by an "object that blogs" in the physical environment interacting with the digital realm. This is covered in Chapter 3. The fourth way is the augmented space. This is considered as the evolution of the simple virtual reality. Whereas the latter can be seen as the overlay of pre-designed digital information (mostly in graphic form: video, texts, animations), the former includes real-time data, the combination of multiple forms of access and the personalisation of the experience to the individual (Crang and Graham 2007).

In this, cities are significantly transformed by the ubiquitous presence of code. "The modern city exists as a haze of software instructions" (Amin and Thrift 2002:125). In being pervasive, the Internet of Things radically transforms not only the intimate nature of the environment, which is characterised now by a combination of physical and digital qualities, but also the relationship between individuals and the environment itself. People communicate with the environment and through it, they exchange information both willingly and often unconsciously, directly and passively. People contribute to the making of the environment and its continuous adaptation and refinement. Conversely, the environment is pervasively present in each individual's life, percolating into the individual dimension (e.g. self-monitoring and tracking), and in the social sphere. In Anne Galloway's words: "when everyday life is understood in terms of specialization, temporalization, and embodiment, ubiquitous computing offers a unique opportunity to evaluate the 'relational' as flows, intensities and transductions that mobilize sociotechnical assemblages" (Galloway 2004:405).

Ambience intelligence and intelligent agents

If computers are everywhere, their computational reach is virtually ubiquitous. The objects existing within this digital environment have similar characteristics to the systems that created and contain them. The very idea of ubiquitous computing in terms of everyware relies on the presence of objects, where the Internet is not exclusively everywhere, but rather "in every thing" (Greenfield 2010:11). Digital objects are, by their nature, disassembled and scattered around the (digital) world. Digital objects are made of information and, as such, are everywhere. Physical objects, on the other hand, that belong to the Internet of Things contain some sort of computational capacity in them. This makes them able to connect to other devices via the Internet to process their tasks. These objects are partially physical and, to some extent, virtual. This means that they are in a hybrid state, whereby some of their components are physically located in a specific place, and other parts are mobile, with strings of codes distributed in several servers across the world and activated as the task requires. Some of these objects are collectors of data (e.g. sensors or cameras), some others are triggers of distributed processes (e.g. movement or temperature sensors). However, it is important to note that the real extent of these objects exceeds their physical dimension, for their other components are scattered through the Internet and several servers. Internet of Things objects are not definable exclusively through their physical extent, but they are better qualifiable as agents of larger processes that take place in a disperse and globally distributed environment. These agents result in "a world of ambient intelligence, happening around us on the periphery of our awareness, where our environment is not a passive backdrop but an active agent in organising daily lives" (Crang and Graham 2007:789). These objects have been otherwise defined as amplified objects (Galloway 2004:390), where the (physical) object does not change its physical properties yet embeds the new qualities coming from the digital dimension. Galloway makes an interesting distinction between the role of an amplified object and virtual objects in virtual reality with regards to the flow of information. In the latter, the user is in control of the information, whilst in the case of the amplified reality, the object is in control of the flow of information about the user and the environment. (Galloway 2004:390).

Within the context of this book, we will consider the definition of intelligent agent given by Wooldridge and Jennings (1995:116–17). This definition is probably the most common and accepted across computer science and urban informatics. An agent is defined as a piece (or more) of hardware and/or software-based computer system that is characterised by: (a) a certain autonomy (it operates without the direct control of humans or other agents and it has certain control over the latter), (b) social ability (the agent communicates with other agents and humans through an agent communication language), (c) reactivity (the agent is context-aware and able to gather input from the physical environment, humans through computer interfaces, other agents, the Internet, etc. and react timely to them as response) and (d) pro-activeness (in addition to responding to external inputs, an agent is able to take initiative in order to pursue certain goals and tasks as per instructions) (Wooldridge and Jennings 1995:116). To this definition, Wooldridge and Jennings (1995:117) add that there may be stronger notion of agency whereby the agent includes traits of human behaviour, such as knowledge, belief, intention, decisions, capabilities, choices, commitments and obligation (Shoham 1993) or even emotional states (Bates 1994). Moreover, Wooldridge and Jennings include the following extra assumptions that characterise a computer-based agent (Wooldridge and Jennings 1995:117):

- Mobility: an agent is able to move around the digital environment.
- Veracity: by its programmed nature, an agent will always return accurate information as output of its processing. In other words, it has not the ability to communicate false information or data on purpose.
- Benevolence: an agent does not have conflicting goals; hence it will process as instructed.
- Rationality: an agent will always process information merely to achieve the goals that have been set for it. It will take the most rational decision in any given situation to achieve the goal.

Considered all together, for Wooldridge and Jennings these characteristics make an agent (which, as such, acts on behalf of humans or some other agent) intelligent, for it has instructions that enable it to gather information and analyse it, evaluate different options and scenarios and eventually take decisions in order to solve a problem, process as instructed or to achieve a predetermined goal.

Intelligent agents are increasingly everywhere. Amongst many other uses, they are largely employed in establishing new geographies through generating updated, real-time and interactive mappings of the world and of human activities, with a particular focus on urban environments. Cars represent a clear example of moving agents in the urban environment where multi-technologies (including motion sensors, ultrasonic sensors, radar sensors, GPS, omnidirectional cameras and Lidar technology) are combined into sophisticated kits that not only provide drivers with useful information on the street, but they continuously scan the city, gathering differing sets of urban data (Mattern 2017), including people's behaviour in the public space (cf. Chapter 3). As a part of the Internet of Things, these agents operate as appendices in a global network of data and information, establishing a sort of interface with the physical world. Mounted on cars, integral parts of building facades or strapped on urban furniture (Chapter 3), these agents are becoming a standard component of all elements in the built environment. It is interesting to consider that the majority of these new maps currently being built and continuously updated and improved by these agents are made for and by machines (Mattern 2017). They have been programmed with the aim of gathering certain sets of data: monitoring atmospheric values (e.g. pollution, noise or humidity levels), analysing urban performances (traffic congestions at a particular crossroad) and monitoring people's behaviours (speed cameras in motorways, crowd control in tube stations, etc.). Their ultimate goal is to provide sufficient data to increase efficiency, monitor performances, reduce crime or support people in their daily activities (for example suggesting driving directions to destinations). By their very nature, agents will solely do this, duly processing their scripts and returning the results as instructed. Following this logic, we should not substitute the plethora of other mapping and investigative methods we developed so far to study the built environment. Shannon Mattern (2017) suggests that: "Ideally, we should balance or juxtapose different modes of knowledge and production: Western scientific and indigenous epistemologies, human and other-species ontologies, mechanical and organic means of experiencing and representing place, cartographic rationalism and empiricism, projection and retrospection".

This leads to the importance of being able to qualify the ambient in which all these agents operate. Malcolm McCullough (2013) provides a series of characteristics to define the notion of ambient in which the embodied information proliferates. For him, the notion of ambient is a complex and multifaceted one. However, he suggests twelve ways of understanding it that include what "that which surrounds but does not distract", the "rampant availability of opportunities to shift attention", a "persistent layer of messages for somebody else", what is "no longer a luxury, but both a necessity and a nuisance", "an emergent effect of embodied interaction design", "an environment replete with non-things", the "semantic information, made more cognitively accessible", an "intrinsic (environmental) information, enlivened by mediation", what is "cognitively unobtrusive media covering the cognitively restorative world", a "change in the nature of distraction", "a new sensibility and not the recovery of some lost sensuality!", and "a continuum awareness and an awareness of continuum" (McCullough 2013:18).

The first suggestion on the list is possibly the more relevant in this context. Ambient is something always running in the background of our activities that does not directly interfere with them. It is something referable to the notion of periphery suggested by Weiser and Brown in their analysis of the calm technology (Weiser and Brown 1996). McCullough adds that important characteristics of the ambient are the question of attention which, in an age of unprecedented distraction (2013:49) poses new challenges for individuals. An example is walking through the city while using a mobile device and interacting with the built environment (and people in it) at the same time. McCullough suggests that "you might wonder just what it is that can be divided (in terms of attention) so acceptably, appealed to so relentlessly, or dissociated from physical context so universally by today's communication media" (2013:48). In such a scenario, one of the keys to maintain attention in a given situation is the notion of embodiment, with embodied knowledge or embodied skills or, in general terms, embodied cognition (2013:69). In looking at the work of Andy Clark (1998), McCullough expands on the idea that our brain works faster and easier if it does not have to recall all elements from memory in a given situation. By rather using pattern recognition techniques, for example embedding knowledge as opposed to retrieving from memory, the brain would react quickly and with less effort to the situation. Clark (1998:83) illustrates the radical shift from the interpretation of the brain's work as intended in classical cognitivism to that suggested in the artificial neural network. Memory passes from being considered as "retrieval from a stored symbolic database, to memory as pattern recreation; the problem solving as logical inference becomes problem solving as pattern completion and pattern transformation; cognition as centralized becomes cognition as increasingly decentralized". Moreover, "the environment is intended as an active resource whose intrinsic dynamics can play important problem-solving roles, and the own body becomes as part of the computational loop" (Clark 1998:83–84).

One of the consequences of pervasive technologies is what has been defined as calm technology (Weiser and Brown 1996). Mark Weiser and John Seely Brown addressed the need to reflect on human relationships in a period radically transformed by the increasing presence of computing technologies everywhere (ubiquitous computing). In so doing, they elaborated the idea of a calm technology in opposition to the frenetic pace often resulting from the extensive use of technology itself: "Pagers, cellphones, newservices, the World-Wide-Web, email, TV, and radio bombard us frenetically. Can we really look to technology itself for a solution?" (Weiser and Brown 1996:1. Designing calm technology). Central to this idea is the distinction between the periphery and the centre of our attention in any human activity. While driving a car, for example, using the car is most likely to be at the centre of our attention as the main focus, whilst music and noises in the background, passers-by, building facades or the sound of the engine are in the periphery of our attention. Weiser and Brown hold that technology (as any other element in a given environment) can easily move from the periphery to the centre and vice versa: "Calm technology engages both the center and the periphery of our attention, and in fact moves back and forth between the two" (Weiser and Brown 1996:2). This continuous shifting from the periphery to the centre is encalming in both directions. When moving elements from the centre outwards, our brain is able to contain more peripheral items at the same time while focusing more on the fewer left in the centre, without overburdening. On the other hand, when we decide to bring to the centre items from the periphery, we can retake control of them, empowering the brain to process a particular item (Weiser and Brown 1996:2). More specifically, the notion of calm technology hinges on the idea of coping with the increasing amount of data and information resulting from ubiquitous technologies, by incrementing the amount of information in our peripheral attuning. This would not only empower each individual's capacity of being aware of different items at the same time (the example given by Weiser and Brown is the video conference as opposed to the teleconference) but, more importantly, it would result in a calmer attitude to technology (Weiser and Brown 1996:7). If digital technologies are so ubiquitous and embedded in our daily lives, they would gradually fade out until they disappear in the background and will be taken for granted, like electricity or other consolidated ubiquitous technologies (Weiser and Brown 1996:2).

The cloud

While looking at a generic streetscape, what can be directly seen is only a portion of what the real human activities are. A significant part of human and machine's communications and activities are happening through data in a new displaced urban and global geography. The cloud becomes the realm where such activities take place.

In layman's terms, the cloud is often presented as an abstract place where data are stored, and from which they are immediately retrieved at any time. By this notion of the cloud, data are virtually infinite in number and volume due to the unlimited capacity of their virtual container. The cloud is invisible and ineffable, constituted by no physical elements. A more realistic and accurate definition is provided by Peter Mell and Tim Grance (2011) whereby cloud computing can be intended as: "a model for enabling ubiquitous, convenient, on-demand network access to a shared pool of configurable computing resources (e.g. networks, servers, storage, applications and services) that can be rapidly provisioned and released with minimal management effort or service provider interaction" (Mell and Grance 2011:3). Benjamin Bratton (2016) provides another relevant definition as: "a terraforming project, covering the globe in subterranean wires and switches and overhead satellite arrays, simultaneously centralizing and decentralizing computing and data storage and the social relations that depend on them" (Bratton 2016:115–16). The cloud is not a single entity, but rather a useful model to describe a combination of technologies and resources based on the idea of dislocation. Such resources should be considered physical on three levels. The first one is due to the fact that data are stored in physical objects such as servers, hard disks, hard drives, etc. and processed by physical machines, to be then sent back to laptops, desktops and mobile devices of any sort. When considering the Internet mechanisms, this principle follows the idea of the materiality of routing (Dourish 2017). The second reason is related to the microscopic nature that characterised data. In order to be stored (or indeed to physically exist), data have to be expressed in a digital form, namely in a series of 0s and 1s at the machine code. A read/write head that moves around the platter of the hard disk is able to read the orientation of each of the magnetised areas into which a disk in a hard drive is divided. Each orientation corresponds to 0s and 1s (magnetised is a 1 and de-magnetised is a 0), so the head is able to read every single datum. The number of atoms necessary to store a bit of information varies significantly depending on the technology used. In the traditional and widespread commercial hard drives, around 1 million atoms are necessary to store 1 bit (Gibney 2017), whereas advanced experiments have

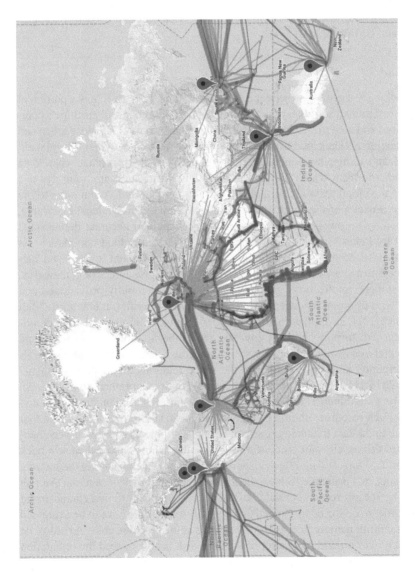

Figure 2.1 Map of the Amazon Web Services (AWS) regional data centres and global connections

Source: http://turnkeylinux.github.io/aws-datacenters/

resulted in 12 atoms per bit (Loth et al. 2012), and even in 1 atom per bit (Natterer et al. 2017). To exist, data require a physical space, albeit at the atomic scale. The third reason why a system of data should be regarded as something with physical qualities is the fact that data are organised in databases, folders, columns and rows following highly organised patterns of spatial configuration (Drepper 2007). If we consider the atomic volume of data, we can understand how large datasets and their communication across different platforms and devices constitute a certain use of space with physical characteristics.

At the macro level, the cloud includes relatively large physical spaces that communicate continuously through very large distances. The programmes that regulate the functioning of the cloud are distributed around the world through servers and data centres. Some parts, data or partial copies of them are hosted in each individual device that is connected. For example, cookies that reside in the memory of a personal computer or the client software in FTP services that partially share data with the respective server. Some part of the cloud is physically inside each device connected to it, whereas the majority is housed in data centres and the various nodes in their network. To this, we should add the growing use of material qualities that are applied to the realm of information technologies in the context of social phenomena. Characteristics like scarcity, resilience, density and durability are increasingly employed to describe social conditions (Dourish 2017:3).

Remediation

The strong binary that categorises the digital city as opposite to the physical space should be reconsidered in light of the notion of remediation. In opposition to the idea that the former is a virtual entity that lacks all physical characteristics that identify the latter, remediation is presented as a long-existing process of access to reality (through perception) by means of a specific medium. According to Bolter and Grusin (2000), the new digital technologies available today do not introduce anything new with regards to the interaction between the digital and the physical. They rather re-mediate the two environments, by re-establishing the function of media between virtual and physical. In this perspective, cyberspace

> is constituted through a series of remediations. As a digital network, cyberspace remediates the electric communications networks of the past 150 years, the telegraph and the telephone; as virtual reality, it remediates the visual space of painting, film, and television; and as social space, it remediates such historical places as cities and parks and such "nonplaces" as theme parks and shopping malls. Like other contemporary telemediated spaces, cyberspace refashions and extends earlier media, which are themselves embedded in material and social environments.
>
> (Bolter and Grusin 1999:182–83)

A new media is the opportunity to enable new relationships between the digital and the physical dimensions. A new phone app, for example, can be seen as the touch point between the two facets of the physical/digital environment, whereby the app functions as an interface.

The spatiality of software

The idea that software is directly related to the production of space or, in other words, that they have an agency in spatial practices has been extensively studied by Rob Kitchen and Martin Dodge (amongst others, Kitchin and Dodge 2005; Dodge and Kitchin 2005; Dodge, Kitchin, and Zook 2009; Kitchin and Dodge 2011). The mechanisms underpinning this agency are analysed in-depth in the following chapters (especially Chapter 3). However, it is useful at this point to discuss the extent to which software is characterised by a sort of spatiality per se, having its own unique topology. I argue that software is characterised by three interconnected aspects: it is (a) discrete in its nature; (b) geographically ubiquitous; and (c) global in its physical extension.

As the result of a systematic set of lines of code, software is inherently discrete. Put simply, a programme runs when the lines of code that compose it are executed. The programme (in this case, an interpreter) reads the lines of the script one by one, duly performing each instruction (creating variables, reading databases, renaming objects, etc.). Lines are executed one by one, with no intermediate commands in-between. In this iterative process, there is no ambiguity or ambivalence, for the programme runs every line after the other. If it encounters an error (e.g. an unclear value or a mistake in the syntax), the programme stops working. The code is run in ordered and subsequent parts, where there is no continuity but only repetition of line executions. Once one line is read and the instructions contained in it executed, the programme goes on to the next line, and so forth until the end of the script. This process describes a space that is paced by the order of the lines of the code. There is a clear sequence, and lines are numbered ascendingly. The spatiality of the code is characterised by a series of sequential lines that automatically progress from the top of the script to the bottom, whereby the number in the sequence determines the time of execution. This space is linear and ordered by a systematic set of discrete movements generated by the interpreter as it goes through the lines.

Once the code has been created, it is usually reused in different variations in different programmes by several coders. In this sense, codes are shared, generally as modules, amongst programmes and programmers. It would be practically impossible to track the origin (or indeed the entire journey) of a single line of code or module once it has been distributed through the Internet. Numerous online repositories (e.g. GitHub) allow code sharing and redistribution across the world. Moreover, the same software is usually installed in servers and personal computers worldwide. This makes it possible for the same line of code to be, possibly, everywhere in the world at the same time. Code is ubiquitous, for it is hosted in a myriad of computers in the world, and global at the same time, since it is potentially everywhere by retaining its original characteristics, with no specific mutation with regards to any locality.

Assemblages

The notion of assemblage is particularly useful in this discussion. From a socio-logical point of view, an assemblage can be intended as a kind of anti-structural description of reality that is helpful to observe phenomena like "emergence, het-erogeneity, the decentred and the ephemeral in nonetheless ordered social life" (Marcus and Saka 2006:101). Drawing from Deleuze (Deleuze and Guattari 1987) and Manuel DeLanda (2002), Marcus and Saka associated the idea of assemblage to a continuous process of unfolding space-time between two (or more) systems:

> assemblages are the causally productive (machinic) result of the intersection of two open systems, and their properties are emergent in the sense in which that concept is deployed in logic, that is, not part of, and so not foreseeable in light of, either one or the other system considered in isolation, but instead only discernible as a result of the intersection of both such systems.
>
> (Marcus and Saka 2006:103)

This idea is helpful in understanding how the three systems involved in the physi-cal/digital environment interact and produce an indiscernible result. Kitchin and Lauriault (2014) expanded this notion to the digital realm, analysing data assem-blages that are defined as: "a complex socio-technical system, composed of many apparatuses and elements that are thoroughly entwined, whose central concern is the production of a data". Data are intrinsically connected to the assemblage that characterises them, underpinned by a set of "contingent, relational and contextual discursive and material practices and relations" (Kitchin and Lauriault 2014). In this perspective, assemblages are presented as a dynamic entity, always evolv-ing and mutating, as they are based on the on-going relationships amongst open systems. The anti-structured characteristic of such a combination of systems well describes the ubiquitous dimension that underpins the tripartite physical/digital environment: individuals, software and the built environment. When taken indi-vidually, these three are describable with a clear structure, each of them very dif-ferent from the others. Individuals follow social and cultural structures, regulated by behaviour and social norms. Software is regulated by the digital logic and computing rules. The built environment is governed by a combination of laws of physics (e.g. gravity), aesthetics (perception of buildings and public spaces) and function (use of specific spaces, typologies and the notion of purpose). When assembled, individuals, software and the built environment become an indistin-guishable combination of characteristics of different nature that do not relate to each other in a direct manner. The only common ground is the fact that they are in a continuous evolution in their relationship. This becomes particularly clear when it comes to the data assemblage. The three elements of the physical/digital envi-ronment have a common purpose: the production and management of data. This occurs at different levels: individuals produce and consume data both consciously and unconsciously by carrying on their daily activities (working, consuming, entertaining themselves, etc.). Programmes are the mechanism by which data are inputted and outputted in a continuous computing process. Finally, the built environment can be seen as the container of such processes. Data are produced and consumed inside it, and it provides an overall framework for the data production and consumption to take place. Individuals are the actors, software is the mechanism and the built environment is the framework. The three entities work as an assemblage that allows the system to keep working and maintain its continuous evolution. In this sense, the data production and consumption are the main vehicles for the three entities to work seamlessly in a continuous data exchange. Data are the only common means of communication amongst the three in the physical and digital environment.

Non-lieux and place-ness

This section reconsiders two of the notions that have widely characterised the urban debates in the 1990s and 2000s: namely Augé's non lieux (Augé 1995) in light of the new knowledge we now have about the digital/physical built environment.

Originally published in 1992 as *Non-Lieux, Introduction a une anthropologie de la Surmodernité*, Marc Augé elaborated the idea that the supermodernity was the acceleration and excess of the symptoms of modernity (Oxford Reference 2018) resulting in the emergence of places that are non-anthropological:

> If a place can be defined as relational, historical and concerned with identity, then a space which cannot be defined as relational, or historical or concerned with identity will be a non-place.
>
> (Augé 1995:77–78)

Those spaces that cannot be comprised within the category of places become, by exclusion, their negative. In such a group, Augé includes urban and architectural spaces that are not completely defined, but rather in a continuous state of incompleteness. These spaces are transitional, where people stay only for short periods of time moving from a determined place to another. Amongst these are:

> the air, rail and motorway routes, the mobile cabins called means of transport (aircraft, trains and road vehicles), the airports and railway stations, hotel chains, leisure parks, large retail outlets, and finally the complex skein of cable and wireless networks that mobilize extraterrestrial space for the purposes of a communication so peculiar that it often puts the individual in contact only with another image of himself.
>
> (Augé 1995:79)

Such places are generic enough for people to avoid any attachment or real identification, neglecting them the status of places. This genericness emerges as a common aspect in the same architectural typologies across the world (Ibelings 1998). Airports, train stations or shopping centres present all a similar degree of genericness across the globe. Many scholars (e.g. Latour 1993; Thrift 1999) are somewhat in disagreement with the static view that Augé presents of these generic spaces and tried to add other layers of interpretation to this phenomenon by looking at more "relational, open, dynamic and inclusive conceptions of place" (Merriman 2011:30).

Looking more closely to these generic spaces, or *non-lieux*, we should consider that everything that concerns the transit of passengers from routing to behaviour control is governed by algorithms. These spaces are conceived and designed through software (see Chapter 3) and monitored and controlled by means of code. Let us take the three main qualities that Augé used to discern the places from non-places.

Firstly, he claimed that such spaces are not relational in that they are unable to generate the human relationships that are constantly restored and resumed over time, with the "millennial ruses of the invention of the everyday" (Augé 1995: 78–79). If we compare the experience that an individual might have by wandering around the Markt square in Delft and one of the passageways that connects the Terminal 1 to the Terminal 2 at the Barajas Airport in Madrid, Augé's point may be proven true. However, if we consider the fact that all the relationships that occur in the built environment are today transported into the digital realm, we can easily see the extent to which these spaces are highly relational. In fact, it is through a large number of algorithmic systems that airport spaces are first designed and extensively simulated, then built and continuously kept under scrutiny by machines. Algorithmic models like crowd control, pedestrian flow simulations and automatic behaviour recognition are programmed around the various types of relations that might occur among people in confined spaces. Moreover, such algorithms are intelligent, for they learn through their daily observations (see Chapter 3). The more they run, the more they acquire knowledge about how people interact in those spaces: what makes someone walk faster or slower, what changes their walking pace, what suggests to them that they stop by attracting them to a specific point of interest, how they react to specific circumstances and so forth. In places like airports, people do not establish relationships to each other, nor they do it with the environment they are in, but these relationships exist at a higher level, within the lines of the code. The other type of relationship that takes place in places like airports is the one related to the individuality of each passenger and his/her instant access to any contacts from everywhere. Through the Internet of Things and the ubiquitous Internet, any passenger can connect with friends, continue working and, more generally, continue her/his relationships independently from the physical place in which she/he is. In this scenario, it is not the place that is conducive to establish relationships, it is rather the individual who carries her/his relationships with her/him everywhere she/he goes. The physical place becomes then the moving background of these relationships. Every individual brings with her/him connections and relations to her/his own world. These are continuously cast on the physical environment as the person moves into buildings, lounges and corridors. In this new hybrid environment, the digital moves with the person and it is continuously fused with the moving physical realm. In this sense, there is no longer "reinvention of the everyday", as Augé put it, because the hierarchy between people and built environment has changed. In the paradigm to which Augé refers, individuals are considered different from the environment, in an utter dichotomous relationship. The individual is different from the environment in which she/he moves, therefore is able to establish relationships with it. Today, individuals are a constitutive part of the environment and they continuously modify it as they live in it. People join software in the agency of the new built environment.

Secondly, Augé uses the history of a place to determine whether it is a place or non-place. As seen previously in this chapter, the discrete logic that is changing our urban life has altered the notion of time. The speed of processing and the continuous adaptation of the environment to better and more performative forms is in contrast with the stratified vision of places that we used in traditional urban studies. In this latter, a place is characterised by several layers of histories, including cultures, dominations, religions, key moments in history or simply the stories of individuals living in that particular place, those of the local communities and particular episodes. Some of these layers have left a visible trace in the built environment (e.g. a celebratory statue, an honorary bench, etc.), and some others need to be unveiled by the careful work of historians. In the digital perspective, all these need to be reconsidered. Computers use databases to map information to places. Databases give the ability to cross-reference different types of information coming from different sources and pertaining to different fields of knowledge. A relevant quality of databases here is that they can be easily updated, with the amount of information in them expanded ad infinitum. In the computer vision, history is no longer a stratified entity to be unpacked. It is more a table of facts and data that can be accessed and manipulated at will. In the traditional view, history is linear and chronological, whereas in the digital perspective it is tabular and characterised by no sense of a univocal timeline. Computers operate through models and simulations, whereas time can be recalled and redeployed with different scales depending on the calculation. Time can run quicker or slower and simulated as any other parameters in the processing. Time is just a factor and, as such, can be modified in view of the desired outcome. History then is not considered as a determined sequence of facts and interpretations based on the sources available. It is considered as something that can be manipulated at any time and continuously adaptable. In particular, the strict distinction between past, present and future is not relevant for computers in their simulation, as they can reload each simulation, interrupt it at any time, modify any factor and roll it back. For computers, a place is a fixed point in a coordinates-based system to which a variable and scalable number of attributes (data) can be appended. In the digital environment, there are no historical places, but rather places that are qualified with more information than others.

Thirdly, Augé regards the notion of identity as crucial to defining a place. In the new digital/physical environment, a place has no identity per se. The only elements with a clear identity are the individuals. Places are points described by coordinates, and a useful way to navigate through space, either the physical or the digital one. By this token, it is impossible for computers to be concerned with the identity of a specific place. Machines map the new environment, which is a seamless combination of the physical and digital world. A specific physical place (say a town) is translated in the same coordinate system together with Internet Protocol Addresses (IPs) or Uniform Resource Locators (URLs) over the Internet. IPs are not qualified with identity by machines, but rather through numerical labels like: 127.255.255.255, exactly in the same way in which a computer would locate a physical place, namely through a set of coordinates (for example lat. 40.785091 and long. -73.968285).

Summarising, for Augé a place was something for which we can define a set of relations, a history and with a clear identity. A space with none of these characteristics is a generic place, or a non-place. In the digital perspective, individuals, software and the built environment are fused together into a new form of environment. In this, identity is only related to individuals, history does not really exist in the same way as we always intended and everything is relational (based on information). The three characteristics that Augé used to define a place need to be updated in the digital perspective. History disappears, identity is only attributed to one of the three components of the new environment and relations become the fabric of everything. We can see how the characteristics of places and non-places are both present in the new definition of environment. This makes it impossible to discern between Augé's two categories. We can infer that there are no places or non-places in the digital perspective, but only a new type of environment which encompasses both of them, replacing them.

References

Amin, Ash, and Nigel Thrift. 2002. *Cities: Reimagining the Urban*. Cambridge, UK: Polity Press.

Augé, Marc. 1995. "Non-place." *Introduction to an Anthropology of Supermodernity*. London: Verso.

Bates, Joseph. 1994. "The Role of Emotion in Believable Agents." *Communications of the ACM* 37 (7): 122–25.

Batty, Michael. 2007. *Cities and Complexity: Understanding Cities with Cellular Automata, Agent-based Models, and Fractals*. Cambridge, MA: MIT Press.

Batty, Michael. 2012a. "Building a Science of Cities." *Cities* 29: S9–16.

Batty, Michael. 2012b. *Smart Cities, Big Data*. London: Sage.

Batty, Michael. 2013. *The New Science of Cities*. Cambridge, MA: MIT Press.

Bolter, Jay David and Richard Grusin. 2000. *Remediation: Understanding New Media*. Cambridge, MA: MIT Press.

Bratton, Benjamin H. 2016. *The Stack: On Software and Sovereignty*. Cambridge, MA: MIT Press.

Carpo, Mario. 2017. *The Second Digital Turn: Design Beyond Intelligence*. Cambridge, MA: MIT Press.

Clark, Andy. 1998. *Being There: Putting Brain, Body, and World Together Again*. Cambridge, MA: MIT Press.

Clough, Patricia Ticineto. 2000. *Autoaffection: Unconscious Thought in the Age of Teletechnology*. Minneapolis, MN: University of Minnesota Press.

Crang, Mike, and Stephen Graham. 2007. "Sentient Cities Ambient Intelligence and the Politics of Urban Space." *Information, Communication & Society* 10 (6): 789–817.

Cuff, Dana. 2003. "Immanent Domain: Pervasive Computing and the Public Realm." *Journal of Architectural Education* 57 (1): 43–49.

Deleuze, Gilles, and Félix Guattari. 1987. "A thousand plateaus, trans. Brian Massumi".

De Roo, Gert, and Jean Hillier. 2016. "Spatial Planning, Complexity and a World 'Out of Equilibrium': Outline of a Non-linear Approach to Planning." In *Complexity and Planning*, 159–94. London: Routledge.

Dodge, Martin, and Rob Kitchin. 2005. "Codes of Life: Identification Codes and the Machine-readable World." *Environment and Planning D: Society and Space* 23 (6): 851–81.

Dodge, Martin, Rob Kitchin, and Matthew Zook. 2009. *How Does Software Make Space? Exploring Some Geographical Dimensions of Pervasive Computing and Software Studies*. London: Sage.

Doel, Marcus A. 1999. *Poststructuralist Geographies: The Diabolical Art of Spatial Science*. Lanham, MD: Rowman & Littlefield.

Dourish, Paul. 2017. *The Stuff of Bits: An Essay on the Materialities of Information*. Cambridge, MA: MIT Press.

Drepper, Ulrich. 2007. "What Every Programmer Should Know About Memory." *Red Hat, Inc* 11: 2007.

Galloway, Anne. 2004. "Intimations of Everyday Life: Ubiquitous Computing and the City." *Cultural Studies* 18 (2–3): 384–408.

Gibney, Elizabeth. 2017. "Magnetic Hard Drives Go Atomic." *Nature*.

Graham, Steve, and Simon Marvin. 2002a. *Splintering Urbanism: Networked Infrastructures, Technological Mobilities and the Urban Condition*. London and New York: Routledge.

Graham, Steve, and Simon Marvin. 2002b. *Telecommunications and the City: Electronic Spaces, Urban Places*. London: Routledge.

Greenfield, Adam. 2010. *Everyware: The Dawning Age of Ubiquitous Computing*. Berkeley, CA: New Riders.

Ibelings, Hans. 1998. *Supermodernism: Architecture in the Age of Globalization*. Rotterdam: Nai Uitgevers Publishers.

Johnson, B. R. 2016. *Design Computing: An Overview of An Emergent Field*. New York: Routledge.

Kang, Jerry, and Dana Cuff. 2005. "Pervasive Computing: Embedding the Public Sphere." *Washington and Lee Law Review* 62: 93.

Kaufmann, Stuart A. 1993. *The Origins of Order: Self-organization and Selection in Evolution*. New York: Oxford University Press.

Kitchin, Rob, and Martin Dodge. 2005. "Code and the Transduction of Space." *Annals of the Association of American Geographers* 95 (1): 162–80.

Kitchin, Rob, and Martin Dodge. 2011. *Code/Space: Software and Everyday Life*. Cambridge, MA: MIT Press.

Kitchin, Rob, and Tracey Lauriault. 2014. "Towards Critical Data Studies: Charting and Unpacking Data Assemblages and their Work." In *Geoweb and Big Data*, edited by *The Programmable City Working Paper 2*; pre-print version of chapter to be published in J. Eckert, A. Shears and J. Thatcher Nebraska: University of Nebraska Press, Forthcoming.

Latour, Bruno, and Catherine Porter. 1993. *We Have Never Been Modern*. Cambridge, MA: Harvard University Press.

Loth, Sebastian, Susanne Baumann, Christopher P. Lutz, D. M. Eigler, and Andreas J. Heinrich. 2012. "Bistability in Atomic-scale Antiferromagnets." *Science* 335 (6065): 196–99.

Mackenzie, Adrian. 2010. *Wirelessness: Radical Empiricism in Network Cultures.* Cambridge, MA: MIT Press.

Manuel, DeLanda. 2002. *Intensive Science and Virtual Philosophy.* London: Bloomsbury.

Marcus, George E., and Erkan Saka. 2006. "Assemblage." *Theory, Culture & Society* 23 (2–3): 101–06.

Mattern, Shannon. 2017. "Mapping's Intelligent Agents." *Places Journal.* Last accessed March 3, 2018. https://placesjournal.org/article/mappings-intelligent-agents/

McCullough, Malcolm. 2013. *Ambient Commons: Attention in the Age of Embodied Information.* Cambridge, MA: MIT Press.

Mell, Peter, and Tim Grance. 2011. "The NIST Definition of Cloud Computing." NIST Special Publication 800–145. Computer Security Division. Information Technology Laboratory. National Institute of Standards and Technology. Gaithersburg, MD.

Merriman, Peter. 2011. "Marc Augé." In *Key Thinkers on Space and Place*, 26–33. Thousand Oaks, CA: Sage.

Natterer, Fabian D., Kai Yang, William Paul, Philip Willke, Taeyoung Choi, Thomas Greber, Andreas J. Heinrich, and Christopher P. Lutz. 2017. "Reading and Writing Single-atom Magnets." *Nature* 543 (7644): 226.

Shoham, Yoav. 1993. "Agent-oriented Programming." *Artificial Intelligence* 60 (1): 51–92.

Thrift, Nigel. 1999. "Steps to an Ecology of Place." *Human Geography Today*: 295–322.

Thrift, Nigel. 2004. "Remembering the Technological Unconscious by Foregrounding Knowledges of Position." *Environment and Planning D: Society and Space* 22 (1): 175–90.

Thrift, Nigel, and Shaun French. 2002. "The Automatic Production of Space." *Transactions of the Institute of British Geographers* 27 (3): 309–35.

Weiser, Mark, and John Seely Brown. 1996. "Designing Calm Technology." *PowerGrid Journal* 1 (1): 75–85.

Wooldridge, Michael, and Nicholas R. Jennings. 1995. "Intelligent Agents: Theory and Practice." *The Knowledge Engineering Review* 10 (2): 115–52.

Part II
The discrete city

3   The production of the discrete city

What and how do computers see?

By nature, computers are instructed to duly compile a set of instructions that programmers write and test. The high level of sophistication that characterises machine learning today makes it possible for scripts to generate, once launched, actions of their own (Paglen 2016). In combination with accurate sensing devices, programmes are built to gather and analyse information from the environment they are in (Ramos et al. 2008), with the objective of learning from it. Through the Internet of Things (IoT) and ubiquitous computing, computers constantly observe, listen to and analyse human activities.

Computers are blind to most of the complexities and nuances that we humans use every day to perceive and interpret phenomena in the physical world. Scripts execute strings of instructions, incorporating new information through physical devices (microphones, cameras and sensors). The biggest challenge that computers are facing today is the semiotics of the data they gather. This is partially due to the fact that semantics (namely the attribution of meaning to objects or phenomena) is an intellectual activity very unique to the human brain. As such, any attempt at interpreting phenomena that we ask computers to perform is somehow alien (if not contrary) to their functioning. When machines are deploying any type of semantics, we are programming them to mimic an associative human function that is inheritably hard-wired in our brains. Computers approach this problem by taking advantage of their computational nature, whereby the storing and accessing of complex and large volumes of information can overcome the associative process to attribute meaning and make sense of the world. Artificial Intelligences (AIs) learn about humans by continuously adding information to a growing database whose goal is to produce an accurate profile of each user. This is especially true with digital personal assistants (DPA) like Siri, Alexa or Google Assistant, where, throughout time, the accuracy of the answers given to users increases at each use. In some instance, DPAs even predict the user's next query before it is formulated.

The computer's logic

Computers read the world through algorithms and work through processes. The reading of the world's phenomena happens through a procedure that "operates in the space of implementation between critical theory, computational logic, and cultural understanding" (Finn 2017:52). Finn argues that the algorithmic reading works through process, abstraction, implementation and imagination (Finn 2017). The logic that underpins the computer reading of the world is that everything (from inputs gathered through ambient sensors to mathematical operations) is obtainable by means of a systematic and organised series of steps described in a given method. Albeit computers are output-driven, namely their algorithms exist as a means to provide solutions to given problems, the core of their nature lies in the process. Finn describes this in terms of surface material presented as output (the final result of a calculation, process, etc.) at any given moment, and the series of "rules and agents that constantly generate and manipulate that surface material" (Finn 2017:53). The emphasis is therefore on the potential production, rather than on the final outcome. We could argue that, for computing logic, the generic possibility of processing is more important than a processed result at any given time. Computers work by means of systems that are in motion: "a sequence of iterations that comes into being as it moves through time" (Finn 2017:53). Machines work through abstraction; whereby significant work is done by algorithms to decide what is included and what is elided in each representation of the world.

The eyes and ears of machines

Computers require inputs in order to process data and return outputs. In order to acquire data from outside the machine itself or the system of which the computer is part, machines need to have a mechanism that allows them to be receptive to the external world. In a very simple system, inputs are prompted manually by an individual who mediates between the facts that describe a certain phenomenon and the computer. The individual selects the data that will be compatible with the algorithm and types them in a form that the computer can use. If the programme is scripted to calculate the average among a series of values, the individual would input the single numbers and run the script. The computer would return the arithmetic mean. In more complex systems, scripts are so sophisticated that they include functions to allow them to scan the environment in which they sit for the necessary inputs. Such programmes enable external devices like microphones or cameras to gather the data they need. The devices substitute the labour that was previously performed by the individual, automating it. The analogy which is often used is the one of senses, projecting human functions like hearing or seeing onto computers. Machines are programmed to receive inputs, filter them in the search for the values necessary to run their scripts with the ultimate goal of returning an output. This is then given to a person or another computer that uses it as input. When these complex systems escalate into networked environments, where different machines are working together to gather and analyse urban data, they are described as sentient cities, sensing cities, smart cities and the like.

Computers sense the world through different techniques that are here sorted in two main groups. The first one includes programmes that run online, automatically searching for data to create databases or profiles without direct contact with the physical world. These are processes that work on a machine-to-machine platform. In the process called Data Crawling, a bot (or crawler) scans web pages looking for metadata in order to collect a series of data through a number of given attributes. Crawlers are an example of Data Scrapers, whereby the former is mainly built to scan web pages and the latter can refer to local machines or databases not necessarily online. In the two similar processes, a crawling agent and a parser scan databases in search of specific data the attributes of which are pre-organised in the script.

When data scraping involves the study of people's behaviour online (and off-line), machines work through automated systems that include data mining and data analysis to harvest large datasets about a particular individual that enable them to generate a highly accurate personal profile. This may include political views, social status, emotional characteristics, inclinations, spending patterns and a plethora of private facets about a person.

The second group of techniques used by computers to generate inputs involves an external action or device that allows data to be acquired and processed from outside the computer itself. The most basic tool is that which prompts inputs from the user. This is performed through a computer interface (e.g. a browser window) where the user is asked to type a datum. The programme will then store that datum into its database and compute it when needed. When cameras and microphones are connected to a computer, video and audio-based data can be input. Whilst in the case of the user inputting queries, the machine receives only the data relevant to the programme; with external devices, the computer will load a range of data, some of which will be useful for the programme and some of which will simply be stored. This process requires a sifting step where algorithms find and select the relevant information in the database.

Trackers are devices that record geolocation-based data, proximities or biometric information about individuals that are then sent to programmes in the cloud that are able to return statistics, averages and trends. With the aid of wearable technologies that monitor daily activities, each individual is capable of self-tracking and having an accurate report of various aspects of her/his life. These include calorie intake, quality and quantity of consumed food, quality of air of the surroundings, noise level, light exposure, hydration levels, number of sleep hours, and also blood oxygen levels, number of steps or miles walked, etc. Wearable computers collect all this information, sending it to a server, which gives back to the individual an accurate picture of health condition, quality of life and, more importantly, stores a valuable amount of data for future use. Data, and wearable devices that allow individuals to collect and control their routines, provide people with what Kevin Kelly (Swan 2013:85–99) termed "exosenses": a new set of senses by which one can experience oneself, as well as the environment in a new way. People may decide to hack their own habits, or create new ones based on the old (Neff and Nafus 2016:90). These may resonate with routines at work (being more efficient), with the social sphere (being more sociable), with health and wellness (being more aware of the impact, for instance, of a sedentary life), as well as with the psychology of each individual (happiness in general terms).

Geolocation trackers like the satnav connect through a GPS signal to a satellite that allows an accurate position of the device to be determined through longitude, latitude and altitude.

More widely, trackers can be associated with practically anything that moves or performs changes in the world. Julian Bleecker (2006) defined such generic tracking devices as Blogjects: "objects that blog" (2006:3). Blogjects are a combination of a moving object (or animal or person) onto which a tracker (a sensor, a GPS tracker, etc.) is mounted. The data received by the tracker are sent through the Internet to servers where they are processed and can be fed into databases for further analysis. Bleecker's idea is that any device can become a means of input for computers and the IoT, extending, to a high level, the extent to which machines can have direct access to world phenomena:

> Once "Things" are connected to the Internet, they can only but become enrolled as active, worldly participants by knitting together, facilitating and contributing to networks of social exchange and discourse, and rearranging the rules of occupancy and patterns of mobility within the physical world.
>
> (Bleecker 2006:2)

Digital Personal Assistants (DPAs) can be seen as an evolved version of the on-screen inputting of data to the computer where, instead of typing, data are acquired through the user's voice and the Conversational User Interface (CUI) works entirely via Natural Language Processing (NLP) and in spoken form. DPAs perform a number of tasks to simplify the user's interaction with her/his device and the Internet, including making and taking phone calls, sending and receiving text messages, controlling media (volume, channels, change tune, etc.), finding information about traffic, news, read emails and many more (Krupansky 2017). DPAs are usually installed in mobile devices and connected to GPS receivers (Dussell et al. 1999). While the user asks the DPA simple queries about the time or the weather, the computer connected to this device will gather a large amount of data, some of which are only marginally pertinent to the question asked. Through the DPA, mobile devices and computers collect data about the user's habits and behaviour, including the unique position of the user, the name and location of the Wi-Fi network to which the device has recently connected and other devices in the range of connection of the user. Moreover, through the DPA, the computer will be able to analyse and interpret the data collected, generating trends, recording the user's habits and learning from them. DPAs gather a number of data that include GPS position, routines, time of actions, data downloaded, search engine queries, etc. These data have a dual function. On the one hand, they are interpolated by the DPA in order to answer the query of the user. An example is the question: "Is it going to rain this afternoon?" and the user would not normally specify the location to which she is referring. A more exhaustive question would be: "Is it going to rain in [the city I am currently in]?" The digital device will combine geolocation data and other sensed data in order to generate a clear set of information in order to answer the question. Interestingly, the DPA will not engage in a conversation with the user by asking for the missing information it needs to complete the query. It would rather automatically complete the query with the sensed data and present the final answer to the user.

The world as a discrete system of points and individuals

Computers utilise a geographical representation of the world that is based on physical location and user identity (Galloway 2004:369). The physical location is interpreted within a scalable representation of the planet Earth where the world is organised into a long list of unique points related to longitude, latitude and altitude. For most of the mapping Applications Programming Interfaces (APIs), including Google Maps and Bing Maps, the world is rendered with a scalable series of tiles. These vary in resolution and detail depending on the user's action of zooming in or out, with the entire world representable as small as a single 256×256 pixels tile (Batty et al. 2010:4).

The second fundamental factor allowing computers to represent the world is the unique identifier (UID), known in information systems as Universal Unique Identifier (UUID) and defined as "an identifier that is unique across both space and time, with respect to the space of all UUIDs" (The Open Group 1997). The UUID is usually an alphanumeric value consisting of 16 octets for a total size of 128 bits (The Open Group 1997) assigned to a single entity within a given environment. Once the entity has been uniquely identified, the machine can assign attributes to it, for example personal information, unique position or links to other databases. An example of a UUID can be:

116h9197-j73a-21y6-h904-009012340987

where the 16 octets are organised in 32 digits (base 16) grouped in 5 parts separated by hyphens (Leach, Mealling, and Salz 2005).

Definitions

Cyberspace

Many studies have successfully analysed and described cyberspace from the human point of view, examining questions of scale, dimensionality, continuity, density, limits (Stone and Benedikt 1991:132), trying to map it (Dodge and Kitchin 2003) and providing a solid framework for further studies (Graham 2004). Very few studies have tried to describe cyberspace from the point of view of the machines which actually produce it and use it from the backend. Many definitions have been given to describe cyberspace. Amongst the 28 and more currently provided (Mayer et al. 2014), Kuehl's appears to be particularly relevant to this discussion: "cyberspace is a global domain within the information environment whose distinctive and unique character is framed by the use of electronics and the electromagnetic spectrum to create, store, modify, exchange, and exploit information via interdependent and interconnected networks using information-communication technologies" (Kuehl 2009:27). This is perhaps one of the most radical cases of humanisation of a machine domain. Strictly speaking, computers do not understand space and, with it, the two subcategories of human and cyber spaces. Any possible definition of space to describe what humans intend and perceive as a spatial condition would be useless to machines. Rather, computers understand space through the mathematical terms of domains, whereby there exists a set of possible values (related to an independent variable) that allow a function to exist. As such, within the context of this work, we should consider the notion of space in its particular acceptation of computer-legible space, or function-based domain (set of values).

Software-sorting

Once data are gathered from the outside world, a series of algorithms sorts the inputs into categories and stores them into databases ready to be accessed by other algorithms. Sorting data implies some degree of automated decision-making and judgement. Although such processes usually involve human decisions at certain stages, it is relevant to note that computers are being gradually trained to increase their autonomy in sorting information. In order to be able to sort data, algorithms need to refer to attributes associated with each single datum and the recognition of sets of values. Software runs assessment cycles against the data collected in order to categorise the information returning organised outputs that reflect the initial values used. In the case of observation of urban phenomena, algorithms return software-sorted geographies (Graham 2005). Algorithms actively categorise urban elements and people's behaviour in cities, whereby the code "directly, automatically and continuously allocates social or geographical access to all sorts of critical goods, services, life chances or mobility opportunities to certain social groups or geographical areas" (Graham 2005:564). The values by which these algorithms run are predetermined by coders and those actors who inform their work, including governmental bodies, police enforcement and private companies. By providing the initial attributes and values for the construction of these algorithms, the actors, as subsequently the coders, embed their own judgments into the code. With it, they also include a certain degree of biases and preconceptions that are inevitably part of the factors that guide the assessment process. This, in part, stems from the idea that classifying is a fundamentally human characteristic (Bowker and Leigh Star 2000:1) that is highly rationalised when programmers write codes. Classifying is made in the attempt to optimise human sorting operations that help to generate intelligible processes. The attribution of values strictly follows a set of rules declared in the code. As eloquently argued by Lash (2007:70), such rules belong to the realm of computer science and are significantly different from those applied in human sciences. In particular, Lash refers to generative rules as: "virtuals that generate a whole variety of actuals. They are compressed and hidden and we do not encounter them in the way that we encounter constitutive and regulative rules" (Lash 2007:71). These rules are the result of an elaborated use of algorithmic logics whereby the output of the script A is used as input in the script B. This generates an evolutionary cycle that is structured to automatically feed itself, building on a series of progressive computations. With this, machines are able to generate an elaborated representation of the world, sorted into classes and categories where the organisational processes are regulated by "inhuman rules of automated flow" (Burrows and Gane 2006:804).

The phenetic fix

The more algorithms are employed to scan the external world, the more a need to generate and control a series of classes and categories emerges. With particular regard to CCTV and surveillance systems in general, this tendency has been studied by David Lyon who coined the term phenetic fix: as the trend "to capture personal data triggered by human bodies and to use these abstractions to place people in new social classes of income, attributes, habits, preferences, or offences, in order to influence, manage, or control them" (Lyon 2002:3). This idea has been studied by several authors including Adey (2002) and Gandy (1993) through his panoptic sort. Algorithms are able to read from CCTV footage people's movements and body language, inferring unusual behaviours and potential threats in public spaces (Carroll-Mayer et al. 2006:5). Codes become the fundamental in the process of surveillant sorting (Adey 2002:508; Gray 2002; Curry, Phillips, and Lyon 2003) and its application in different fields, especially in those spaces where mobility becomes a fundamental characteristic (Thrift 1994; Cresswell 2001). This includes train stations, transportation hubs and airports (Adey 2002:500).

AI and machine learning

Programming can be defined as: "making a specific automatic system, simply by describing it appropriately for a general purpose system" (Haugeland 1989:127). When programming evolves to predict human reactions in a machine-human interaction, the machine operates an intelligence that emulates the cognitive behaviour of the human brain. Initially, in AI developments, the programmes followed similar learning patterns to the human brain (Haugeland 1989:170). An example can be found in Shapiro (1979:123) while describing a deductive question-answering programme based on Raphael's Semantic Information Retrieval (SIR) (Raphael 1964). Raphael describes the extent to which a computer would be able to understand as: "A basic assumption here is that understanding can be demonstrated by dialogue; i.e., a computer should be considered able to 'understand' if it can remember what it is told, answer questions, and make other responses which a human observer considers reasonable" (Raphael 1964:577). The programme presented by Shapiro contains a class of English words (e.g. "bye") which trigger a response. The programme runs the inputted and outputted sentences until it reads the trigger words, to which it returns "good bye" (Shapiro 1979:124). Shapiro shows how the script runs with a similar behaviour while expecting punctuation marks (!, ?) or keywords (person, man, fireman, etc.) to which it returns sentences according to a pre-compiled rule list. Interestingly, the rules consist of four parts: a pattern (a list or a symbol), a list of variables (related to the pattern), a list of tests (to be run against the variables), and actions to be carried out if the "pattern matches and the variables pass the test" (Shapiro 1979:124). This early stage version of artificial intelligence is based on the prediction of human answers to the computer's question. The programme returns actions based on a continuous comparison between the human input and its database (list of sentences, trigger words, patterns, etc.).

With the further development of new techniques and computational powers, the algorithms that underpin AI programmes started to be machine-focused instead of human-focused. Computers need to learn about human behaviours and habits in order to instruct other computers. With this final goal in mind, we can reverse this scenario and see that computers are utilising machine-based learning processes to generate inputs from the outside world. Computers are no longer working as human brains, they are rather capitalising on their superior computational power based on calculation and iterative processes. Machines are synthesising our reality to feed themselves in order to be able to perform the tasks for which they have been programmed. Machine learning algorithms are today classified through the level of human intervention in their learning tasks. They range from supervised learning, where the algorithm learns through examples to map inputs to outputs, to independent learning, where the algorithm generates its own rules through an inductive process by learning from previous experience (Ayodele 2010:19).

Supervised learning implies the presence of a programmer who teaches the machine to create correlations between inputs and outputs in a general context. The computer should then be able to apply the rules learned to any specific computational case it may be asked to process drawing on its experience. There exist a number of variants of supervised learning. The technique whereby the computer is given only part of the necessary information to be able to produce the correct mapping is called semi-supervised learning.

Active learning describes that technique where the amount of training is limited and unlabelled data are abundant. In this scenario, the machine learning algorithm can choose the specific data to compute to perform its learning (Settles 2012).

When the input data are not pre-scripted, but are provided to the machine in the form of feedback within a real-life scenario as a result of the interaction with other agents in the outside world (people, opponent in a videogame, physical obstacles, etc.), the approach is usually called **reinforced learning**. In this model, the programme deploys an agent that is connected to its environment capable of both perception and with the freedom of action (Kaelbling, Littman, and Moore 1996:238). The process is recursive and the agent receives certain data about the current status of the environment as input. The programme sets a fixed value of parameters that the agent compares with the input at each step of the interaction. The agent chooses an action that will modify the environment. The second iteration of this process takes the modified environment as input and then computes it once more against the given initial value (reinforcement signal). Through a variable number of iterations, the algorithm will find the closest input value generated by its own actions through a trial and error process (Kaelbling, Littman, and Moore 1996:238).

In **unsupervised learning**, the computer runs programmes that allow it to generate its own rules as the result of a series of computations against a given context or scenario. Unsupervised learning is helpful when the computer needs to discover certain information (e. g. hidden structures or patterns) in unlabelled data (Chandrashekar and Sahin 2014:22). An example of unsupervised learning is represented by the clustering techniques, where an algorithm discovers patterns (groups) of data in a series of objects without any initial information about class labels or attributes (Chandrashekar and Sahin 2014:22). An illustrative example of the unsupervised learner is provided by the Self Organizing Feature Map (SOFM). As for any other unsupervised network, this system is able to associate classes of data with certain similarities and recognise data clusters within a given dataset (Ayodele 2010:37), without the need to relate inputs to outputs as part of its learning technique. SOFM networks are also able to recognise new data (by comparison with the previously used training data), thus determining the discovery of a new data cluster. SOFM are recursive regression processes "automatically organized into a meaningful two-dimensional order in which similar models are closer to each other in the grid than the more dissimilar ones" (Kohonen 1998:1). Therefore, the SOFM algorithm is an incremental-learning system based on regression, whereby a sample value of a variable is recursively computed against an initial value within a given equation (Kohonen 1998:2). At each iteration (epoch) the selected value, that is the one closest to the initial given value (or input case), is used as input in the following iteration and adjusted through the weighted sum of the previous value and the given one (Ayodele 2010:37). The algorithm progresses through several iterations and thus a topological map is generated. This includes a number of neighbouring values that are progressively nearer to the given value. The number of neighbouring values in the topological map is reduced in number as the iterations progress, indicating the progressive refining of the calculated values and the approximation to the wining value (Ayodele 2010:38).

The machine learning model works through the implementation of a number of different algorithms that perform different tasks at different stages of the learning process. If we focus on the output and ultimate task of these algorithms, they can be taxonomised as follows. The **classifiers** are those algorithms that sort unlabelled input data into classes. Once the classes have been created, along with a set of rules for classification, the new data coming into the system will be assigned into one or more class. Usually the classifiers use classes created by the programmer prior to the run of the scripts. The **clustering** algorithms measure similarities among groups of data, organising them into groups (clusters). Clusters of data are collections of objects that are considered together for their similarity (same attributes, same class, same label, or same size, format, source, etc.). By extension, these algorithms also recognise dissimilarity of clusters with other data groups within the same environment (Su and Khoshgoftaar 2009:9). The clusters generated as output are the final result of the algorithms, so considered as a finding, rather than a given class. This is one of the reasons why the clustering algorithms are usually utilised in unsupervised learning machine models. The **regression analysis** category includes those algorithms that calculate the correlations between

Table 3.1 Main types of machine learning algorithms. A complementary table of data mining tasks and techniques can be found in Miller and Han (2009:7) and Kitchin (2014:104).

Supervision	Type	Algorithm	Brief description
Supervised (and semi-supervised) Learning	Regression analysis	Logistic regression	
	Regression analysis	Ordinary least squares regression (OLSR)	
	Regression analysis	Linear regression	
	Regression analysis	Multivariate adaptive regression splines (MARS)	
	Regression analysis	Stepwise regression	
	Classification/ regression	K-nearest neighbours algorithm (KNN)	Non-parametric. Instance-based algorithm
	Classifiers	Learning vector quantization (LVQ)	Instance-based algorithm
	Classifiers	Naive Bayes	
	Classifiers	Hierarchical classifier	
	Classifiers	Binary classifier	
	Classifiers	Linear classifier	
	Classifiers	Linear discriminant analysis (LDA)	
	Classification/ regression	Decision trees	
	Classification/ regression	Support Vector Machines	
	Classification/ regression	Random Forest	
	Association rule learning	A priori algorithm	
Unsupervised Learning	Clustering	Hierarchical clustering	
	Clustering	K-means	
	Clustering	Mixture models	
	Neural Networks	Self-organising map (SOM)	Instance-based algorithm
	Neural Networks	Auto-encoders	
	Neural Networks	Deep Belief Nets	
	Neural Networks	Hebbian Learning	
	Neural Networks	Generative Adversarial Networks	
	Latent variable models	Expectation – maximisation algorithm (EM)	
	Latent variable models	Method of moments	
	Latent variable models	Blind signal separation	

variables (dependent and independent) in a given system. More specifically, these algorithms are based on mathematical models that allow to calculate the value of some variables while the other variables are changing in a dynamic system with a deterministic and a stochastic part of the model (Bates and Watts 1988).

Object-oriented ontology (OOO)

Computers classify everything as objects. As such, they have an inherited object-oriented approach to the exterior world. At macro level, machines work, by their very nature, by processing bits of information organised into undividable elements. This can be a byte, a single string of data, a packet, a block and so forth. Computers can only process discrete elements that can be considered as objects. The object-oriented ontology (OOO) is one of the current philosophical theories that is proving useful in providing a clear framework for this approach. Ian Bogost (2009) provides a clear definition of OOO, which can be used as a starting point:

> Ontology is the philosophical study of existence. Object-oriented ontology ("OOO" for short) puts things at the center of this study. Its proponents contend that nothing has special status, but that everything exists equally – plumbers, cotton, bonobos, DVD players, and sandstone, for example. In contemporary thought, things are usually taken either as the aggregation of ever smaller bits (scientific naturalism) or as constructions of human behavior and society (social relativism). OOO steers a path between the two, drawing attention to things at all scales (from atoms to alpacas, bits to blinis), and pondering their nature and relations with one another as much with ourselves.
>
> (Bogost 2009)

Levi Bryant holds that "the sole criteria for being an object-oriented ontologist lies in holding that the universe is composed of units" (Bryant 2013). Graham Harman holds that the entire world is made of objects and these "must be given equal attention, whether they are human, non-human, natural, cultural, real of fictional" (Harman 2018:9). These objects, to which the entire existence is reduced, are equal, including those entities that cannot be described as physical or real (Harman 2011:5).[1]

By enabling a "ruthless rejection of the concept of Nature" (Morton 2011:164), OOO advocates for a view of the world as flat ecology where everything (from people to pebbles, from sounds to colours) is considered an object. Moreover, Morton (2013) speculates on the existence of hyperobjects: objects that are so ethereous and extended as to have no boundaries and be considered everywhere. Examples are radioactive materials or global warming. In particular, Morton uses the notion of viscosity to qualify OOO objects: "all objects are caught in the sticky goo of viscosity, because they never ontologically exhaust one another even when they smack head-long into one another" (Morton 2013:36). Morton's objects are everywhere and continuously intertwined with each other. Objects are also characterised by being molten (their size is so large that they exceed space-time),

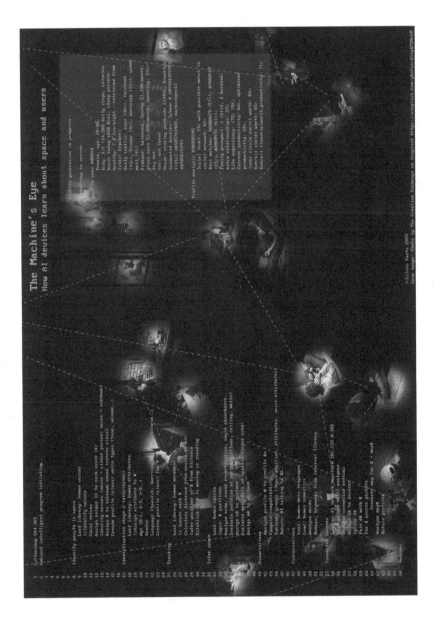

Figure 3.1 The Machine's Eye. Simulation of an AI machine in action in a public space

nonlocal (their real extent cannot be related to any particular locality) and by inter-objectivity (they are the result of relations/interactions amongst other objects).

Bogost takes this notion of democratic or flat ontology even further by suggesting the notion of tiny ontology (a very simple version of ontology that does not require a treatise to be explained) (Bogost 2012:21–22). We can infer that computers proceed by ontologising the realm of existence by flattening everything as objects, treating them with the same importance and simplifying them in order that they can be easily processed.

This provides a clear analogy for understanding the mechanisms by which computers scan the world. As illustrated in case study 3.4, computers are made aware of the existence of different elements (objects) in the external world through different sensing mechanisms, and assign to each of them a unique identifier. In the case study of the Machine's Eye (3.4), we can see how a new voice, a sudden new lamp switched on or new access to the local area network (LAN) triggers the attention of the sensing machine, which records and classifies every new input in its database. Once stored and organised, all these entries are ready to be retrieved and processed in future computations. Inputs, their classification, and the correlations that the computer generates are the main objects of the world as the machine sees it.

Blockchain

A sophisticated application of distributed object systems can be found in the blockchain. Based on the principle that data can be clustered and organised in blocks, this technology operates a significant step forward in the relationship between blocks with the aim of "totally order[ing] transactions on a distributed ledger" (Vukolić 2015:113). Using a Merkle tree, the Blockchain technology operates through a series of organised blocks, whereby each of them contains a number of transactions (relationships among blocks) along with a timestamp, transaction data (Tasca, Thanabalasingham, and Tessone 2017) and the key that relates to the preceding block. This latter is a function (hash) which is used to map data within a system. The blockchain consists of a hashchain of blocks, starting with the initial one called the genesis block (Vukolić 2015:113). This technology is considered particularly useful in avoiding any intermediation in the data transfer and exchange, "removing the constant need for actively intermediated data synchronization and concurrency control" (Mattila 2016:4).

Machine semantics

After the sensing of direct input from the exterior world, and the process of classifying it into categories suitable for a database, computers process these data with the goal of generating meaning. The production of meaning for computers is not the same as intended by the human brain. Naturally, the human brain establishes links amongst objects and phenomena, generating patterns, relationships and sequences in order to produce meaning.

John Haugeland (1989) created a parallel between the creation of meaning and the act of talking: "we do think what we say" (Haugeland 1989:90). By the same token, one may argue that, as machines do not speak, they do not express any thought and they do not produce any meaning. Haugeland adds another layer of complexity to the reflection around the semantic properties of machines. The creation of meaning is operated through the formulation of language, and this latter is overall a symbolic system (Haugeland 1989:91). He qualifies symbols as simple (like words), arbitrary and complex (like sentences) of which meaning is related to their composition in a systematic manner (Haugeland 1989:91). While making sense of a certain phenomenon (an event, a sentence, a text, etc.), an interpreter (human or machine) needs to understand the individual meaning of the single symbol (the word, an act, etc.) and all other symbols in the system. After this, the interpreter needs to determine the meaning of each symbol in its position and role in the system. In the understanding of a sentence, the single word must be contextualised within the rest of the individual meanings of the other words. Grammatical and syntactical rules support the generation of meaning for each individual word (the word "name" after an article is most likely to be a name, whilst after a subject it is most likely a verb). These rules constitute the logical grid around which sense is generated. However, sense-making is characterised by some level of uncertainty and approximation. This is guided by a degree of ambiguity caused by the linking of the meaning of the individual symbol with its context. The human brain deals with this by tapping into its experience, recalling previous interpretations and looking for some common pattern between past examples. Haugeland describes this as the need for coherence (Haugeland 1989:94), where an ordered text (a phenomenon organised in a certain sequence) is understood in such a way that it makes reasonable sense, where the meaning is acceptable to the interpreter once compared to previous interpretations.

As "interpreted automatic formal systems . . . and symbol-manipulating machines" (Haugeland 1989:106), computers can be considered a very powerful subset of the sense-making ability that characterises the human brain. In abstract terms, they are programmed to make sense of phenomena, which are represented by data. Zhuge (2011) holds that machines have two main limitations in this regard. The first one is about the limited number of links that machines have as a pre-set in their scripts to describe the physical, socio and psychological spaces, so that "it is not realistic to expect machines to discover laws and solve problems in these spaces" (Zhuge 2011:988). The second limitation is about the fact that – by their procedural nature – computers cannot take the initiative in their analytical processes. By specifically referring to cyberspace, Zhuge raises a relevant point here by explaining that the action that computers can have is limited to the processing of instructions that are pre-designed (Zhuge 2011:988). Computers fail to underpin the real extent of the human notion of linking (rules, habits, phenomena, facts, etc.). To overcome this impasse, Zhuge considers the possibility of linking the different types of spaces that machines have difficulties in connecting while computing data about them (or in them) separately. This complex and multi-disciplinary entity is defined as the Cyber-Physical-Physiological-Psychological-Socio-Mental

Environment (CP3SME) and it is meant to flatten these different spaces into one same level, so computers and human intelligences can comprehend it in a similar way (Zhuge 2011:994).

Case studies

Case Study 3.1 ANPR at work

A clear example of how computers sort data following algorithmic-governed processes can be seen in the way Automatic Number Plate Recognition (ANPR) cameras work. In the United Kingdom, there are around 8,500 ANPR cameras distributed around the entire country that collect between 25 and 35 million instances every day, sending them to the National ANPR Data Centre (NADC) to be cross-checked against existing databases to monitor and control the movements of individuals in the motorway national system.[2]

This case study shows the work conducted by Xiaojun Zhai, Faycal Bensaali and Reza Sotudeh at the School of Engineering and Technology University of

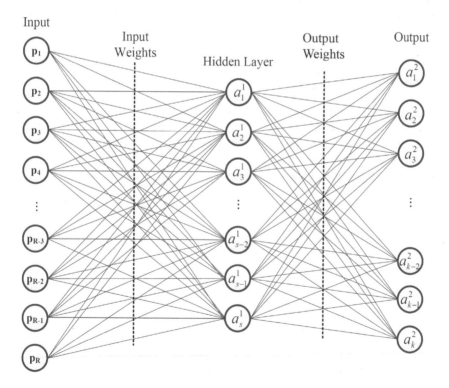

Figure 3.2 The OCR architecture used in this ANPR recognition system

Source: Zhai, Bensaali, and Sotudeh (2012)

Hertfordshire in 2012 on an OCR-Based Neural Network for ANPR (Zhai, Bensaali, and Sotudeh 2012).

The OCR system used in this project works with a two-layer feed-forward neural network in order to convert the images on the plate (alphanumeric digits) into an encoded text readable by the computer. The inputs from the external world are vectors and indicated with the letter R, the neurons of the system with S and the outputs with the letter K. Each layer contains a series of neurons and the corresponding transfer function. The 2D image captured by the camera associated with the ANPR system is transformed into a 1D vector (p) with R elements and it is used to feed the neural network. In this, the pixels of the image are scanned line by line. The neural network produces a series of vectors (a) as an output of which number (33) matches the number of characters on the UK number plate system (25 letters and 9 numbers, with exceptions for I and O).

The neural network is trained with a Scaled Conjugate Gradient (SCG) algorithm (Møller 1993), which is faster than the standard back propagation algorithm (BP) (Rumelhart, Hinton, and Williams 1986), the CGL conjugate gradient algorithm (CGL) (Goodman et al. 1990) and the one-step Broyden-Fletcher-Goldfarb-Shanno memoryless quasi-Newton method (BFGS) (Battiti and Masulli 1990). The proposed algorithm can process one character image in 8.4ms with a successful recognition rate of 97.3% when using a database of 3,700 character images.

Case Study 3.2 Self-organising maps

As a subcategory of unsupervised neural networks, a *self-organising map* (SOM) is a clustering technique designed to find categories in large datasets. In SOMs, neurons are configured in a hexagonal or rectangular 2D grid (Ng and Soo 2017). This algorithm gradually groups the neurons in the system around points in the grid with more concentration of values (data points), indicating areas with clusters in the dataset. In their website[3] and book (Ng and Soo 2017), Annalyn Ng and Kenneth Soo provide a clear example of how an SOM works.

Table 3.2 Self-organising map

Step 0	Randomly position the grid neurons in the dataspace.
Step 1	Select one data point, either randomly or systematically cycling through the dataset in order.
Step 2	Find the neuron that is closest to the chosen data point. This neuron is called the Best Matching Unit (BMU).
Step 3	Move the BMU closer to that data point. The distance moved by the BMU is determined by a learning rate, which decreases after each iteration.
Step 4	Move the BMU's neighbours closer to that data point as well, with farther away neighbours moving less. Neighbours are identified using a radius around the BMU, and the value for this radius decreases after each iteration.
Step 5	Update the learning rate and BMU radius, before repeating Steps 1 to 4. Iterate these steps until positions of neurons have been stabilised.

Source: Ng and Soo (2017). https://algobeans.com/2017/11/02/self-organizing-map/

Step 0: Position neurons (orange) in data space.

Step 1: Select one data point (blue).

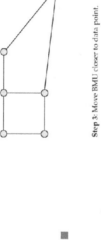

Step 2: Identify best matching unit (red).

Step 3: Move BMU closer to data point.

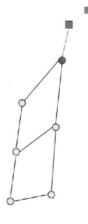

Step 4: Move BMU's neighbors closer to data point, with farther neighbors moving less.

Figure 3.3 Example of iterative process of SOM

Source: Ng and Soo (2017)

SOMs represent an efficient technique to reduce data dimensions (for a map) and find similarities in data clusters. The algorithm underpinning this technique is trained by a set of inputs in the form of vectors with different weights. The vector with the values closest to the current object is selected as the winner and becomes the active unit (the new current object). The process is repeated until the approximation is considered satisfactory. During the iterations, the values of the variables in the inputs are gradually adjusted in order to maintain the existing spatial relationships between the neighbouring elements (Ahn and Syn 2005).

Case Study 3.3 Spam filtering

Spam filtering programmes are based on the comparison between the content, form and appearance of genuine emails (ham) and malicious emails (spam). In order to automatically determine the difference between the two groups, programmes work through a series of logical steps.

The first is the preparation of the training data. The programme requires a set of spam and genuine emails to be analysed. The content of these sample emails needs to be simplified in order to be easily computed. Elements of the text that do not contribute to the categorisation are removed. For example, punctuation marks or special characters are common to both ham and spam emails, so they are not included in the data analysis. Similarly, prepositions (of, at, to, etc.) and articles (the, a, an) are widely present in each of the two sets, so their analysis becomes irrelevant. Finally, several words can be considered as different inflections of the same term. In order for a group of words like "combination", "combine", "combined", "combines", etc. to be considered as the same entity, the programme needs to lemmatise them before processing.

The second step is the creation of a word dictionary, which enables the programme to extract the words from the texts of the emails and calculate their frequency. The third step is the extraction of the words from the dictionary in preparation of the training phase. The fourth step is the training of the classifier, where a piece of code will sort all the words of an email into two categories (spam/ham), calculating the probability of these words belonging to one of the two groups.

The most common types of spam filters work through two combined techniques. The first is based on the algorithmic implementation of the Bayes' Theorem through the Naïve Bayesian classifier. The second is based on the bag of words model. The Bayes Theorem can be summarised in the formula below:

$$P\left(\frac{A}{B}\right) = \frac{P\left(\frac{B}{A}\right)P(A)}{P(B)}$$

where A and B are events; P(A) and P(B) represent the probability of observing A and B without regard to each other; P(A|B) is a conditional probability, namely the probability of observing A if B is true; and P(B|A) is the probability of observing B while B is true.[4] The Bayes' Theorem is helpful when, given a hypothesis about an event A as the starting point for which we don't have enough information, we acquire new data about a second event B which is related to the first one. This theorem helps us to calculate the likelihood of an event to be true, based on the evidence of another related event. In other words, Bayes' rule is a powerful tool for computers to update an initial hypothesis based on new information gathered. This process can be iterative, allowing for an exponential increase of data acquisition in a given system.

The bag of words model is based on the idea of deconstructing a system of objects (for example a text) into its elements (for example words), disregarding any rule of logical construction that underpins that system (Zhang, Jin, and Zhou 2010). In the case of a text, this module would ignore syntax, classical, grammatical or logical rules that assign meaning to the words in the text. This model extracts each word from its context in order for the Bayes's algorithm to be able to classify it based on a number of occurrences in the text using its calculation of probability. In spam filter programmes, this is based on the assumption that spam email would contain certain words more often than genuine emails (hams). The spam filtering programme is trained through the consequential analysis of spam and non-spam emails, using the Bayes classifier. The following piece of code represents a working filter where the programme has been already trained:[5]

Box 3.1   Trained classifier filter

```
#classifies a new email as spam or not spam
def classify(email):
 isSpam = pA * conditionalEmail(email, True) # P (A | B)
 notSpam = pNotA * conditionalEmail(email, False) # P(¬A | B)
 return isSpam > notSpam
```

Source: https://hackernoon.com/how-to-build-a-simple-spam-detecting-machine-learning-classifier-4471fe6b816e. Last accessed 24 May 2018.

Case Study 3.4 The Machine's Eye

This visual illustrates how a generic AI device sees the public space of a coffee shop, in a generic working day morning, exchanging data with other computers. The complex and multi-faceted picture that we all would have in a similar situation is utterly blank to computers. This machine would start learning about the space it is in by sensing sounds, recognising words and thus inferring the nature of the relationships among people in the cafeteria. At the start, voices are isolated inputs within a space that is limited by the catchment area of the microphone.

From these, which are the only initial data available, the AI device will rapidly assign a unique number to each voice in the space, calculating its position and mutual distances. Analysing the behaviour of sound waves in the room (factoring echo, reverberation and refraction time of the voices), the computer will calculate where walls, ceiling and floor are. The AI is now able to assign a unique position to each voice (person) within the given space, generating an accurate physical description of the coffee shop. The AI will then start assigning attributes to each voice, inferring gender, age and language. This initial profiling is possible through a comparison between the sensed data and comprehensive libraries hosted in the server to which the device is connected. The sensed data are then correlated with the information gathered through the other devices connected to the local Wi-Fi network in the coffee shop. The AI device is now able to compute an accurate profile where data from mobile phones, trackers and laptops are combined with the physical data sensed in the observed space. This visual shows the accurate, yet blunt picture that AI machines generate while watching humans in their daily activities. Whilst most of us think of AIs as aids that ease our daily routines, we should start to consider the fact that these machines are co-habiting our world. They continuously scan and analyse all inputs available to them, inferring activities, generating profiles and returning a machine-based view of the world. In this world, we are simply predictable datasets, instrumental to greater data analysis capability.

The script that the ideal AI machine uses in this demonstration has not been generated using any specific programming language, but it follows a high-level generic programming logic for the lines of code (a sort of pseudocode).

Box 3.2   Script of the AI machine applied to the coffee shop

Coffeeshop 014.389
Ambient intelligent programme initiating . . .
. . .
Identify people in space
    Load library: human voices
    >>Identify voices
    Count voices
    Assign unique ID to each voice (#)
    Identify noises (noise = silent person; noise = unknown)
    Assign # to unknown sound (create class)
    Create profile (class) voice types (tone, volume . . .)
Identification stage 2 (attributes)
    Load library: human attributes
    >>Assign attribute to #
    Age (0–1, 1–3, 3–5 . . .)

<pre>
        Gender
        Language (Spanish, American English, Chinese . . .)
        Create profile (class) for #
Tracking
        Load library: human movement
        >> locate each #
        Calculate distance from source to mic
        Infer position of # from distance
        Establish if # is moving or standing
Infer space
        Load: human spaces
        Input: # positions
        Analyse echo, sound reverberation, sound absorbance . . .
        Evaluate position of surfaces (floor, ceiling, walls)
        Assign s# to surface
        Evaluate materials of surface (input echo)
        Assign m# to surface
Associations
        Analyse profile # to profile #n
        Compute compatibility
        Evaluate groups (input position, attributes, voice attributes)
        Return: #1 talking to #2. . .
Conversations
        Load: human main languages
        Load: human semantics
        Analyse words
        Return: keywords from internal library
Connected devices
        Load wi-fi network map form 187.720.0.345
        Load packet sniff analyzer
        Analyse connected devices
        Assign d# to devices
        Locate d#
        Pair d# with #
        For # access packets
                Generate map for # = map#
        Analyse map#
        Return profile#
Actions
Profile generation in progress . . .
. . .
Connecting to server . . .
. . .
</pre>

Profile user #00000145
>   Female, age: 30-40,
>   body: fit (14,500 daily steps, calories burnt today 1650 Kcal, sleep pattern: healthy: 7.5 hrs/night – retrieved from fitbit tracker)
>   Daily traffic: asos (35%), facebook (42%), tinder (9%), whatsapp (12%), yahoo email (4%)
>   Finance: balanced. Saving $1,200/month; gross earn $3,800/month; spending: $35/day out.
>   Car: not found
>   House: renting postcode 123456, Brooklyn
>   Connected devices: Iphone X d#9984359953, fitbit d#585768403, macbookpro13 d#585675943

Profile analysis #00000145
>   Social level: 73% with possible match in social network: 62%
>   Best matches: #0000875 (67%), #0000510 (65%), #0000998 (61%);
>   Family prospect: 1 child, 1 husband; extra relationships: 37%
>   Life expectancy: <75; >56;
>   Current productivity: 82%, optimised productivity: 89%;
>   Inner circle social worth: 84%
>   Overall social worth: 65%
>   Overall financialworth.productivity: 71%

Case Study 3.5 Semantics

An interesting project developed by Alexander Trott, Xiong Caiming, and Richard Socher (2017) can shed light on the way meaning is created at the algorithmic level, so as to be understood by machines. Trott and colleagues introduced a method called the Interpretable Reinforcement Learning Counter (IRLC), which enables a computer to count objects in a given image through a sequential decision process. This approach becomes very helpful when it comes to machine context-specific reasoning based on the analysis of images through the process known as visual question answering (VQA). The IRLS method allows objects to be identified and isolated in an image and counted.

Figure 3.4 illustrates the algorithm in action. The process is iterative and at each step an object is selected and the total count of objects in the scene updated. Subsequently, the model used for selecting the objects in the image is changed in order to prioritise the unselected objects (Trott 2017:1). The steps continue and the total count is updated until all objects are identified and processed.

In order to localise the objects in the scene, Trott et al. (2017) used a deep neural network model developed by Teney et al. (2017), which is developed around a Fast Region-based Convolutional Network method (Fast R-CNN) for object detection (Girshick 2015). This method finds a series of regions in a given image

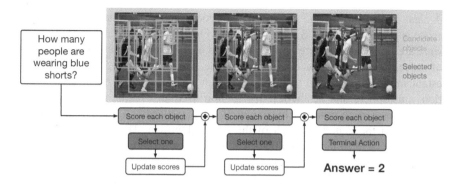

Figure 3.4 Sorting algorithm in action

Source: Naik, Philipoom, Raskar, and Hidalgo (2014)

where objects are identified. It identifies a set of bounding boxes, which are related to the objects that are most likely contained in them. In Trott et al.'s method, each question is encoded and compared to the objects identified through a scoring function (Trott 2017:5). This will output a scoring vector per each object in the image, with a parameter to measure the relevance of the scoring vector compared to the initial question. In their model, Trott and colleagues "aim to learn how to count by learning what to count" (Trott 2017:5). This approach works under the assumption that for each counting question posed to the programme, the series of algorithms is able to identify a subset of the objects in the image that meet a set of variable criteria which have been previously set. The model's goal is to quantify the subset of objects (Trott 2017:5–6).

Case Study 3.6 Cover

One of the first concrete examples of architecture entirely conceived and designed by computers can be found in the work of the company Cover Technologies Inc. Founded in 2014 in Los Angeles, this company provides consulting, design, building and installation of entire backyard houses. The design process is entirely automated, whereby a number of questions about life style, needs and preferences are asked of the client and input into machine learning software to generate a unique user profile. A number of design solutions are then generated and proposed to the client through a second cycle of user's input, based on comments on the proposed schemes. A number of algorithms are employed to optimise the space planning and building layout based on the client's feedback. This process involves a combination of direct feedback and automatically retrieved data, such as geospatial data, geolocation, orientation and environmental data (wind, light, sun path, etc.).

Case Study 3.7 Evolving floorplans

A clear application of the active role of code in the determination of physical space is provided by Joel Simon's Evolving Floorplans.[6] The outputs of this software are floorplans that are purely generated using a high degree of optimisation of space, flows and use as the main rationale. This extreme approach disregards established approaches to architecture design, such as theory, meaning, perception, atmosphere and aesthetics. Joel Simon used an existing school in Maine (USA) as a starting point for his exploration. He utilised two types of algorithms to establish the genetic growth of the initial floorplan. The first is the graph-contraction: a technique to reduce "a rooted ordered (data) tree to its root by a sequence of independent vertex removals" (Abrahamson et al. 1989:287). One type of contraction algorithm is the Karger's algorithm. In 1995 Karger defined his recursive algorithm by stating:

> the minimum spanning forest algorithm intermeshes steps of Borůvka's algorithm (used to find a minimum spanning tree in a graph for which all edge weights are distinct) called Borůvka steps, with random-sampling steps. Each Borůvka step reduces the number of vertices by at least a factor of two; each random-sampling step discards enough edges to reduce the density (ratio of edges to vertices) to fixed constant with high probability.
>
> (Karger, Klein, and Tarjan 1995:324)

The algorithm contracts the graphs by overlapping the vertices and deleting the unnecessary edges, until a simplified version of the initial graph is achieved. In particular, the Karger's algorithm can be described by this abstract form (Karger 1993:2):

(premises)

- Let us assume we have a multigraph $G(V, E)$ with n vertices and m edges
- Let us contract two vertices v_1 and v_2 by replacing them with a new vertex v
- Let the set of edges incident on v be the union of the sets of edges incident on v_1 and v_2

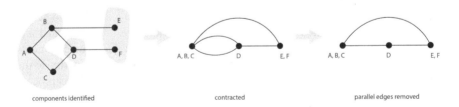

| components identified | contracted | parallel edges removed |

Figure 3.5 Contraction of the graphs using graph connectivity

Source: Diagram based on Blelloch and Hardwick (1993)

Figure 3.6 A Karger series of minimum cut contractions with two sets of five vertices and three edges

Source: Thore Husfeldt. Licence: e GNU Free Documentation Licence

- Do not merge edges connecting v_1 and v_2 which have the same other endpoint
- Let us give v multiple instances of those edges
- Let us remove edges which connect v_1 and v_2 to eliminate self-loops

(implementation)

1. repeat until two vertices remain
2. choose an edge at random
3. contract its endpoints

The second type of algorithm used is the ant-colony pathing. This is an optimisation technique based on probability to generate optimised paths (connections amongst vertices) through graphs. This algorithm was initially developed in the early 1990s by Marco Dorigo et al. (Colorni, Dorigo, and Maniezzo 1991) as a way to understand the combination of the "low-level interactions among many cooperating simple agents that are not aware of their cooperative behaviour" (Colorni, Dorigo, and Maniezzo 1991:134). The ant algorithm is underpinned by this logic (Colorni, Dorigo, and Maniezzo 1991:138):

Box 3.3   Script of the ant algorithm

1 Initialize:

     Set t:=0

     Set an initial value $\tau_{ij}(t)$ for trail intensity on every path$_{ij}$

     Place $b_i(t)$ ants on every node i

     Set $\Delta\tau_{ij}(t,t+1):= 0$ for every i and j

2 Repeat until tabu list is full {this step will be repeated n times}

     2.1 For i:=1 to n do {for every town}

              For k:=1 to $b_i(t)$ do {for every ant on town i at time t}

                       Choose the town to move to, with probability p_{ij} and move the k-th ant to the chosen location

Insert the chosen town in the tabu list of ant k
Set $\Delta\tau_{ij}(t,t+1):=\Delta\tau_{ij}(t,t+1)+\Delta_{\tau ij}^{k}(t,t+1)$ computing $\Delta\tau_{ij}^{k}(t,t+1)$

2.2 Compute $\tau_{ij}(t+1)$ and $p_{ij}(t+1)$

3 Memorize the shortest path found up to now and empty all tabu lists

4 If not(End_Test)

then

set t:=t+1
set $\Delta\tau_{ij}(t,t+1):=0$ for every i and j
goto step 2

else

print shortest path and Stop
{End_test is currently defined just as a test on
the number of cycles}.

Source: Colorni, Dorigo, and Maniezzo (1991:138), © *1992 Massachusetts Institute of Technology, published by the MIT Press*

At the start of the process (time = 0) all agents (ants) are located in different positions with no information about the reciprocal positions. After t = 0, each agent starts moving in different positions (from i to j). This movement is described by a probability function and the following two parameters: trail (τ_{ij}) indicating the number of agents that have already used the same path, and visibility (η_{ij}) that indicates the degree of desirability of the final destination (the closer to the agent position, the more desirable). At each cycle of the algorithm run (determining an iteration of the agents' move) the value for trail (τ_{ij}) is captured, stored (indicating a certain path used) and used to compute new values of the path simulation. Probabilistic functions (Colorni, Dorigo, and Maniezzo 1991:136–37) are used to predict the new trails and then computed again and again until the end of the given cycles. Once the number of pre-set iterations has been exhausted, the shortest path to connect each set of points is found, giving the output of the computation.

As we can see, Simon's evolving floorplan uses a combination of statistical computations to find out the shortest path between two points in a system (from the ant colony optimisation – ACO) and reduction of the number of possible paths (by contracting the graphs that represent the system). In order to control the automated generative process of forming the floorplans, Simon utilises Stanley and Miikkulainen's NeuroEvolution of Augmenting Topologies (NEAT) (2002): a technique designed to generate evolution of neural network topologies based on the weight of their elements. NEAT is based on the presence of historical markings, speciation and incremental growth from minimal structure (Stanley and Miikkulainen 2002:116). NEAT simulates and computes the crossover of two genomes and their network connectivity. Each genome has information

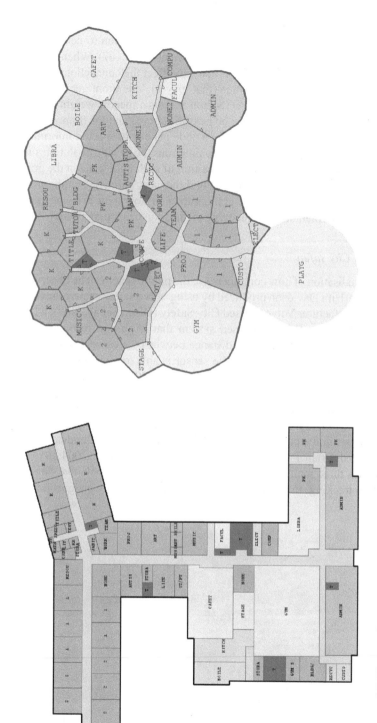

Figure 3.7 The transformation from an existing floorplan into a new phenotype, as the result of a custom growth process that uses physics and ant colony simulations and the NEAT evolutionary algorithm

Source: Simon (2018)

about possible connections with another genome, with each node gene including a list of inputs, hidden nodes and the weight of the connection to determine the outputs of their encounter (Stanley and Miikkulainen 2002:107). When genomes are computed, genes undergo a mutation that can affect the connections amongst genes, the internal structure of genomes (that may include more genes) and the overall network structure. Using NEAT, Simon assigns a specific weight to rooms and connections (e.g. room A needs to be next to room B and far from room C). Each part of the building is represented by a node gene with specific information that will determine the mutation. The programme runs the genetic evolution simulation reconfiguring the connections and position of each node gene in the graph.

Once the final graph has been computed and the most optimised configuration has been reached, Simon converts the graph into an orthographic drawing, generating an evolved floorplan, using a genotype to phenotype mapping (Simon 2018).

Case Study 3.8 City safety

An explicit visualisation of how computers see the public space can be observed in the work that Barbara Davidson produced by using Volvo safety cameras mounted on cars. Car manufacturer Volvo utilised City Safety (Distner et al. 2009): a Light Detection and Ranging (LIDAR)-based system that is able to recognise other vehicles on the road and calculate the distance between the camera and the other objects (Fields and Green 2012:497). The sensor is able to recognise vehicles in the range of approximately 10 metres (Distner et al. 2009:3). A precursor of this system has been designed by Grubb et al. (2004) as 3D vision sensing for improved pedestrian safety. Mounted onto a car, this combination of hardware (camera and sensors) and software (automated recognition) is able to recognise pedestrians as the vehicle moves in the city. The software detects and tracks individuals in real time using a Pedestrian Protection System (PPS) (Grubb et al. 2004:19). This system operates three main functions: obstacle detection, obstacle classification and pedestrian tracking. In particular, for pedestrian tracking, two algorithms are

Figure 3.8 View from a Waymo car

Source: Waymo (2018)

utilised: Kalman filters (Kalman 1960) to compute distances between the vehicle and pedestrians, and Bayesian probability (see Case Study 3.3 Spam filtering) to classify the behaviour of pedestrians over time (Grubb et al. 2004:19–22).

Case Study 3.9 Waymo

A more comprehensive application of sensible technologies in cars can be founded in Waymo: the independent self-driving technology company which originated as Google's self-driving car project in 2009. The Waymo technology is a combination of LiDAR, firing a large number of laser beams in a 360-degree direction to scan the surrounding environment and radar technologies to detect other objects, with their position and speed of movement. The data gathered by sensors and radars are input into a number of machine learning algorithms that generate semantics for these data, rendering a real-time version of the urban environment (Russell et al. 2004). Waymo cars are able to assess whether to operate through a manual driving or an autonomous driving mode. A processor "assesses the status of the vehicle's environment, the vehicle and systems of the vehicle, and a driver and identifies one or more conditions . . . to generate a set of tasks" (Cullinane et al. 2017). Waymo uses a number of algorithms. For example, one of the main elements that allows Waymo cars to modify the operational mode of the radar system in various configurations is the sensor fusion algorithm (Brown 2016). This allows a host device to determine the combination of its position and orientation having as input the raw measurements from at least two different types of sensors (Perek et al. 2013). A Waymo car is also able to read the environment, capturing any changes (Ferguson and Dolgov 2015) and predicting any behaviours of detected objects (Zhu Ferguson and Dolgov 2014.) The object detection algorithm, which we partially discussed in Case Study 3.5 Semantics, underpins this function.

Case Study 3.10 City scanner

What Waymo is trying to build through its own vehicles is extended to the extent of an existing infrastructure by the Senseable City Lab's City Scanner project. A sensing kit was mounted on top of local garbage trucks and sets of drive-by data were collected over a period of eight months around the streets of Cambridge, Massachusetts. This turned the garbage collection trucks into elaborated Vehicular Sensor Networks (VSNs) with almost real-time data sensing and elaboration through IoT. The kit utilised in this project is a multi-purpose sensing platform that collects a variety of environmental data at the same time. It includes non-intrusive sensors like "thermal cameras, WiFi scanners, accelerometers, GPS, air quality, temperature, and humidity sensors" (Anjomshoaa et al. 2018:7). As a part of their usual routine, the garbage trucks covered a constant network of streets and alleys with a weekly frequency. This allowed the researchers to harvest data about the same routes over time, therefore being able to observe the variation of the parameters during a given time. This allows for the possibility of interpreting the data by highlighting trends, variations and anomalies. Once sensed, these urban data can then be used for a range of analyses feeding into different services. Senseable City

Lab's researchers indicate this range by using the acronym FEELS to represent the combination of Fluid (Ambient Fluid Properties), Electromagnetic Properties, Envelope (Urban Envelope Properties), Light (Photonic Properties) and Sound (Acoustic Properties) (Anjomshoaa et al. 2018:3). Table 3.3 provides a clear overview of the variety of data that can be captured by a multi-purpose sensing kit.

Once gathered by the sensing platform, data are transmitted via Wi-Fi to a core unit, which then forwards them to a cloud-based server via a Transmission Control Protocol (TCP) standard. In the cloud, data are automatically sorted by algorithms into a number of categories depending on the type of data and the type of

Table 3.3 2327–4662 (c) 2018 IEEE. See www.ieee.org/publications_standards/publica tions/rights/index.html for more information.

Type	Sensor	Potential applications
Ambient fluid	Particulate matter	• Monitoring the distribution of fine particulates (e.g. PM2.5, PM10)
	Chemical pollutants: CO_x, NO_x, SO_x, O_3	• Monitoring the distribution of various pollutants
	Methane sensor	• Detecting methane leaks
	Nanosensors (no commercial sensors yet)	• Detecting explosive material • Detecting chemical substances
	Temperature, humidity, air pressure	• Monitoring urban heat island phenomena
	Particle radiation	• Monitoring the airborne particulate radioactivity
Electromagnetic	Wi-Fi, Bluetooth	• Crowd and station mapping by scanning Wi-Fi and Bluetooth signals
	GPS	• Localisation and annotating sensor data • Inferring mobility aspect of vehicles (e.g. mobility mode of people or traffic status)
	RFID scanner	• Tracking and managing assets in urban areas (e.g. trees) • Sensing of spatial information by implanted beacons (e.g. road conditions)
	Isotropic sensors, Magnetometers	• Monitoring the electromagnetic field level (e.g. for studying irradiation impacts on citizens)
Urban envelope	LiDAR, Ultrasonic	• Generating 3D model of cities • Monitoring the street surface quality • Monitoring road-side parking spots
	Wave radar, ground penetrating radar	• Monitoring the street surface quality • Identifying the pavement material and quality • Detecting black ice formation • Mapping the subsurface infrastructure (e.g. pipes, cables, tunnels)
	Accelerometer, Gyroscope, Odometer	• Monitoring the street surface quality • Monitoring road traffic and identifying hazardous road segments • Monitoring driving behaviour • Monitoring bridge vibrations

Type	Sensor	Potential applications
Photonic	Visual camera	• Real-time imaging of urban areas and creating panoramic views • Monitoring of crowd and vehicles for event management and security purposes • Monitoring of traffic
	Thermal camera	• Monitoring energy efficiency of built environment • Monitoring the anthropogenic heat pollution • Detecting natural gas and CO_2 emissions • Monitoring crowd • Monitoring infrastructure (e.g. powerlines, street surface) • Detecting black ice formation
	Photosensor	• Monitoring street lighting, infrastructure quality, blazing light and reflections
Acoustic	Audio sensor, Microphone	• Monitoring noise and identifying activity patterns • Mapping the soundscape of cities • Monitoring the impact of noise controlling measures (e.g. noise-absorbtion walls)

Figure 3.9 Numina sensor view of multimodal traffic along the Fulton Mall between Hanover Pl and Flatbush Ave in Downtown Brooklyn, New York

Source: Numina (2018)

analysis needed (using the FEELS categorisation). These analyses include data visualisation, storage and sorting, or they can be used to feed more sophisticated processes such as data analytics and AIs (Anjomshoaa et al. 2018:7). The potentials presented by this approach are very promising. The project resulted in an output of 1.6 million measurements and could, if needed, in combination with other data sources, be used for various purposes such as analysing the thermal efficiency of building façades, detection of certain infrastructural failures (e.g. the overheating of power lines), studying thermal pollution/heat-island phenomena in urban areas and studying the impact of microclimate on pedestrian comfort.

(Anjomshoaa et al. 2018:7)

Case Study 3.11 Numina

Urban planning and traffic data are increasingly a focus of machine learning-based automation and intelligence deployed in cities. Numina, a "deploy-anywhere sensor solution that gives cities unprecedented traffic data" (Numina 2018), provides a leading example. The Numina sensor mounts to street infrastructure like light poles and uses computer vision to sense the volumes, movements and interactions of cyclists, pedestrians, vehicles of all classes and other travellers and objects (wheelchairs, strollers, street furniture, trash bags and more) in streets. Numina's image processing takes place in real time and onboard the sensor itself, and all images are destroyed after analysis. The only data that is transmitted from the sensors is minimal, anonymised metadata about each object (its type, a count of each object type, location and timestamp). Numina uses cellular networks to transmit measurements every minute, and to deploy new system updates and classifiers over the air. Users interface with Numina data through a cloud-based Web dashboard and developer API.

Numina data can be applied to a variety of transportation planning use cases, as exemplified in Numina's research in Jacksonville, Florida conducted between 2016 and 2017. In order to develop a better, more accurate understanding of pedestrian mobility and safety in Jacksonville's urban core, Numina installed 22 sensors at 11 high-risk urban intersections. This allowed the company to gather "counts, times, and street-level travel behaviors of pedestrians" and derive quantitative crash rates for each intersection (Numina 2018; Goodman et al. 1990).

Case Study 3.12 Streetscore

Streetscore is a binary classifier algorithm developed by Nikhil Naik at MIT to rate the appearance of safety in the context of street views (Naik et al. 2014). This machine learning system was trained to perceive safety (as it would appear to a human) by analysing images and comparing them, attributing a final score as output. Three thousand training images have been interpolated with perceived safety (Streetscore 2018) from Place Pulse, an MIT project that "quantitatively measures urban perception by crowdsourcing visual surveys to users around the globe" (PulseMedia 2018). As a part of the training process, each image has

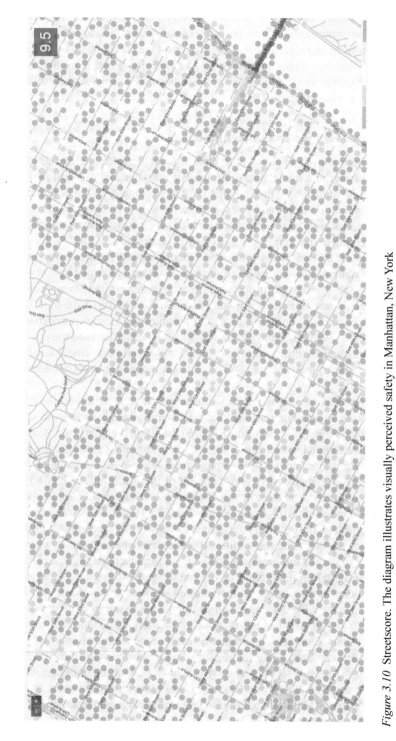

Figure 3.10 Streetscore. The diagram illustrates visually perceived safety in Manhattan, New York

Source: Streetscore (2018)

been translated into a number of attributes based on colours, textures and shapes contained. The attributes have then been interpolated with the scores from Place Pulse. Once trained, the algorithm was able to repeat the process with new images by "decomposing this image into features [attributes] and assigning the image a score based on the associations between features and scores learned from the training dataset" (Streetscore 2018).

What do designers see from machines?

In the paragraphs above, we have observed how computers detect elements of the real world and use these partial data to generate interrelated and sophisticated pictures to describe human activities and the built environment. In the design practice, this information is acquired by designers as a starting point or data to support their work. Increasingly, urban planners, architects, urbanists and digital designers in general utilise the framework provided by computers in their projects. In this logic, the external world is processed twice. The first process involves the recreation of some of its relevant characteristics that are determined by software-sorting processes. The second process involves the interpretation that architects produce based on sensed data. Computers output a description of the built environment that is taken by designers as a starting point for their own understanding of the world. Whereas in the pre-digital era architects processed the physical world through their own analogue tools, like traditional surveying, sketching, photographs, etc., in the CAD era, the world is a digital construct rendered by computers. An example is the 3D scanning of an existing building. Advanced survey techniques, such as LiDAR, and image-matching techniques allow software to generate an accurate representation of the physical characteristics of the building (Ackermann 1999; Nex and Rinaudo 2009) or the landscape (Cureton 2016:44). Once scripted, tested and debugged, the algorithms governing the scanning process run autonomously, going through several cycles of computations in order to produce a high-fidelity representation of the given building. After this operation is completed, and the software has returned a high-resolution file that is scaled, filtered and adjusted (Nex and Rinaudo 2009:13), architects are able to see that building through the result of the computational work of machines. Architects in this instance are not using the traditional methods of physical surveying, their own analogue tools, and the cues gathered while in person on the site. Conversely, they trust the digital representation of the building. An illustrative example of this can be found in the project Transformation, realised by the ScanLAB Projects, where about 1600 3D scans have been produced to document the move of the Bartlett School of Architecture to a vacant building at 22 Gordon Street on UCL's Bloomsbury Campus. The project consists of the combination of two sets of scans: the first captures the building in the days before the start of the building works, whilst the second set was taken two years later with the building in use, during the Bartlett Summer Show. The two sets of scans have been overlapped in order to create two 3D digital models based on a pointcloud with more than a billion measured points (UCL 2017).

Figure 3.11 ScanLab – Transformation project

Source: ScanLab (2017)

Another example is in the form of the urban environmental data acquired by sensors, whereby architects create a picture of the city through sensed data. City dashboards are a very strong example of this. The underpinning idea is that a plethora of complex and often time-isolated datasets are converted into one system that is able to interpret and present these data under combined categories. One can see here the computational capacity of machines in action, whereby computers can process an enormous quantity of data rendering some useful sense for humans.

More and more cities are their own dashboards, including London, New York, Chicago, Sao Paolo and many more. Dashboards can be considered to be data aggregators. This concept is clearly explained through the CityDashboard project. This online interface has been developed by the Bartlett Centre for Advanced Spatial Analysis (CASA) research lab at UCL in 2012. CityDashboard gathers statistical and spatial data for a number of cities in the UK, including Birmingham, Glasgow, Leeds, London and Manchester, and automatically visualises them into a series of maps, tables and diagrams.[7] This project retrieves publicly available data from a plethora of sources, including governmental-level departments (e.g. the Department for Environment Food and Rural Affairs, the National Oceanic and Atmospheric Administration, Port of London Authority, Transport for London and ScotRail), online resources and digital companies (OpenStreetMap, Yahoo! Developer Network, MapTube, Google and Twitter) and educational institutions (e.g. London School of Economics and UCL CASA).

One system that may be representative of them all could be the Dublin Dashboard: a collaborative project led by Rob Kitchin and developed by The Programmable City project and the All Island Research Observatory (AIRO) at Maynooth University in collaboration with Dublin City Council (Dublin Dashboard 2018). This online dashboard offers designers and decision makers, as well as the general public, "real-time information, time-series indicator data, and interactive maps about all aspects of the city [that] enables users to gain detailed, up to date intelligence about the city that aids everyday decision making and fosters evidence-informed analysis" (Dublin Dashboard 2018). Through the lens of this dashboard, the city of Dublin can be read and interpreted under different strands. One can know the traffic condition of any junction at any time, or the available parking bays in a specific area. There are a number of sophisticated environmental indicators, including the water and sound level at any given time in specific urban areas, or temperature, humidity, precipitation level and wind speed, as well as air quality and pollution levels for different city parts. The Dublin Dashboard also includes social indicators, unemployment rates, average monthly residential rent, average cost of new-build housing or health and crime information: number of theft and related offences, number of pupils in each school, average of people with a higher degree, number of patients in each hospital, etc.

Another illustrative project is Whereabouts London: a Future Cities Catapult's initiative that remaps all London's boroughs, retracing the demographics of the city. By combining a number of datasets from 235 different sources (including the Greater London Authority's London Datastore, the Food Standards Agency, the Office for National Statistics, Land Registry, OpenStreetMap, Flickr and Transport for London), this project has resulted in an interactive online map that provides accurate and updated statistical and spatial information about London and its inhabitants. The city of London is categorised into eight zones (or whereabouts), with distinctive characteristics, including density, commuting type, average degree level of the population, crime rates, average of ownership or rental properties, etc.

Machines have the ability to have a large overview of complex situations that can then be condensed and simplified into graphics that are easily readable by humans, like in the case of dashboards or urban informatics projects. On the other extreme of the spectrum, computers are able to observe and analyse the environment at the microscopic level. Projects like Citizen Sense's Dustbox illustrate how urban sensing technologies can be used to monitor the particles in the air and software can be used to visualise the magnified particles of pollen and carbon detected by the sensors (Citizen Sense 2016).

What do architects do with these data?

In this chapter, we implicitly divided designers into two categories: those who use computers to read the city, unveil hidden patterns, and discover new insights on urban phenomena, and those who use these readings in order to generate new projects. This section explores the second group, whereby the machine output produced as a final result by the first group is here considered the initial input. In terms of workflow, architects receive a picture of the urban phenomena made up predominantly of data and their interpretation. As seen previously in this chapter, such data can be in the form of point clouds, CCTV footage, number of interactions amongst agents, or tracked paths of selected users. The first problem that the designers of the second group need to address is the management of this information, followed by its correct interoperability amongst different systems. These data need to be converted into various formats in order to be processed by different software and platforms. By the same token, information systems that facilitate the use of data across platforms, practices and data systems are increasingly playing a crucial role in helping designers to manage the initial information about cities.

BIM

The most common information system that enables architects and urban designers to analyse, manage, share and coalesce all types of input from different sources into the same platform is the Building Information Modelling BIM.

CAD software is primarily used to represent a real building, where line types, thicknesses, colours and symbols are used to identify a specific type of material or object, along with their position in the drawings. Every element in a CAD drawing is representational and does not contain any data except its visual expression. CAD drawings are based on the sharing of drawing conventions and annotations,

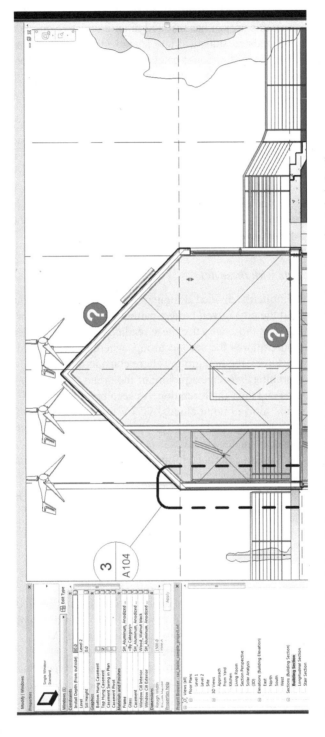

Figure 3.12 Generic sectional view of a house in BIM. "Autodesk screen shots reprinted courtesy of Autodesk, Inc."

Source: Autodesk (2018)

whereby every user is able to decode the meaning of each line or element. Conversely, in the BIM environment, every item contains information that can be manipulated by all users of the file. Whilst a wall may be represented in CAD by two parallel lines, in BIM the wall is a specific entity, with its own attributes and parameters. Once inserted in the BIM environment, the wall is uniquely identified and hence traceable at any point in the design process. Its characteristics can be updated at any stage of the design process by any other user. Similarly, the parameters of the wall can be recalled at any point. In this way, the user is able to ask the software about the physical properties of the wall, by knowing qualitative (type of wall, finish, layers included, final look, etc.) and quantitative (extension, dimensions, thickness, thermal mass, insulation, k-value, etc.) characteristics. A BIM model is based on the use of intelligent modelling and object-oriented parametric techniques, whereby each element in the model is related dimensionally and in its position with the others (Azhar, Khalfan, and Maqsood 2015:16). If any user at any point of the workflow modifies the attributes of an element, the rest of the connected elements will be affected, and transformed accordingly.

CIM

Whilst BIM has predominantly been employed for the design and management of data regarding complex buildings, more recently designers have been using this system as an application for smart cities and the management of cities in general (Kupriyanovsky et al. 2016). This expansion involves including new parameters in the managing system, like operational infrastructures as well as social and behavioural performance criteria (Al Sayed et al. 2015). This new type of BIM usage would be better described through the notion of City Information Modelling (CIM) (Al Sayed et al. 2015:8; Beirão et al. 2012).

For Xu et al. (2014), CIM is the combination of a number of urban sub-modules: transportation module (including spatial characteristics of roads, stations and transportation hubs), city furniture module (those urban elements which are considered ancillary to the city, like gardens, public utilities and services), building module (information about buildings and their characteristics: this is usually covered by a normal BIM system), water body (all parts of the urban and landscape infrastructure that pertains to the water system, including lakes, rivers, water basins, etc.) and mechanical, electrical and plumbing (MEP) module (this part is usually covered by BIM-based systems) (Xu et al. 2014:293, 294). From a purely data processing perspective, a CIM system is fed by a set of data that comes from BIM and GIS databases, so it is an integrated system that includes both geo-referenced data and building data. A clear visualisation of a CIM system can be achieved by using two semantic models: the Industry Foundation Classes (IFC) and the City Geography Markup Language (cityGML) (Xu et al. 2014:293–96). Whereas the IFC is the information model that underpins the BIM structure (Thein 2011), the cityGML is the XML-based standard based on an open data model that allows designers to visualise (represent) 3D models of cities and exchange the data globally. CityGML has a twofold function. Firstly, it supports designers in generating the physical appearance of urban models (e.g. massing and volumes) in a 3D environment and, secondly, it "specifically addresses the object semantics and the representation of the thematic properties, taxonomies and aggregations" (Kolbe 2009:15). In addition to including a comprehensive range of functional aspects of cities, CIM also includes facets of urban life. One way to include these is suggested by Stojanovski (2013) as a combination of layers of accesses and connections amongst a city's blocks. Within a CIM environment, we can easily record social interactions by means of tagging activities (e.g. meetings) in relation to urban elements (e.g. buildings). All activities considered within a certain observation are identified with a unique ID number and stored in a database. The activities are linked with the online realm of the Internet and might include hashtags, news feeds, events, stories, shared pictures and video. These are then interpolated with the urban blocks and buildings in the system and to each correlation a number of attributes are assigned (Stojanovski 2013:6). In this sense, CIM is the interactive and real-time evolution of GIS and BIM logics, whereby all static and offline characteristics are superseded by live and continuously evolving data. What BIM and GIS probably do not include in their systems are the liveness of individuals in the public realm, their complexity and unpredictability, with continuous adaptation to events (e.g. people sheltering under a canopy in response to a sudden downpour). This notion is encapsulated by the idea model of urban design ontology (UDO), whereby the ontology of the urban life would be included, factored and represented by a CIM system (Montenegro and Duarte 2009:259).

Using data

The case studies that follow illustrate how the urban sensed data are used by architects. In particular, it is worth noting that data are used to improve existing buildings (INDICATE project) or building models (KPFui), making buildings and cities smarter.

The INDICATE project (Indicator-based Interactive Decision and Information Exchange Platform for Smart Cities) is a collaboration among a set of different partners, including public bodies, academic institutions and small and large private companies. The project provides a series of tools to transform existing cities into smart cities. Each building in the analysed area has a number of attributes attached to it that describe the smartness of the building, including connectivity, energy performance, energy consumption, production of CO_2 etc. (Indicate 2018). The software that is developed as a part of this project (an interactive cloud-based tool) is a simulation tool that helps designers to evaluate the current status and performance of existing buildings and to test and monitor the improvements based on the proposed changes. This is done through interpolation of the building characteristics (including level of occupancy and usage) and a number of infrastructural systems, including the electricity grid, and Renewable Technologies and Information Communication Technologies (ICT) (Indicate 2018). In a sense, INDICATE is a good example of how a CIM may work with particular attention to the building performances and energy usage.

When a data-rich system is used to inform the design process through a logic parametric process, we can observe how a consolidated urban block as the Blooms-bury in London can become much smarter (KPFui 2018). A study conducted by KPF Urban Interface (KPFui), the digital research strand of the global architec-tural practice, illustrates this rationalisation process through a consistent digital logic. The input data for this process are the Floor Area Ratio (FAR), the local density, the historical development of the urban block from Georgian architecture to date, daylight access for residential units and ambient daylight in public spaces. A workflow based on a number of generative algorithms provided the designers with an iterative testing tool to determine the characteristics that a building block should have in order to perform at its best. The system tested a number of possible solutions parametrically. Some of the parameters have remained constant (resi-dential and public space daylight levels), while the variables include orientation of the block in its context and the ideal density (to be maximised). This system allowed for a clear framework to benchmark any possible variation of a given block in a given urban context. A number of algorithms have been scripted to allow the machine to compute tens of thousands of possible outcomes assessed against the initial criteria of optimal density and quality of residential and public spaces. The system generated a discrete range of ideal scenarios where urban planners can have high performing block configurations yet with a certain degree of leeway.

Once the most performing configuration has been identified, the process is then applied to a generic urban area where algorithms provide a strict set of rules of variations for the developable area, the street area, the average block perimeter, the total GFA (Gross Floor Area), podium area ratio and total surface area. All parameters are in a system and related to each other, whereby each value changes according to the others in a harmonious manner. By observing several iterations, one can notice that the variations are discrete, as the building blocks or streets move within a grid-like fashion, occupying slits in an invisible matrix of rigid boxes.

The third case study is Sidewalk Labs's project for a smart city conceived "from the Internet up" (Doctoroff 2016). This is part of a larger concept of envisioning the future of cities, whereby "a combination of digital technologies – ubiquitous connectivity, social networks, sensing, machine learning and artificial intelli-gence, and new design and fabrication technologies – would help bring about a revolution in urban life" (Doctoroff 2016). The most extensive study has been carried out on the Quayside area of Toronto, where a new type of neighbourhood has been designed where the physical and digital dimensions are combined. Inter-estingly, in a city from the Internet up, the majority of traditional urban elements are different. For example, the grid that characterises most of the contemporary developments as efficient urban schemes is replaced by a more dynamic and fluid structure.[8] Similarly, main roads, avenues and promenades have a meandering and undulating shape, where building fronts have curved facades to stimulate people's engagement with the public space. The building blocks have a high degree of mixed-use programmes, where: "a radical mixed-use environment means that the

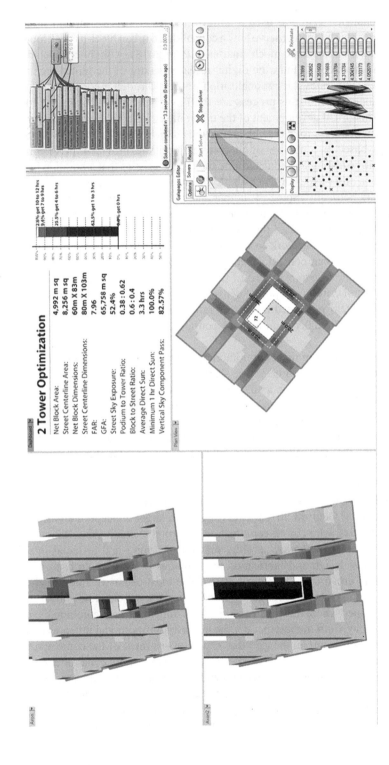

Figure 3.13 Testing of different options in search of the highest performing block configurations

Source: KPFui (2018)

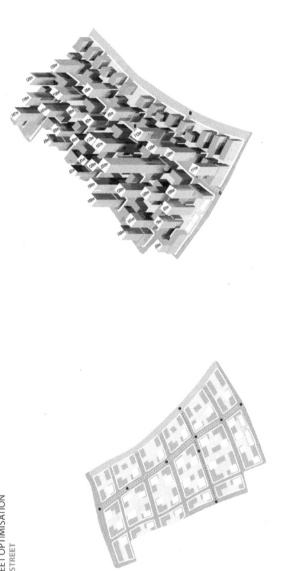

Figure 3.14 Schematic diagram of the mutual change of parameters in testing the optimum density for urban blocks

Source: KPFui (2018)

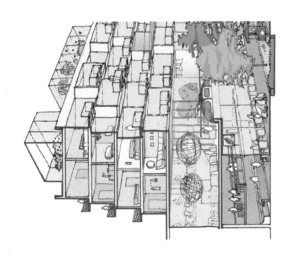

New Neighbourhood

Traditional Neighbourhood

Figure 3.15 Sidewalk Labs – Quayside Toronto. Urban fabric from the Internet-up

Source: Sidewalk Labs (2017:26)

neighbourhood is always in flux, creating a dynamic community and enabling needs to be met at a much quicker pace" (Sidewalk Labs 2017:27). All utilities and urban infrastructures are placed underground, including telecommunications and waste collection. On top of any elements constituting the built environment, Sidewalk Labs places a ubiquitous digital layer. "A Sense feature knits together a distributed network of sensors to collect real-time data about the surrounding environment, enabling people to measure, understand, and improve it", where there is a "map component [which] collects location-based information about the infrastructure, buildings, and shared resources in the public realm" (Sidewalk Labs 2017:66).

The new area is imagined as a living laboratory for data harvesting, urban analytics and future software development, whereby people are at the centre. "A vastly expanded array of fixed-sensor inputs and control outputs will generate an enormous amount of data on the built environment that developers, students, and residents will be able to use to reimagine and reinvent how the city works" (Sidewalk Labs 2017:71).

Data are continuously produced by individuals who are always connected to an overarching cloud system. Individuals and everything else in the built environment are tracked and sensed by beacon sightings, LiDAR and cameras, and sensors. These are controlled by APIs that recognise entities and categorise them by recording spatial and temporal characteristics (location, speed, number of occurrences, frequency, etc.). These data are then located in an historical database for future retrieval and analytics, and, at the same time, they feed real-time databases used to compute quick queries (Sidewalk Labs 2017:73). Since the whole sensing

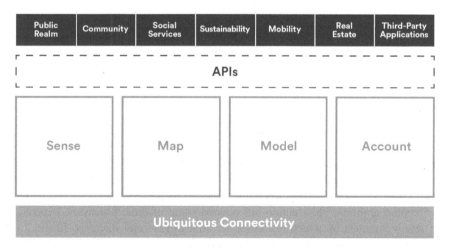

Figure 3.16 Sidewalk Labs – Quayside Toronto. Map of the APIs based on a ubiquitous connectivity

Source: Sidewalk Labs (2017:67)

Figure 3.17 Sidewalk Labs – Quayside Toronto. The presence of sensors in the urban environment

Source: Sidewalk Labs (2017:67)

infrastructure is controlled by the same agency (Alphabet), data are comprehensively collected and their storage and analysis are centralised. This can be seen as an ultimate version of the IoT controlled by one party.

Conclusions

This chapter has explored some of the mechanisms by which machines scan, read and try to interpret the world, in contrast with the sensible ways in which humans perceive it. Whilst people see the world through their senses and attribute meaning to it through their intelligibility, computers perform routines that are in part based on their computational and iterative nature, and in part a simulation of human abilities. This section has opened some of these processes, exposing a few techniques by which machines are able to read and interpret. In the following chapters, we describe how these practices, as they are increasingly more extended, have a significant impact in determining the perception and the use that people have and make of the built environment. In the realm of urban design, this process of discretisation starts from the ways in which designers work with the environment. They start the design process with data that have been produced and rationalised by computers. They use a set of tools that are entirely digital and, as such, based on a computational system. The initial data, intended here as the context of the design process, and the digital design tools are considered within a conceptual and operational framework which has now become characteristic of today's design processes. This framework is inheritably digital, as it is operated by following a digital logic, whereby phenomena are translated into data, discretised in a highly elaborated series of 0s and 1s, and output into blocks that take the form of pixels, lines of codes, voxels, digits, numbers and letters, etc. All these are regulated by algorithms, underpinned by mathematical formulae. In some cases, the results of these designs patently show the digital aspects, where the underpinning discrete logic corresponds to aesthetical values and discrete shapes (e.g. voxel-based geometries). In some other cases, the final result is not a visual carrier of the discrete logic. This is the case for those architectures that appear fluid and seamless. In Chapter 5, we discuss in-depth this point, proposing a number of characteristics that qualify the architectural space resulting from the digital logic. The aim of this chapter is to identify and bring to the fore the discrete logic that is behind any digital design today.

Notes

1 To be precise, Harman generates a model that reduces the realm of the existence into two types of qualities (real and sensual) and two objects (real and sensual), analysing their mutual relationships in his ontography (Harman 2011:124).
2 www.npcc.police.uk/FreedomofInformation/ANPR.aspx. Last accessed 9 April 2018.
3 https://algobeans.com/2017/11/02/self-organizing-map/. Last accessed 9 April 2018.
4 www.eecs.qmul.ac.uk/~norman/BBNs/Bayes_rule.htm. Last accessed 9 April 2018.
5 https://hackernoon.com/how-to-build-a-simple-spam-detecting-machine-learning-clas sifier-4471fe6b816e. Last accessed 24 May 2018.
6 www.joelsimon.net/evo_floorplans.html. Last accessed 7 November 2018.
7 http://citydashboard.org/about.php. Last. Last accessed 24 May 2018.
8 See the report: Vision Sections of RFP Submission at page 22 https://sidewalktoronto. ca/wp-content/uploads/2018/05/Sidewalk-Labs-Vision-Sections-of-RFP-Submission. pdf. Last accessed 1 September 2018.

References

Abrahamson, Karl, Norm Dadoun, David G. Kirkpatrick, and T. Przytycka. 1989. "A Simple Parallel Tree Contraction Algorithm." *Journal of Algorithms* 10 (2): 287–302.

Ackermann, Friedrich. 1999. "Airborne Laser Scanning: Present Status and Future Expectations." *International Society for Photogrammetry and Remote Sensing (ISPRS)* 54 (2–3): 64–67.

Adey, Peter. 2002. "Secured and Sorted Mobilities: Examples from the Airport." *Surveillance & Society* 1 (4).

Ahn, Jae-Wook, and Sue Yeon Syn. 2005. "Self-organizing Maps." Accessed May 28, 2018. www.pitt.edu/~is2470pb/Spring05/FinalProjects/Group1a/tutorial/som.html.

Al Sayed, Kinda, Mark Bew, Alan Penn, Dan Palmer, and Tim Broyd. 2015. "Modelling Dependency Networks to Inform Data Structures in BIM and Smart Cities." In *Proceedings of the 10th Space Syntax Symposium (SSS10)*, edited by H. Karimi, L. Vaughan,

K. Sailer, G. Palaiologou, and T. Bolton, 90:1–90:15. London: Space Syntax Laboratory, The Bartlett School of Architecture, University College London.

Anjomshoaa, A., F. Duarte, D. Rennings, T. Matarazzo, P. de Souza, and C. Ratti. 2018. "City Scanner: Building and Scheduling a Mobile Sensing Platform for Smart City Services." *IEEE Internet of Things Journal*: 1–1. doi:10.1109/JIOT.2018.2839058.

Ayodele, Taiwo Oladipupo. 2010. "Types of Machine Learning Algorithms." In *New Advances in Machine Learning*. IntechOpen. Last accessed March 1, 2018. https://www.intechopen.com/books/new-advances-in-machine-learning/types-of-machine-learning-algorithms.

Azhar, Salman, Malik Khalfan, and Tayyab Maqsood. 2015. "Building Information Modelling (BIM): Now and Beyond." *Construction Economics and Building* 12 (4): 15–28.

Bates, Douglas M., and Donald G. Watts. 1988. "Nonlinear Regression: Iterative Estimation and Linear Approximations." *Nonlinear Regression Analysis and Its Applications*: 32–66.

Battiti, Roberto, and Francesco Masulli. 1990. "BFGS Optimization for Faster and Automated Supervised Learning." *International Neural Network Conference*. Dordrecht: Springer.

Batty, Michael, Andrew Hudson-Smith, Richard Milton, and Andrew Crooks. 2010. "Map Mashups, Web 2.0 and the GIS Revolution." *Annals of GIS* 16 (1): 1–13.

Beirão, José, José Duarte, Rudi Stouffs, and Henco Bekkering. 2012. "Designing with Urban Induction Patterns: A Methodological Approach." *Environment and Planning B: Planning and Design* 39 (4): 665–82.

Bleecker, Julian. 2006. "A Manifesto for Networked Objects – Cohabiting with Pigeons, Arphids and Aibos in the Internet of Things." Last accessed March 1, 2018. http://nearfuturelaboratory.com/files/WhyThingsMatter.pdf.

Blelloch, Guy E., and Jonathan C. Hardwick. 1993. *Class Notes: Programming Parallel Algorithms cs 15–840b (Fall 1992)*. Pittsburgh: School of Computer Science, Carnegie-Mellon University.

Bogost, Ian. 2009. "What is Object-Oriented Ontology?" Accessed May 24, 2018. http://bogost.com/writing/blog/what_is_objectoriented_ontolog/.

Bogost, Ian. 2012. *Alien Phenomenology, Or, What It's Like to be a Thing*. Minneapolis, MN: University of Minnesota Press.

Bowker, Geoffrey C., and Susan Leigh Star. 2000. *Sorting Things Out: Classification and Its Consequences*. MIT press.

Brown, Adam. 2016. "Adaptive Algorithms for Interrogating the Viewable Scene of an Automotive Radar." *Google Patents*.

Bryant, Levi. 2013. "Object-Oriented Ontology, Lacan, and the Subject." Last accessed March 1, 2018. https://larvalsubjects.wordpress.com/2013/06/18/object-oriented-ontology-lacan-and-the-subject/.

Burrows, Roger, and Nicholas Gane. 2006. "Geodemographics, Software and Class." *Sociology* 40 (5): 793–812.

Carroll-Mayer, Moira, N. Ben Fairweather, Bernd Carsten Stahl, and Ben Fairweather. 2006. *From the Far Side of the Looking Glass: The Distortion, Uglification and Derision of Justice through 21st Century Surveillance Technologies*. Sheffield: Crime, Justice and Surveillance.

Chandrashekar, Girish, and Ferat Sahin. 2014. "A Survey on Feature Selection Methods." *Computers & Electrical Engineering* 40 (1): 16–28.

Colorni, Alberto, Marco Dorigo, and Vittorio Maniezzo. 1991. "Distributed Optimization by Ant Colonies." In *Toward a Practice of Autonomous Systems: Proceedings of the*

First European Conference on Artificial Life, edited by Francisco J. Varela, and Paul Bourgine, 134–142. Cambridge, MA: MIT Press, 1992.

Cresswell, Tim. 2001. "The Production of Mobilities." *New Formations* (43): 11–25.

Cullinane, Brian Douglas, Philip Nemec, Manuel Christian Clement, Robertus Christianus Elisabeth Mariet, and Lilli Ing-Marie Jonsson. 2017. "Engaging and Disengaging for Autonomous Driving." *Google Patents.*

Cureton, Paul. 2016. *Strategies for Landscape Representation: Digital and Analogue Techniques.* Abingdon, Oxon: Taylor & Francis.

Curry, Michael R., David Phillips, and David Lyon. 2003. "Privacy and the Phenetic Urge: Geodemographics and the Changing Spatiality of Local Practice." In *Surveillance as Social Sorting: Privacy, Risk, and Automated Discrimination.* London: Routledge.

Dashboard, Dublin. Accessed 2018. www.dublindashboard.ie/pages/index.

Dashboard, Dublin. 2018. www.dublindashboard.ie/pages/DublinRealtime.

Distner, Martin, Mattias Bengtsson, Thomas Broberg, and Lotta Jakobsson. 2009. "City Safety – A System Addressing Rear-end Collisions at Low Speeds." *Proceedings 21st International Technical Conference on the Enhanced Safety of Vehicles.* Stuttgard: ESV.

Doctoroff, Daniel. 2016. "Reimagining Cities from the Internet Up." https://medium.com/ sidewalk-talk/reimagining-cities-from-the-internet-up-5923d6be63ba.

Dodge, Martin, and Rob Kitchin. 2003. *Mapping Cyberspace.* London: Routledge.

Dussell, William O., James M. Janky, John F. Schipper, and David J. Cowl. 1999. "Position based Personal Digital Assistant." *Google Patents.*

Ferguson, David I., and Dmitri A. Dolgov. 2015. "Systems and Methods for Determining Whether a Driving Environment has Changed." *Google Patents.*

Fields, Anna, and Richard Green. 2012. "Characteristic-based Vehicle Recognition for Collision Detection." In *Proceedings of the 27th Conference on Image and Vision Computing New Zealand*, edited by Brendan McCane, Steven Mills, and Jeremiah D. Deng. Dunedin: ACM.

Finn, Ed. 2017. *What Algorithms Want: Imagination in the Age of Computing.* Cambridge, MA: MIT Press

Galloway, Anne. 2004. "Intimations of Everyday Life: Ubiquitous Computing and the City." *Cultural Studies* 18 (2–3): 384–408.

Gandy Jr, Oscar H. 1993. *The Panoptic Sort: A Political Economy of Personal Information (Critical Studies in Communication and in the Cultural Industries).* Boulder, CO: Westview.

Girshick, Ross. 2015. "Fast r-cnn." *arXiv preprint arXiv:1504.08083.*

Goodman, Dennis M., Taylor W. Lawrence, J. Patrick Fitch, and Erik M. Johansson. 1990. "Bispectral-based Optimization Algorithms for Speckle Imaging." *Proceedings SPIE 1351, Digital Image Synthesis and Inverse Optics.* San Diego, CA: SPIE.

Graham, Stephen D. N., Ed. 2004. *The Cybercities Reader.* London: Routledge.

Graham, Stephen D. N. 2005. "Software-sorted Geographies." *Progress in Human Geography* 29 (5): 562–80.

Gray, Mitchell. 2002. "Urban Surveillance and Panopticism: Will We Recognize the Facial Recognition Society?" *Surveillance & Society* 1 (3): 314–30.

Grubb, Gant, Alexander Zelinsky, Lars Nilsson, and Magnus Rilbe. 2004. "3D Vision Sensing for Improved Pedestrian Safety." *Intelligent Vehicles Symposium, 2004 IEEE.* IEEE, Parma, Italy.

Harman, G. 2011. *The Quadruple Object.* London: Zero Books.

Harman, G. 2018. *Object-oriented Ontology: A New Theory of Everything.* London: Penguin.

Haugeland, John. 1989. *Artificial Intelligence: The Very Idea.* Cambridge, MA: MIT Press.

Indicate. 2018. www.indicate-smartcities.eu/.

Kaelbling, Leslie Pack, Michael L. Littman, and Andrew W. Moore. 1996. "Reinforcement Learning: A Survey." *Journal of Artificial Intelligence Research* 4: 237–85.

Kalman, Rudolph Emil. 1960. "A New Approach to Linear Filtering and Prediction Problems." *Journal of Basic Engineering* 82 (1): 35–45.

Karger, David R. 1993. "Global Min-cuts in RNC, and Other Ramifications of a Simple Min-cut Algorithm." *Proceedings of the 4th Annual ACM- Society for Industrial and Applied Mathematics Symposium on Discrete Algorithms*, 21–30. Philadelphia, PA: Society for Industrial and Applied Mathematics, January

Karger, David R., Philip N. Klein, and Robert E. Tarjan. 1995. "A Randomized Linear-time Algorithm to Find Minimum Spanning Trees." *Journal of the ACM (JACM)* 42 (2): 321–28.

Kitchin, Rob. 2014. *The Data Revolution: Big Data, Open Data, Data Infrastructures and their Consequences.* London: Sage.

Kohonen, Teuvo. 1998. "The Self-organizing Map." *Neurocomputing* 21 (1–3): 1–6.

Kolbe, Thomas H. 2009. "Representing and Exchanging 3D City Models with CityGML." In *3D Geo-information Sciences*, edited by Jiyeong Lee, and Siyka Zlatanova, 15–31. Berlin, Germany: Springer.

KPFui. 2018. http://ui.kpf.com/projects/#london-block.

Krupansky, Jack. 2017. "What is an Intelligent Digital Assistant?" *Medium.* Last accessed May 3, 2018. https://medium.com/@jackkrupansky/what-is-an-intelligent-digital-assist ant-3f601a4bb1f2.

Kuehl, Daniel T. 2009. "From Cyberspace to Cyberpower: Defining the Problem." *Cyberpower and National Security*: 24–42.

Kupriyanovsky, Vasily, Sergey Sinyagov, Dmitry Namiot, Petr Bubnov, and Julia Kupriyanovsky. 2016. "The New Five-year Plan for BIM-infrastructure and Smart Cities." *International Journal of Open Information Technologies* 4 (8): 20–35.

Labs, Sidewalk. 2017. "Vision Sections of RFP Submission." https://sidewalktoronto.ca/wp-content/uploads/2018/05/Sidewalk-Labs-Vision-Sections-of-RFP-Submission.pdf.

Lash, Scott. 2007. "Power after Hegemony: Cultural Studies in Mutation?" *Theory, Culture & Society* 24 (3): 55–78.

Leach, Paul J., Michael Mealling, and Rich Salz. 2005. "A Universally Unique Identifier (Uuid) Urn Namespace." Last accessed May 3, 2018. https://tools.ietf.org/html/rfc4122.

Lyon, David. 2002. "Surveillance Studies: Understanding Visibility, Mobility and the Phenetic Fix." *Surveillance & Society* 1 (1): 1–7.

Mattila, Juri. 2016. *The Blockchain Phenomenon: The Disruptive Potential of Distributed Consensus Architectures.* Berkeley, CA: Roundtable on the International Economy (Brie). University of California

Mayer, Marco, Luigi Martino, Pablo Mazurier, and Gergana Tzvetkova. 2014. "How Would You Define Cyberspace." *First Draft Pisa* 19: 2014.

Miller, Harvey J., and Jiawei Han. 2009. *Geographic Data Mining and Knowledge Discovery.* London: CRC Press.

Montenegro, N., and José P. Duarte. 2009. "Computational Ontology of Urban Design." *Proceedings of the 27th Conference on Education in Computer Aided Architectural Design in Europe (eCAADe'09).* Istanbul, Turkey: eCAADe.

Morton, Timothy. 2011. "Here Comes Everything: The Promise of Object-oriented Ontology." *Qui Parle: Critical Humanities and Social Sciences* 19 (2): 163–90.

Morton, Timothy. 2013. *Hyperobjects: Philosophy and Ecology after the End of the World.* Minneapolis, MT: University of Minnesota Press.

Møller, Martin Fodslette. 1993. "A Scaled Conjugate Gradient Algorithm for Fast Supervised Learning." *Neural Networks* 6 (4): 525–33.

Naik, Nikhil, Jade Philipoom, Ramesh Raskar, and César Hidalgo. 2014. "Streetscore-predicting the Perceived Safety of One Million Streetscapes." *Proceedings of the IEEE Conference on Computer Vision and Pattern Recognition Workshops*, 779–785. New Jersey: IEEE.

Neff, Gina, and Dawn Nafus. 2016. *Self-tracking*. MIT Press.

Nex, F., and Fulvio Rinaudo. 2009. "New Integration Approach of Photogrammetric and LIDAR Techniques for Architectural Surveys." In: *Laser scanning 2009*. The International Archives of the Photogrammetry, Remote Sensing and Spatial Information Sciences (IAPRS), edited by F. Bretar, M. Pierrot-Deseilligny, and G. Vosselman, Vol. XXXVIII, Part 3/W838 (3). Paris, France.

Ng, A., Soo, Kenneth. 2017. *Numsense! Data Science for the Layman: No Math Added*. Amazon Media.

Numina. Accessed May 6, 2018. www.numina.co/.

Paglen, Tevor. 2016. "Invisible Images (Your Pictures Are Looking at You)." In *The New Inquiry*. Last accessed May 1, 2018. https://thenewinquiry.com/invisible-images-your-pictures-are-looking-at-you/.

Perek, David R., Michael A. Schwager, Sharon Drasnin, and Mark J. Seilstad. 2013. "Sensor Fusion Algorithm." *Google Patents*.

PulseMedia. 2018. Accessed May 6, 2018. http://pulse.media.mit.edu/vision/.

Ramos, Carlos, Juan Carlos Augusto, and Daniel Shapiro. 2008. "Ambient intelligence—The Next Step for Artificial Intelligence." *IEEE Intelligent Systems* 23 (2): 15–18.

Raphael, Bertram. 1964. "A Computer Program Which Understands." Proceedings of the October 27–29, 1964, Fall Joint Computer Conference, Part I. New York: ACM.

Rumelhart, David E., Geoffrey E. Hinton, and Ronald J. Williams. 1986. "Learning Representations by Back-propagating Errors." *Nature* 323 (6088): 533.

Russell, Mark E., Michael Joseph Delcheccolo, Walter Gordon Woodington, H. Barteld Van Rees, John Michael Firda, and Delbert Lippert. 2004. "Safe Distance Algorithm for Adaptive Cruise Control." *Google Patents*.

ScanLab. 2017. "Transformation." https://scanlabprojects.co.uk/work/bartlett-transformation/.

Sense, Citizen. 2016. "Dustbox". https://citizensense.net/dustbox-and-airsift-data-toolkit/.

Settles, Burr. 2012. "Active Learning." *Synthesis Lectures on Artificial Intelligence and Machine Learning* 6 (1): 1–114.

Shapiro, Stuart Charles. 1979. *Techniques of Artificial Intelligence*. Van Nostrand Reinhold Company.

Simon, Joel. 2018. "Evolving Floorplans." Accessed November 7, 2018. www.joelsimon.net/evo_floorplans.html.

Stanley, Kenneth O., and Risto Miikkulainen. 2002. "Evolving Neural Networks through Augmenting Topologies." *Evolutionary Computation* 10 (2): 99–127. Cambridge, MA: MIT Press.

Stojanovski, Todor. 2013. "City Information Modeling (CIM) and Urbanism: Blocks, Connections, Territories, People and Situations." In *Proceedings of the Symposium on Simulation for Architecture & Urban Design*, edited by Liam O'Brien, Burak Gunay and Azam Khan. San Diego, CA: SIMAUD.

Stone, Allucquere Rosanne, and Michael Benedikt. 1991. "Cyberspace: First Steps." *Streetscore*. Accessed May 6, 2018. http://streetscore.media.mit.edu/faq.html.

Su, Xiaoyuan, and Taghi M. 2009. Khoshgoftaar. "A Survey of Collaborative Filtering Techniques." *Advances in Artificial Intelligence* 2009.

Swan, Melanie. 2013. "The Quantified Self: Fundamental Disruption in Big Data Science and Biological Discovery." *Big Data* 1 (2): 85–99.

Tasca, Paolo, Thayabaran Thanabalasingham, and Claudio J. Tessone. 2017. "Ontology of Blockchain Technologies: Principles of Identification and Classification." *arXiv preprint arXiv:1708.04872*.

Teney, Damien, Peter Anderson, Xiaodong He, and Anton van den Hengel. 2017. "Tips and Tricks for Visual Question Answering: Learnings from the 2017 Challenge." *arXiv preprint arXiv:1708.02711*.

The Open Group. A Universally Unique IDentifier (UUID) URN Namespace. 1997. retrieved from https://www.ietf.org/rfc/rfc4122.txt

Thein, Volker. 2011. "Industry Foundation Classes (IFC)." *BIM Interoperability through a Vendor-independent File Format*. White Paper. Bentley. last accessed May 1, 2018, http://www.consultaec.com.au/white-paper-ifc-bim-interoperability-through-a-vendor-independent-file-format/.

Thrift, Nigel. 1994. "Inhuman Geographies: Landscapes of Speed, Light and Power." *Writing the Rural: Five Cultural Geographies*: 191–248.

Trott, Alexander, Caiming Xiong, and Richard Socher. 2017. "Interpretable Counting for Visual Question Answering." *arXiv preprint arXiv:1712.08697*.

UCL. 2017. "3D Scan Film Shows the Bartlett's Transformation." www.ucl.ac.uk/bartlett/architecture/news/2017/nov/3d-scan-film-shows-bartletts-transformation.

Vukolić, Marko. 2015. "The Quest for Scalable Blockchain Fabric: Proof-of-work vs. BFT Replication." In *Open Problems in Network Security*, edited by J. Camenisch, and D. Kesdoğan. iNetSec 2015. Lecture Notes in Computer Science, Vol 9591. Cham: Springer.

Whereabouts London. 2018. http://whereaboutslondon.org/#/map.

Xu, Xun, Lieyun Ding, Hanbin Luo, and Ling Ma. 2014. "From Building Information Modeling to City Information Modeling." *Journal of Information Technology in Construction (ITcon)* 19: 292–307.

Zhai, Xiaojun, Faycal Bensaali, and Reza Sotudeh. 2012. "OCR-based Neural Network for ANPR." Imaging Systems and Techniques (IST), *IEEE International Conference on Imaging Systems and Techniques Proceedings*. New Jersey: IEEE.

Zhang, Yin, Rong Jin, and Zhi-Hua Zhou. 2010. "Understanding Bag-of-words Model: A Statistical Framework." *International Journal of Machine Learning and Cybernetics* 1 (1–4): 43–52.

Zhu, Jiajun, David I. Ferguson, and Dmitri A. Dolgov. 2014. "System and Method for Predicting Behaviors of Detected Objects." U.S. Patent No. 8,660,734. 25 Feb.

Zhuge, Hai. 2011. "Semantic Linking through Spaces for Cyber-physical-socio Intelligence: A Methodology." *Artificial Intelligence* 175 (5–6): 988–1019.

4   Perception of the discrete city

Visibility

The first fundamental aspect that influences the perception of individuals in the new digital/physical environment is the visibility. As we see in Chapter 2, the new environment is characterised by the merger of physical and digital qualities, with some of them more visible than others to the human eye. To some extent, the relationships between these aspects are still unclear and need to be fully explored. What can be directly seen by individuals determines a certain level of understanding. For instance, data cannot be seen, so their understanding by laymen relies on trust in the system and a number of quantitative indicators (e.g. the monthly count of downloaded data on a mobile device, or the speed of an Internet connection). Along with digital infrastructures per se (e.g. the Internet), we consider here within the large category of digital environment all the infrastructures that are, in part or entirely, characterised by digital systems. These tend to be invisible or silent and difficult to distinguish from the rest of the environment (Graham and Marvin 2002:50). The digital telecommunication infrastructures include underground and aerial, radio and satellite networks that work in combination with each other to generate, translate and transport data and information across the world (Graham and Marvin 2002:51).

Contra, the visible objects in the built environment, say buildings, are unequivocally perceived by individuals for their main visual characteristics: location, mass, volume, height, decorative features, style, colours and materials. Whilst the digital infrastructures have been largely under-considered in comparison with the physical infrastructures (Graham and Marvin 2002:50), these have now become the fabric of urban life (Castell 1996). To better illustrate the difference between the visible and invisible infrastructures, and the digital and physical networks, we can compare two orders of maps created by Blum (2012) and Cheshire and Uberti (2013:143). Blum's work on mapping the physical infrastructure that makes the Internet possible describes the extent to which what is considered a network (probably today par excellence) is in reality a network of networks, whereby: "one company might own the actual fiber-optic cables, while another operates the light signals pulsing over that fiber, and a third owns (or more likely rents) the bandwidth encoded in that light" (Blum 2012:19). Whilst Blum's account is entirely text-based and descriptive, the information networks described by James Cheshire and Oliver Uberti are chiefly graphical.

Their maps visualise a series of urban data retrieved from a variety of sources to unveil patterns of behaviour (Cheshire and Uberti 2013:201), spatial and social aspects of the urban life (Cheshire and Uberti 2013:35) and use of the urban infrastructures (2013:111) of people living in London. In particular, the map that describes the routes taken by 67,000 minicabs (Cheshire and Uberti 2013:142) through 1.5 million journeys presents an interesting merger of the physical and digital systems. The map is based on the physical infrastructure of the urban and suburban road system, along with the motorways that connect the city to the major airports. However, by using GPS-based tracking technologies, the taxi drivers follow the routes indicated by SatNav applications (e.g. Google Maps and Waze). This map shows the overlap of the road network that connects Greater London as seen by computers, through community detection algorithms that establish clusters in datasets (Manley 2014) with the physical road system.

While considering the seamless functioning of invisible networks, the theme of disruption might become an element that influences the visibility and perception of such networks in people. Graham (2010) explains that digital infrastructures are invisible until the effects of their failing emerge: "the unexpected absence of functioning infrastructure works to underline the very (albeit useless) presence of the vast stretched-out system that usually remains so invisible" (Graham 2010:18). In case of failure or disruption within the digital environment, people perceive their presence immediately. Some examples can be the momentary absence of a Wi-Fi signal or problems with an Ethernet cable or Internet provider. In all these cases, people momentarily have no access to the Internet, therefore no contact with their relationships in the digital realm.

In search of patterns of use in the urban environment, the combination of physical and digital elements allows us to unveil new aspects of cities and urban life. Louise Amoore explores this potential while examining the geography of the cloud that provides the "means to map and to make perceptible the geography of our world in particular ways" (Amoore 2018:3). However, if the combination of the two realms might result in powerful tools to discover new facets of the built environment, we should also consider that their merger is not always immediate and easy. The aspects in fact function by almost opposite principles, are perceived through different means and present opposite manifestations. The physical is perceived by humans through their senses. People can measure the physical dimension of the environment in order to understand its characteristics (for example the extension of an area or the distance between two locations). The digital is read by machines, which translate the input they gather from the physical dimension into their digital realm (see Chapter 3). People have knowledge and experience as a result of their understanding of the urban environment. Computers produce data as their main output. If we concentrate on the point of view of people, and on the ways in which they experience the built environment, the notion of visibility becomes crucial to reconciling the two dimensions of the digital and the physical. Through the new tools provided by the digital technologies, people can see aspects that only computers are normally able to process. This augmented sight that people can have through computers is one of the manifestations of the new digital/physical environment. People can naturally perceive the built environment, while visualising information processed by computers at the same time. Through the new environment, "visibility both literal and metaphorical is transformed. What was opaque becomes transparent, yet what makes the hidden accessible is itself invisible" (Cuff 2003:43). The ubiquitous presence of computers allows people to increase their knowledge, not only in terms of quantity and quality, but also with regard to time (Cuff 2003:45). The speed of access to knowledge is in fact an important factor, whereby individuals can access information about what they are observing in almost real time. Pervasive computing can "open up the workings of an otherwise inaccessible mystery" (Cuff 2003:45).

Urban interfaces

The cloud is an entity that is at the same time nowhere in particular, but everywhere in general, for it is a highly distributed system the configuration of which is displaced by its nature. In topological terms, the cloud is an invisible place that is now developed alongside the traditional physical place. The relation between the cloud and the built environment is particularly relevant in this discussion. For the layman, the cloud is invisible and somewhat existing and functioning in disconnection from the physical dimension of the built environment. There is a significant separation between the two, whereby one is tangible, visible and controllable, and the other is ineffable, unperceivable and it runs by complex rules if not almost automatically. If the visibility acquires a crucial role in the appreciation of the new environment, the mechanisms that underpin the visualisation become paramount.

People access the digital world through interfaces: apparatuses that establish a common visual plane between individuals and machines. Interfaces have a dual nature: they can be read by people on one side and interpreted by machines on the other. They translate in real time two languages (human and machine code) otherwise incomprehensible to each other and they relate two incompatible systems. The British sociologist Norman Long defined, in the 1980s, the interface in sociological terms as:

> a critical point of intersection or linkage between different social systems, fields or levels of social order where structural discontinuities, based upon differences of normative value and social interest, are most likely to be found. The concept implies some kind of face-to-face encounter between individuals or units representing different interests and backed by different resources.
> (Long 1989:2)

This notion is now perfectly extendable to the individual-machine encounter: two systems that need a shared element of communication to be related.

Human-computer interfaces have been developed in different forms, from joysticks (Baer et al. 1982) and light-emission pistols (Yokoi 1976) in the game industry, to keyboards (David 1985) and mice (English and Engelbart 1967) in home computing. The common goal is to make it easier and intuitive for the user to interact with the software that the computer is running (Tulbert 2010). More recently, while mice and keyboards are still widely used, especially in the context of classrooms and offices, new technologies have emerged that increase the level and the sophistication of the interaction between human and machine. These include touch screens (Sears 1992), speech recognition (Pinola 2011) and, more interestingly, Personal Digital Assistants PDAs (Viken 2009). These represent a milestone in human-computer interaction development for they generate a hybrid interface that functions as a computer (retrieving information from the Internet, opening emails and suggesting directions through GPS networks), yet they carry some qualities that make them similar to humans (voice, humour and learning abilities). With PDAs, we can see a computer simulating and trying to replicate human behaviour. Since digital assistants have functions that work at a very high level in order to communicate with humans, the real computer logic with which they operate comes to the fore and it is extremely easy to read. In fact, whilst in other interface devices, such as a screen, the user needs to adapt to the machine outputs, trying to interpret the information required, with PDAs this direction is inverted. With digital assistants, it is the machine that tries to lean towards the user to better facilitate the communication. In other devices, the range of sequential translation of languages goes from machine code to user-friendly outputs (e.g. a text or image on the screen). In PDAs this range is wider, and it extends out to an attempt at a higher level of communication in the form of a verbal interaction. The ultimate goal would be for machines to hide their logics and functioning in the background completely, appearing and behaving *as human* at the other end of the interface. Thrift (2000, 2002, 2004) presented an optimistic view of this relationship in the hypothesis that in the future machines will become so aware of human needs and idiosyncrasies that they will shape their behaviour to adapt to people:

> through the advent of "soft computing", better understanding of affect, and new kinds of human-centred interfaces, computing is increasingly adapted to and modulated by the user. It will increasingly second-guess the user, becoming a part of how he or she decides to decide. "Computing" will therefore no longer be seen as a primary task but as a subsidiary part of many different practices, just as many mundane tools already are.
>
> (Thrift 2004:183)

However, we have discussed so far just one method of human-machine communication through interfaces, namely from humans to machines. The interaction in the other direction, that is computers to people, occurs via those inputting mechanisms that are characteristic of computers: sensors, microphones, cameras, GPS trackers, etc. (see Chapter 3). A digital camera lens is the interface through which a computer sees the world. That lens is a surface standing in-between the digital and the physical realms. Moreover, the camera itself is the vehicle by which the world's phenomena and the computer's understanding of them can actually happen. Computers themselves operate a number of stages of translation with different degrees of "concreteness and abstraction" with interfaces in-between each of these "layers in this stack" (Mattern 2014). For instance, between the machine binary code, expressed in sequences of 0 and 1, and a high-level programming language, which uses English words and mathematical symbols, there are compilers that translate the two languages. Between a high-level language and a lower level language there are interpreters, and between lower level language, in the form of letters and symbols with basic instruction, and the machine language there are assemblers (Earley and Sturgis 1970; Henz 2012). Amongst these, we should also include encoders and decoders that translate from one code to another more in general terms (see for example Koenen 1999). At an even higher level we could mention the Application Programming Interfaces (API). These are instructions, protocols and tools that connect two or more languages across different systems, as they are independent of any specific language, and they create an interface between applications (application software) and libraries (programming library (Unrein, Odenwald, and Rose 2013). All these translations from higher levels to the most basic machine code are operated by virtual interfaces that make the contact between two languages possible.

A second level of interface between humans and computers, with particular application in urban contexts, is the city dashboard (Mattern 2015). As cities and governments open up their urban data to the general public, dashboards, in the form of public websites, are the main vehicle by which people can access these open data and have insights into the city's performance. Dashboards are simplified and user-friendly platforms that convert complex and large datasets (chiefly big data) gathered from a variety of sources and in different formats, into information that is easy to read by the layperson. These dashboards are software and represent an interface: a place where the complexity of datasets incomprehensible to people but easily managed by computers is transformed into a high-level language that people are able to appreciate intuitively. On the one hand, we have long and complex datasets (Assunção et al. 2015). On the other hand, we see a graphical language accompanied by brief descriptive texts and values that express urban trends, characteristics and performances. One of the interesting aspects of dashboards is the direction of information between computers and people. In principle, this type of interface simplifies human to machine communication, in the translation of the two languages. However, considering this question from a social perspective, one might note that the relationship established between the two parties is utterly unbalanced. Whilst it is true that the software translates complex datasets for people to easily access information about their own city, it is also true that people are relegated to a passive and inquisitive role, whereby they can only ask the software for a specific range of information that relates to utilisation and performance of the urban resources. Shannon Mattern explored this question arguing that: "these interfaces to the smart city suggest that we've traded in our environmental wisdom, political agency and social responsibility for corporately-managed situational information, instrumental rationality and personal consumption and convenience" (Mattern 2014).

Tracking the self

One the most effective ways in which people interact with the digital world is through the use of digital technologies, more specifically tracking devices, to access information that would be otherwise unknown about themselves. A tendency that epitomises the discretisation of today's society can be found in the Quantified Self movement (Lupton 2016). With the aid of wearable technologies (e.g. sensors, beacons and trackers) that monitor daily activities, each individual is capable of self-tracking and having an accurate report of various aspects of her/his life. These include detailed calories intake, quality and quantity of consumed food, quality of air of the surroundings, noise level, light exposure, hydration levels, number of sleep hours, and also blood oxygen levels, number of steps, or miles walked, etc. Wearable computers collect all this information, sending it to a server, which gives back to the individual an accurate picture of health condition, quality of life and, more importantly, stores a valuable amount of data for future use. Deborah Lupton describes this entanglement of objects, data and people as a type of assemblage (Marcus 2006): human-body-device-sensor-software-data configuration (Lupton 2016:40).

Data, and wearable devices that allow individuals to collect and control their routines, provide people with what Kevin Kelly (Swan 2013:85–99) termed "exosenses": a new set of senses by which one can experience oneself, as well as the environment in a new way. Self-tracking allows for new awareness about ourselves. People may decide to hack their own habits, or create new ones based on the old (Neff and Nafus 2016:90). These may resonate with routines at work (being more efficient), with the social sphere (being more sociable), with health and wellness (being more aware of the impact, for instance, of a sedentary life), as well as with the psychology of each individual (happiness in general terms). Individuals are embracing the possibilities offered by the growing computational capacity to augment their own lives, increasing their self-awareness, in a quest to understand in greater detail both the world and themselves.

When one tracks her/himself, one is under the assumption that one's data are somehow held in a private channel. While logging the food consumed in a day through the phone, the app works as an interface, sending the inputs to a server where they are processed and outputs containing information (e.g. daily calories intake) and statistics (how many calories in the week, or how many steps are needed to burn those calories) are sent back to the user. The individual is interacting with her/his own phone, logging personal information which is shared with software. There is no sense of social communication with other individuals, except when voluntarily sharing results and targets met through social media associated with the person's account. Some tracking application associated with tracking devices offer targets to users that are expressed in numbers of miles or steps per day, week or month. This not only helps monitor individual performance over time, allowing trends to be created and speculating on them, but it acts as an incentive to walk, run and burn more. The idea of individual targets accentuates the perception for individuals that they are operating in a completely private way, whereby targets are suggested and assessed by software, and not a person at the other end of the app.

However, this assumption does not reflect the reality of individual data usage. The data sent by each individual to the tracker servers for their analytics are processed at two levels. The first one is individual, whereby the single dataset (e.g. how many steps on a given day) is processed and quantified outputs are sent back to the user (e.g. how many calories burnt corresponds to those steps). The second level relates to analytics in a broader sense and within the more general idea of big data. To each individual user a unique and anonymised identifier is assigned and the information coming from each person through the app is considered in aggregation. Crawford, Lingel, and Karppi (2015) describe this passage eloquently:

> from the data collected, the wearables company can aggregate and analyze massive data sets of users in different neighborhoods, cities and countries. They can conduct detailed analysis on the different patterns according to the demographics that the user is asked to offer up: gender, age, eating patterns, moods, level of daily exercise. Yet, the user only receives an individual report of their data, day after day.
>
> (Crawford, Lingel, and Karppi 2015:493)

The individual data, considered both as input (individual to software) or output (software to individual) makes sense for the individual her/himself, for it provides useful information about the self, otherwise unknown. However, such data at the exclusive scale of the individual are restricted in their use and meaning. In the larger picture of the digital environment, an individual contribution is considered in aggregation with all other contributions gathered in the software, and furthermore factored along with other databases where relevant. Crawford and colleagues consider the tracker-tracked relationship to be unbalanced, for the user who voluntarily sends personal information only receives a portion of the analytics that are produced by the software and, to a certain extent, of the value of the information with which she/he fed the system. Conversely, computers seem to have a bigger gain in this relationship, as they use the individual contributions to infer general knowledge about cities and people.

> From this perspective, when people start using these devices they enter into a relation that is an inherently uneven exchange – they are providing more data than they receive, and have little input as to the life of that data – where it is stored, whether it can be deleted and with whom it is shared. They are also becoming part of an aggregated data set that is compared against other forms of data: medical and otherwise.
>
> (Crawford, Lingel, and Karppi 2015:493)

We should distinguish here about who the final recipient of this knowledge really is. If we consider computers as a final destination of the aggregate knowledge resulting from millions of tracking devices, we should also remember that machines are exclusively driven by the execution of their instructions in view of a predetermined goal. In this sense, knowledge for computers has no intrinsic value, nor is it the ultimate goal of their functioning. They rather treat knowledge as instrumental to determine their outputs. Conversely, if the real recipient of the new knowledge acquired by machines is people, in the form of governmental agencies or private companies, then the unbalanced relationship should be reconsidered. This would be the case in the governmental use of private data, in terms of their value and concerns related to privacy.

Another aspect to be noted in the consideration of individuals considering their self-tracking as a personal and private experience is the idea that self-tracking can, in some instances, bleed into social life. This occurs when the individual voluntarily shares attainments and targets met through social media, entering some sort of gamified version of the tracking activity. "Such quantification practices using monitoring technologies become co-producing when individuals constitute themselves as subjects engaging in self-tracking, self-care, and self-governance" (Klauser and Albrechtslund 2014:275).

At the personal level, self-tracking can be, in some instances, considered a coping mechanism that individuals employ in response to the information they learn from their devices. A "self-tracking device does not function as a commitment device, but is a re-focusing tool that summons coping tactics [which] are mechanisms that the users adopt because they want to maintain a status quo and circumvent the potential or actual experience of failure, when exposed to unsatisfactory data" (Sjöklint 2015:212). If the individual does not like or recognise herself with the results obtained, she might choose to disregard the profile of herself generated by the software and soften the expected rational approach in favour of a preferred image of the self (Sjöklint 2015:215).

In exploring the perception that people have of the digital/physical environment through the pervading discrete logic, a number of case studies are particularly helpful. They illustrate the ways in which the environment affects individuals at different scales.

The perception might vary depending on the technologies employed and the characteristics of the environment observed. For example, they can range from the simple use of a mobile phone to integrate on-site sketches and notes with the accuracy of the GPS track in certain urban paths (Fraser et al. 2013), to the use of robotic vision to enhance the perception of the urban environment (Vitor 2014).

In his experiments in the use of music in the urban context, Michael Bull analysed the effects of certain types of tunes on people, discovering how their choices may be influenced, if not determined, by sound. Bull's vision of the city is rooted in Augé's idea of genericness and non-lieux (see Chapter 2), whereby urban spaces can appear to be lacking in identity to people and the characterisation of places coming from individuals can have a positive impact: "the more we warm up our private spaces of communication the chillier the urban environment becomes, thus furthering the desire and need to communicate with absent others or to commune privately with the products of the culture industry. Media technologies simultaneously isolate and connect" (Bull 2015:9).

Another experiment carried out by Eric Paulos, R. J. Honicky, and Ben Hooker is helpful here to see the different levels of people's perceptions in the context of tracking technologies. In the attempt to study the perception of air quality in urban contexts, they employed a range of different techniques with a growing level of sophistication, and progressive reliance on digital tools. In the first instance, they gathered opinions from a sample of residents in a given area. In this process, a general mistrust emerged about the source of air quality data and their management by governmental parties (Paulos, Honicky, and Hooker 2009:426). The second stage was the employment of a text-based sharing tool working on mobile phones called ERGO: "a simple SMS system that allows anyone with a mobile phone to quickly and easily explore, query, and learn about his or her air quality on-the-go" (Paulos, Honicky, and Hooker 2009:426). Once inquired about through a text message with a determined post code, this system sends back to the users the most updated air quality reports in the area identified by the post code. This high-level software-user interaction allows people to have information in real time, as they find themselves in a particular place. A third part of this study consisted of providing taxi drivers and students with a "dash mounted GPS logger and a tube to hang from their passenger window that contained a carbon monoxide sensor (a sulfur dioxide sensor or a nitrogen dioxide sensor)" (Paulos, Honicky, and Hooker 2009:427). Although the sensors and trackers were not meant to be read by the participants, quite soon individuals started to take an active role in the experiment, interpreting the readings on the sensor and trackers and formulating their own explanations about air pollution areas in the town. A further development was the construction of a mobile-based sensor that:

> combines a carbon monoxide, nitrogen dioxide, and temperature sensor with Bluetooth wireless communication to the mobile phone. . . . These sensors have a direct response to volume concentration of gas rather than partial pressure and are ideally suited for integration into mobile devices.
> (Paulos, Honicky, and Hooker 2009:429)

This mobile phone-based sensor is to be connected via Bluetooth to a device that makes it easy to read the values of air pollution as the sensor captures them, in real time (Paulos, Honicky, and Hooker 2009:430). The last phase of this experiment consists of a sharing platform, where people can input their geo-referenced readings and see those logged by other participants: "this promotes reflection about your exposure compared to others through the day" (Paulos, Honicky, and Hooker 2009:430).

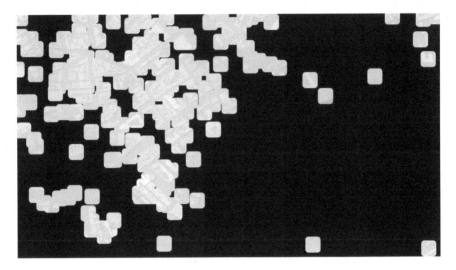

Figure 4.1 Map of open Wi-Fi coverage in central London

An example of discrete environment

As a growing number of electromagnetic waves ubiquitously cover the surface of the world, we could think of the built environment as the combination of these waves and whatever generates interference or obstacles for them. This idea has been described by William Mitchell as the Hertzian landscape (Mitchell 2004), whereby "every point on the surface of the earth is now part of the Hertzian landscape – the product of innumerable transmissions and of the reflections and obstructions of those transmissions" (Mitchell 2004:55). The Hertzian landscape is characterised by the infrastructure (generating and maintaining the transmission systems) and by the users, namely those individuals who, by utilising the available signals to tap into the several networks, establish communications. In particular, data networks are interesting to observe how people use the public space in the urban context. By accessing data networks, people become an active element in the generation of a Hertzian landscape that "overlays and overflows topographical, geographical differences between points" (Mackenzie 2006:141).

People make great use of public and open Wi-Fi networks in big cities and where available. This technology has rapidly become one of the most common ways of accessing the Internet by the general public: "increasingly, it is viewed as not just a newfangled networking gadget, but rather as the vehicle that will usher in a new era of untethered broadband Internet access for the general population" (Henry and Luo 2002:66). In 2016 the Wi-Fi Alliance calculated that around 450 million households and more than 47 million global public hotspots worldwide have been connecting through certified Wi-Fi (Wi-Fi Alliance 2016). The Wi-Fi system is underpinned by the IEEE Standard 802.11 (and all the relevant updates).[1] In general terms, the purpose of the IEEE 802.11 is to: "provide wireless connectivity for fixed, portable, and moving stations within a local area. This standard also offers regulatory bodies a means of standardizing access to one or more frequency bands for the purpose of local area communication" (IEEE 2016).

In simple terms, a router emits a radial signal through radio waves in the area. The router is associated to a Wireless Local Area Network (WLAN) and represents its access point, also popularly known as a hotspot. Any mobile device with a Wi-Fi receiver and IEEE 802.11 protocols is able to intercept the signal broadcast by the router and connect to the wireless network. Each network is identified through an SSID and often requires a password. Once the device has recognised a network, the user needs to choose to connect to the network and input the password in order to access the Internet. Mobile devices are equipped with applications that by-pass the manual choice of the SSID and password, connecting automatically when a recognised network is in range. Users normally have an app per each major Wi-Fi network provider.

In the attempt to better understand the Wi-Fi coverage in the urban context and its use by the general public, we mapped out the presence and, by extension, the absence of Wi-Fi open and public Wi-Fi networks. We concentrated on the central area of London, Covent Garden and the Strand (Figure 4.2). All the official wireless hotspots provided by the major Wi-Fi networks owned by telecommunication companies (these include FON, British Telecom, Sky Wi-Fi, The Cloud and O2), have been located on the map. This study excludes the Wi-Fi networks offered inside tube stations and other stations, as it concentrates on the public space at street level. The exact coverage of a Wi-Fi radio signal that originates from an Access Point (AP) can only be determined empirically (Alizadeh-Shabdiz and Pahlavan 2011), for it is subject to a number of factors, including the type of 802.11 protocol that the router and receivers run, the type of antennae of the transmitter and receiver and their strength, the number of users in the network, interferences with other networks and disturbing signals in the area, and the physical characteristics of the space. The first main difference is, in fact, if the router is located inside or outside a building. The second difference is in the type of materials used in the building and surroundings, their transmittance, propagation and reflectance values (Sugahara, Watanabe, and Ono 2009). Overall, between extreme values of Wireless Local Area Network radio coverage of 60 and 700 metres (Alizadeh-Shabdiz and Pahlavan 2011), we decided to use an average of 30 metres, considering the building structure that mainly characterised the area. Around each Access Point (or hotspot), we identified an area of 30 square metres and all the Wi-Fi signals which covered portions of map have been merged together (Figure 4.2). The results indicate that there are zones which are extensively covered by a number of networks (see for example around Leicester Square and St. Martin's Lane), whilst others are blind spots. Some of these areas with no public access wireless connection coincide with large residential blocks, private buildings, large theatres in the area, open spaces and the River Thames. This is related to the fact that the majority of public-access Wi-Fi networks are associated with commercial outlets, like coffee shops, restaurants and other shops. Therefore, the number and density

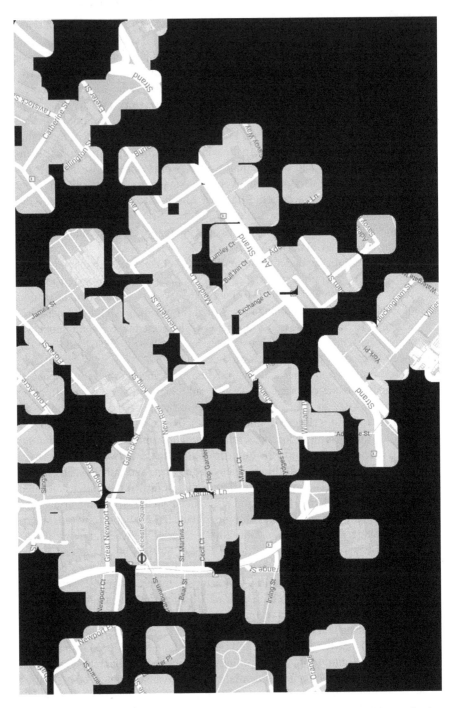

Figure 4.2 Map of open Wi-Fi coverage in central London. Close-up on Covent Garden and the Strand

of access points is directly proportional to the characteristics of specific streets, where some of them are more or less shop-oriented. For instance, the area around St. James's Park and Pall Mall presents a very low concentration of hotspots. Interestingly, we found blind spots that are in-between two buildings which cover a large portion of a street. The individuals looking for free Internet connection will be more likely to avoid these areas, using their mobile phone and the Wi-Fi signal reception icon as a navigation tool. Through this, they perceive the urban context as a discrete dimension characterised by the presence or the absence of a Wi-Fi signal. From this perspective, people understand the urban space as a combination of Wi-Fi and no Wi-Fi areas, with no continuity or fluidity in between. The binary logic of our mobile devices plays a crucial role in this. The radio antenna is reactive and certainly not predictive with regard to the urban context. If the radio signal is present and above a certain strength, the Wi-Fi icon on the screen will show a certain number of signal bars; if the signal is below a certain value, the phone will inform the user about the absence of any Wi-Fi available in that particular position.

A second example can be provided by a recent experiment with the location of taxis in New York. If big data systems are applied to the urban scale, we can observe that the computational logics utilised in smart cities generate an image of the urban spaces characterised by a complex and interrelated system of discrete values. Kitchin et al. (2015) explained this point eloquently by discussing the importance of urban indicators and real-time dashboards, whereby "they enable one to know the city as it actually is through objective, trustworthy, factual data that can be statistically analysed and visualised to reveal patterns and trends and to assess how it is performing vis-à-vis other places" (Kitchin et al. 2015:13). Similarly to all other applications of large datasets, urban big data involve a high degree of granularity, whereby the increased amount of information per unit in the observed phenomenon (for example individuals in the public space) is able to change the overall understanding of the phenomenon. This provides new insights into the system observed, where the information gathered "can be aggregated up to the societal level, and also disaggregated at the level of individual agents, offering fine-grained detail on millions, or even billions, of actions, choices and behaviours" (Rabari and Storper 2014). A clear example of this can be found in the study conducted by Ferreira et al. (2013) about TaxiVis: a visual exploration of a large set of urban data of over 520 million taxi trips in New York.

This study resulted in the production of a user-friendly visualisation tool where a number of queries can be deployed about time (passengers' pick-ups and drop-offs, trip duration, number of trips per specific day, month and time, etc.) and space (trip length, routes, etc.). The visualisation tool can provide accurate information about each taxi trip with data included in the database. This query-able tool is a clear example of how discrete systems operated by big data processes can cherry-pick any information at any time, in any given parameter of the phenomenon observed. TaxiVis is able to return the exact number of taxis in a particular street at a specific date and time, along with their unique identity. Systems where big data are not involved may be able to provide answers based on approximation

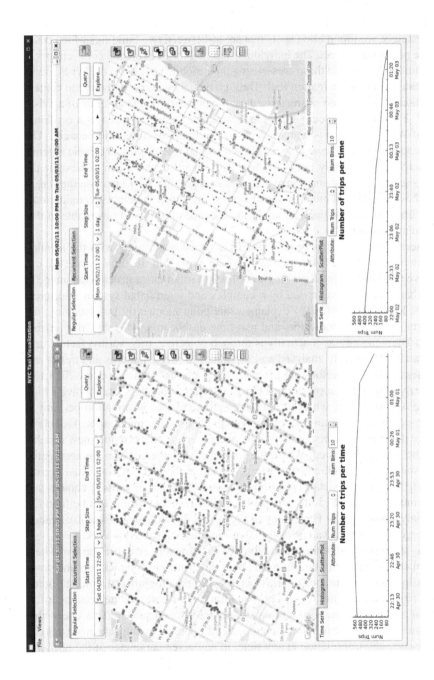

Figure 4.3 TaxiVis. Visualisation of a generic query in Manhattan

or data interpolation. If the former provides a highly accurate level of detail based on the identity of the element in the whole system, with precise datum related to space and time, the latter lacks granularity.

Perceiving a discrete environment

The discrete environment is qualified by a high degree of complexity. As the combination of physical and digital characteristics, whereby the underpinning mechanisms are governed by digital logics, this new environment is chiefly fully understandable by machines. In other words, this environment is partially generated by computers, heavily influenced by them, and operated by them. Strictly considered from the people's perspective, the new environment cannot be comprehended, for it follows a set of rules and logics that are non-human. The main argument of this chapter is that, although people cannot fully understand the complexity of this new environment, they can unveil it by means of digital techniques. This process of occasional insight in the computing complexity of the environment occurs when individuals employ computers to see into them. When people borrow the computer's eye (Chapter 3), they are temporarily exploring reality not through their own senses, but by means of digital techniques. People can only perceive this new reality, where computers are pervasive, and the machine logic is ubiquitous and pervasive, in a discontinuous (discrete) manner.

In this chapter, we analysed two aspects that play a crucial role in the process of unveiling the new environment: the notion of visibility and the practice of self-tracking. The former revolves around the idea of using digital techniques (considered here as exosenses) to be able to see aspects of reality that are invisible to the naked eye. Through computers, people can see how computers operate, see and manage the environment. This practice has been simplified by many as a form of augmented reality, whereby people's views and understanding of reality can be enhanced by the use of computers. This interpretation is here considered partial, for it considers the new environment as human-centric, primarily focusing on what people can and cannot see directly. This view disregards the fact that people share with software and the built environment the role of dynamically making the new environment (see Chapter 2). The enhanced visibility through which people can see new aspects of the environment is to be considered an important part of the process of the transductive making of the environment itself. With the idea of seeing through the software's eye, people can move more comfortably within the digital realm, better grasping the mechanisms that regulate it.

The second key aspect analysed in this chapter is self-tracking. With this, individuals have the ability to peep into the real complexity of the environment in which they live. Through looking into their own personal spheres, individuals perceive a reality that is the aggregate of different complexities, including those of other people and that dictated by the digital logic of computers.

The process of unveiling is here described through the mechanism of the interface. Previously in this section, we saw how different types of interfaces connect two very different dimensions otherwise incompatible with each other. Interfaces work as a medium between the complexity of the digital world and human reality. As such, they operate a mediation between computers and individuals. Danah Boyd expresses this notion by generalising the mediatory role of interfaces: "we live in a technologically mediated world" (Boyd 2014:180).

While discussing one the most used interfaces today to access the digital realm, namely the mobile phone, Cooper et al. (2002) reflect upon an:

> unprecedented level of integration of what might be called virtual and everyday life. . . . However, the precise form that this brave new socio-technological world might take will depend on a whole range of factors including: the practicalities of the production process, the relation between the different players (manufacturers, operators, service and content providers), the economic and regulatory context, the usability of devices, the cultural and symbolic meanings that they acquire in different social contexts, the possible social disadvantage of non-ownership, and the merging norms of acceptable use and social obligation.
>
> (Cooper et al. 2002:289)

Note

1 https://ieeexplore.ieee.org/document/7786995/. Last accessed 28 July 2018.

References

2016. "IEEE Standard for Information Technology – Telecommunications and Information Exchange between Systems Local and Metropolitan Area Networks – Specific Requirements – Part 11: Wireless LAN Medium Access Control (MAC) and Physical Layer (PHY) Specifications." *IEEE Std 802.11–2016 (Revision of IEEE Std 802.11–2012)*: 1–3534. doi:10.1109/IEEESTD.2016.7786995.

Alizadeh-Shabdiz, Farshid, and Kaveh Pahlavan. 2011. "Estimation of Position Using WLAN Access Point Radio Propagation Characteristics in a WLAN Positioning System." U.S. Patent No. 7,916,661. 29 Mar.

Alliance, Wi-Fi. 2016. "Predictions." *Wi-Fi Alliance*. http://span.s1 {font: 5.0px Helvetica}. www.wi-fi.org/news-events/newsroom/wi-fi-alliance-publishes-6-for-16-wi-fi-predictions.

Amoore, Louise. 2018. "Cloud Geographies: Computing, Data, Sovereignty." *Progress in Human Geography* 42 (1): 4–24.

Assunção, Marcos D., Rodrigo N. Calheiros, Silvia Bianchi, Marco A. S. Netto, and Rajkumar Buyya. 2015. "Big Data Computing and Clouds: Trends and Future Directions." *Journal of Parallel and Distributed Computing* 79: 3–15.

Baer, Ralph H., Leonard D. Cope, Oliver D. Holt, and Howard J. Morrison. 1982. "Interactive Game and Control Therefor." *Google Patents*.

Blum, Andrew. 2012. *Tubes: A Journey to the Center of the Internet*. New York: Ecco.

Boyd, Danah. 2014. *It's Complicated: The Social Lives of Networked Teens*. New Haven: Yale University Press.

Bull, Michael. 2015. *Sound Moves: iPod Culture and Urban Experience*. Abingdon, Oxon: Routledge.

Castells, Manuel. 1996. *The Information Age: Economy, Society and Culture. Volume I. The Rise of the Network Society*. Oxford: Wiley-Blackwell.

Cheshire, James, and Oliver Uberti. 2013. *London: The Information Capital*. London: Particular Books.

Cooper, Geoff, Nicola Green, Ged M. Murtagh, and Richard Harper. 2002. "Mobile Society? Technology, Distance." *Virtual Society? Technology, Cyberbole, Reality*: 286.

Crawford, Kate, Jessa Lingel, and Tero Karppi. 2015. "Our Metrics, Ourselves: A Hundred Years of Self-tracking from the Weight Scale to the Wrist Wearable Device." *European Journal of Cultural Studies* 18 (4–5): 479–96.

Cuff, Dana. 2003. "Immanent Domain: Pervasive Computing and the Public Realm." *Journal of Architectural Education* 57 (1): 43–49.

David, Paul A. 1985. "Clio and the Economics of QWERTY." *The American Economic Review* 75 (2): 332–337.

Earley, Jay, and Howard Sturgis. 1970. "A Formalism for Translator Interactions." *Communications of the ACM* 13 (10): 607–17.

English, William K., Douglas C. Engelbart, and Melvyn L. Berman. 1967. "Displayselection Techniques for Text Manipulation." *IEEE Transactions on Human Factors in Electronics* 1: 5–15.

Ferreira, Nivan, et al. 2013. "Visual Exploration of Big Spatio-Temporal Urban Data: A Study of New York City Taxi Trips." *IEEE Transactions on Visualization and Computer Graphics* 19 (12): 2149–2158.

Fraser, Danaë Stanton, Tim Jay, Eamonn O'Neill, and Alan Penn. 2013. "My Neighbourhood: Studying Perceptions of Urban Space and Neighbourhood with Moblogging." *Pervasive and Mobile Computing* 9 (5): 722–37.

Graham, Stephen. 2010. *Disrupted Cities: When Infrastructure Fails*. New York: Routledge.

Graham, Stephen, and Simon Marvin. 2002. *Telecommunications and the City: Electronic Spaces, Urban Places*. London: Routledge.

Henry, Paul S., and Hui Luo. 2002. "WiFi: What's Next?" *IEEE Communications Magazine* 40 (12): 66–72. IEEE, New Jersey.

Henz, Martin. 2012. "Programming Language Implementation." www.comp.nus.edu. sg/~cs4215/notes/notes_01.pdf.

Klauser, Francisco R., and Anders Albrechtslund. 2014. "From Self-tracking to Smart Urban Infrastructures: Towards an Interdisciplinary Research Agenda on Big Data." *Surveillance & Society* 12 (2): 273.

Koenen, Rob. 1999. "MPEG-4 Multimedia for Our Time." *IEEE Spectrum* 36 (2): 26–33.

Long, Norman. 1989. *Encounters at the Interface*. Wageningen, Netherlands: Agricultural University of Wageningen.

Lupton, Deborah. 2016. *The Quantified Self*. Cambridge, UK: Polity.

Mackenzie, Adrian. 2006. "From Cafe to Park Bench: Wi-Fi® and Technological Overflows in the City." In *Mobile Technologies of the City*, 145–59. Abingdon, Oxon: Routledge.

Manley, Ed. 2014. "Identifying Functional Urban Regions within Traffic Flow." *Regional Studies, Regional Science* 1 (1): 40–42.

Mattern, Shannon. 2015. "Mission Control: A History of the Urban Dashboard." *Places Journal*. Last accessed May 3, 2018. https://placesjournal.org/article/mission-control-a-history-of-the-urban-dashboard/.

Mattern, Shannon. 2014. "Interfacing Urban Intelligence." *Code and the City*: 49–60.

Mitchell, William J. 2004. *Me++: The Cyborg Self and the Networked City*. Cambridge, MA: MIT Press.

Neff, Gina, and Dawn Nafus. 2016. *The Self-Tracking*. Cambridge, MA: MIT Press.

Paulos, Eric, R. J. Honicky, and Ben Hooker. 2009. "Citizen Science: Enabling Participatory Urbanism." In *Handbook of Research on Urban Informatics: The Practice and Promise of the Real-time City*, 414–36. Hershey, PA: IGI Global.

Pinola, Melanie. 2011. "Speech Recognition through the Decades: How We Ended Up with Siri." *Web Log Post. TechHive. IDGTechNetwork* 2.

Rabari, Chirag, and Michael Storper. 2014. "The Digital Skin of Cities: Urban Theory and Research in the Age of the Sensored and Metered City, Ubiquitous Computing and Big Data." *Cambridge Journal of Regions, Economy and Society* 8 (1): 27–42.

Sears, Andrew. 1992. "A New Era for High Precision Touchscreens." *Advances in Human-Computer Interaction* 3: 1–33.

Sjöklint, Mimmi. 2015. *The Measurable Me*. PhD Series, No. 37.2015. Frederiksberg, Denmark: Copenhagen Business School.

Sugahara, Hiroto, Yoshinori Watanabe, and Takashi Ono. 2009. "Radio Wave Propagation Characteristic Estimation System, and Its Method and Program." *Google Patents*.

Swan, Melanie. 2013. "The Quantified Self: Fundamental Disruption in Big Data Science and Biological Discovery." *Big Data* 1 (2): 85–99.

Thrift, Nigel. 2000. "Afterwords." *Environment and Planning D: Society and Space* 18 (2): 213–55.

Thrift, Nigel. 2004. "Remembering the Technological Unconscious by Foregrounding Knowledges of Position." *Environment and Planning D: Society and Space* 22 (1): 175–90.

Thrift, Nigel, and Shaun French. 2002. "The Automatic Production of Space." *Transactions of the Institute of British Geographers* 27 (3): 309–335.

Tulbert, David J. 2010. "Human-machine Interface." *Google Patents*.

Unrein, Jason, Louis Henry Odenwald, and Rose George. 2013. "Application Programming Interface (API) Router Implementation and Method." *Google Patents*.

Viken, A. 2009. The history of personal digital assistants 1980–2000. Agile Mobility. Retrieved from http://agilemobility.net/2009/04/thehistory-of-personal-digital-assistants1.

Vitor, Giovani Bernardes. 2014. *Urban Environment Perception and Navigation Using Robotic Vision: Conception and Implementation Applied to Automous Vehicle*. PhD thesis. Compiègne, France: Université de Technologie de Compiègne.

Yokoi, Gunpei. 1976. "Light Ray Gun and Target Changing Projectors." *Google Patents*.

Part III

The new public realm

5　The new public space – a spatial account

Production of space: an update

In 1974 Henri Lefebvre introduced a new type of space where mediation becomes a crucial factor in its making:

> the action of groups, factors within knowledge, within ideology, or within the domain of representation. Social space contains a great diversity of objects, both natural and social, including the networks and pathways which facilitate the exchange of material things and information. Such "objects" are thus not only things but also relations.
>
> (Lefebvre 1991:77)

This seminal notion opened up new directions of research whereby the social space is considered to be the result of the combined action of physical elements (things) and immaterial factors (relations). In Chapter 2, we discussed how the ubiquitous presence of computing is related to an automated production of space. In this section, we will examine the spatial characteristics of both the physical objects (Lefebvre's things) and the relations that underpin the making of the social space. The idea underpinning this section is that Lefebvre's notion of production of space should be reconsidered in the light of the ubiquitous presence of information and software in space. The overall notion of social space should include an updated consideration of "things" and "relations", whereby software plays a major new role.

There are two main aspects to consider when observing the impact that relations have on space. The first one is represented by the invisible layer of information. In the practice of production of space, more than the actual information that concerns a specific part of the built environment, say a building, the important aspect is the access to that information. In the pre-information age, access to information was widely disconnected from the object of the inquiry itself. Information about a building, for example, its history, the architect who designed it, the total cost of construction, details of the owners or the purpose for which it has been built, and the activities happening in the building were usually found in different places (libraries, local archives, land registry, etc.) and through different means (books, registers, archives, oral knowledge, word of mouth, etc.). More likely, this information was dislocated from the building itself, making most of the buildings and the other elements in the urban context cryptic and difficult to understand. Conversely, in the information age, any information can be virtually accessed from anywhere. This implies that the location in the physical context of both the building and the source of information about it is totally irrelevant in the process of accessing the knowledge around the building. If information (and the access to it) is dissociated from the specificity of a physical place, the information and space become two separate and independent entities. This means that space and information can either be in the same place (overlapping) or their relationship can take place remotely, whereby the two entities can be in two opposite parts of the world. Moreover, if we assert that information can be (and is) everywhere, we can also assume then that every place has an invisible patina of information inside it. This patina is the space where relations take place through the access to information.

The second is related to the presence of software. As seen in Chapters 2 and 3, ubiquitous computing and pervasive code result in software (considered here as a generic entity) being omnipresent and virtually everywhere. This means that software has ramifications in any aspect of our lives, either incidentally or in a direct manner. Software, therefore, becomes a ubiquitous agent that not only structures the new environment through its digital and discrete logic, but also influences its spatiality. One of the ways of considering this point would be through McArthur's view that today: "we might cede our control in the space we inhabit to digital technologies without realising it" (McArthur 2016:29). In his account of digital proxemics, intended as the "digital inscribed negotiation of personal space through the mutual mediation of actions between space and user" (McArthur 2016:30), McArthur identified four types of interactions with which software (or digital technologies in McArthur's terms) interacts with the environment and humans. Software embedded in a space can inform a person by converting existing spatial data or gathering new contextual data into useful information for the person. Moreover, software can play an active role in the environment by altering the behaviour of the person, and ultimately, it can control her/his actions through influencing the emotional and behavioural spheres of the individual (McArthur 2016:29–30).

The influence that software has on the spatiality of the new environment should be considered from three different angles. Firstly, software influences people's perception of space. As seen in Chapter 4, people perceive the urban environment through the mediating functions of their mobile devices. They explore the city and its activities navigating through the buildings, squares and other physical urban elements through information accessed via the Internet. Where information is accessible and available, the built environment can be accessed and discovered. The invisible layers of information attached to each built element (e.g. a shop) completes and qualifies the building, unlocking (or unveiling) the knowledge around that particular space.

Secondly, software dictates the production of space by designers (see Chapter 3). Architects and planners survey, analyse and understand space through software. Their perception of spatiality is today heavily influenced by the digital logic that governs the design software. The spaces designed by architects are a direct response to the spatial mechanisms inside the software that they employ. The designed spaces are the reflection of such mechanisms in spatial terms. The rules governing the architectural composition of these spaces obey the software logic.

The third aspect to be considered is the fact that the software is one of the three agents that produces the new environment, actively influencing it. "Objects are transitory, spaces can be virtual or physical, while communication and interactions are varied and changing constantly, all affecting social and political norms" (Poldma 2011:6). As such, not only does it have a direct and indirect influence on space, whether is designed or perceived, but it is a constitutive part of the environment's spatiality. As seen in Chapter 2, software is characterised by its own spatiality that is discrete in its form, ubiquitous in its topology and global in its extension. Moreover, software is scalable. This means that it adapts to the context of reference at any specific time and case. It can be applied to the global scale as in the Internet of Things (IoT), as well as to the local and static dimension of a building. When applied, for instance, to a single coffee shop, software is contained in the physical envelope of the interior of the shop, yet it connects globally through the Internet. If software is inside the envelope of the shop, and it is working within its boundaries, it is manipulating that space (see Case Study 3.4 The Machine's Eyes in Chapter 3). The software interacts with the ambient by means of the telecommunication networks, using the WLAN present in the establishment, permeating into any message or data exchanged through Bluetooth devices (iPhones' AirDrop being an example), through 3G and 4G networks, voice communications, radio waves or trackers. Software is present in the coffee shop through networks as well as off-line. Regardless of whether a device is connected to a network or not, different software are installed in each device, from those worn by individuals, like smart watches, phones or tablets, to the various installations in the building: this includes security cameras, anti-theft systems, points of sale (POS) and cashier machines, heating and aircon controllers, lighting switches and even electric doorbells. Software, in fact, can be as sophisticated as an overall system that connects and controls multiple devices through the Internet, as well as being as simple and primitive as the circuits inside a light switch.

In her study on how Wi-Fi networks influence people's behaviour in public spaces, Laura Forlano (2009) provides an interesting point on how software interacts with the physical space. She explains that

> it should be noted that a WiFi network does not map onto existing physical or architectural boundaries. Instead, it reconfigures them in a number of ways by permeating walls, bleeding into public spaces, and breaking down some traditional notions of privacy and property while reinforcing others.
>
> (Forlano 2009:349)

From this perspective, software seamlessly flows into any space, both physical and digital. This idea is emphasised even more and applied to the urban scale by Adrian Mackenzie (2006) who, drawing from Callon et al. (2002), introduces the notion of overflow as characteristic of the data flow in the city. Overflow indicates, for example, "the flows of data and the re-positioning of everyday practices associated with Wi-Fi" (Mackenzie 2006:142). Data flow through the urban context in various ways and, by doing so, they shape the form of the city (Mackenzie 2006:142). Data flows, holds MacKenzie "are relational entities [that are] never contained. The ontological instability of flow consists in overflow" (Mackenzie 2006:143). This idea "incorporates the notion of flow and circulation as structuring the city, as folding data into places" (Mackenzie 2006:142). Data flows are associated with a degree of excess: "Data flow needs overflow, proliferation or excess of identities, figures and practices" (Mackenzie 2006:149–50).

New dimension of objects

In Chapter 2, we assume that the binaries digital/physical, virtual/real or tangible/cyber should be reconsidered in the light of a new hybridised environment where these two dimensions are not in a dichotomic relation, but rather can be seen as constitutive parts of the same entity. Cyberspace, intended in the 1990s to be dimensionless and immaterial (Negroponte 1995), is now considered within a more complex envelope, in the study of the mutual relationships that the digital world has with the built environment (Graham 2004:17).

Within this new construct, objects assume a new materiality that is not entirely physical, nor immaterial, but rather a combination of qualities from the two categories. This notion is twofold. One the one hand, an object is constituted by material and immaterial elements at the same time. For example, a museum as a general entity has both physical extents, in its built form, spatial characteristics, volume, interior and exterior spaces, etc., and digital extents, including its direct online presence through websites, newspapers, etc., and indirect presence, through the stories shared by individuals over time on social media. One might argue that the two presences (the tangible and the online) are equally crucial in defining the museum itself. However, at this point, it would be reductive to analyse the two identities of the museum as antithetic and distinct. Today a museum cannot probably exist with just one of the two dimensions. It rather needs to extend into the digital and the physical realms altogether and seamlessly. In other terms, the museum needs to cast its existence into the new hybrid environment, where the two dimensions of the tangible and immaterial are part of the same indivisible entity.

On the other hand, what were previously considered purely digital and physical elements, for example a website and a pebble respectively, are now objects hybridised by the layer of information that entangles them at the global scale. The website bears qualities that belong to the physical realm: length, extension, duration, time, etc., whereas the pebble is probably somewhat mapped and logged in some database accessible through the Internet. More significantly, the website and the pebble have an informational dimension in common that relates them.

This takes the form of the software. As seen in Chapter 2, software, considered as a generic computing entity that is ubiquitous and pervasive, is the common denominator that regulates the existence and the functioning of everything that is senseable, measurable and learnable by computers. The website and the pebble are both objects that stand equally within the new hybridised environment. In their analytic processing, computers would probably treat the two objects in the same way, for they both have characteristics that are physical and digital, and they both belong to the same environment.

In discussing the materiality of objects and the conceptualisation of space, Edward W. Soja provides an eloquent image that is helpful here to illustrate the difference between the two extremes of physicality and virtuality of objects (1989:120). Soja puts this in terms of opacity and transparency, distinguishing between a situation of myopia (where the focal point is too close to the object) and hyperopia (with the focal point being too far away from the object). In the first case, we have a short-sighted version of spatiality, whereby we focus only on the immediate surface of objects, limiting our sight to the superficial and opaqueness of reality. In this instance: "spatiality is accordingly interpreted and theorised only as a collection of things, as substantive appearances which may ultimately be linked to social causation but are knowable only as things-in-themselves" (Soja 1989:122). This spatiality is chiefly based on what can be experienced through senses, more specifically sight. Reality, and so the environment, is mainly what can be grasped through our senses. In the second instance, we have a "hyper-metropic illusion of transparency" whereby we can see "right through the concrete spatiality of social life by projecting its production into an intuitive realm of purposeful idealism and immaterialised reflexive thought" (Soja 1989:124). This type of spatiality is "reduced to a mental construction alone, . . . an ideational process in which the image of reality takes epistemological precedence over the tangible substance and appearance of the real world" (Soja 1989:125).

The two illusions discussed by Soja provide us with a polarised version of objects as seen in the new environment. We have an opaque and superficial qualification of objects, whereby they are identified with their appearance and, in contrast, a transparent and esoteric view, which goes through the envelope of objects to identify them in their ontology, through their more invisible and intangible facets. Within the new environment, objects are not intended to be in either extreme position of such polarisation. Being in their dimension hybrid, which makes them partially physical and digital at the same time, objects are chiefly characterised by the informational dimension. This, considered to be the characteristic that does not discern objects but rather assimilates them, supersedes all other aspects that belong to the realm of the digital or the physical. The informational layer qualifies, over every other aspect, objects in the hybrid environment.

Permeable boundaries

One way of studying space is by looking at it as a confined entity whose extension exists within boundaries. Borders and boundaries then become one of the main characterising elements of a certain spatiality, for they define the space contained in it. Changes in boundaries imply modification of space. At the urban scale, boundaries and borders define the way spatiality is unrolled into the city. They define not only the built environment but, more importantly, they determine the movement and flow of people and information in the city. Wood and Graham explain that: "mobility has always been configured by borders and boundaries composed of a multiplicity of hybrid objects, from infrastructure and technology to law and culture" (Wood and Graham 2006:177). These boundaries are not fixed, and they vary according to multiple factors that are related to the governance of the city. One aspect that determines the way boundaries function is the enforcement of the idea of ownership and right to physical places. A party wall, a fence or a gate are clear examples of the manifestation of such rights implemented through architectural forms. All these boundaries allow some level of permeability, as a mechanism to control the passage through the areas defined by the property lines. By definition, a wall creates an inside and an outside part, explicitly generating two distinct areas. These are connected and can be crossed through openings through the wall (doors, gates, etc.). As doors and openings are a typological subcategory of walls, the notion of permeability is built-in inside the notion of boundary itself.

From a social perspective, boundaries can be considered permeable "to different degrees creating societies that are differentiated by speed and access, and the values attached to both" (Wood and Graham 2006:177). Moreover, this permeability is "imprecise" and "differential" (Wood and Graham 2006:181), as it allows different groups of people to move differently and at a different speed through boundaries (2006:181). This notion relates to the idea that borders and boundaries, considered here as discerning mechanisms that regulate the functioning of flows in the city, discriminate people in the crossing of their limits. An example here can be some semi-private areas in the city that can be accessed only by individuals who have a membership card, or urban gardens accessible only for people who have a key to open the closed gate (e.g. Bedford Square Garden in London). Another example is represented by the kinetic elite (Sloterdijk 1988): a select group of people in the global society, including businessmen and political leaders who constantly travel around the world for work, spending significant amounts of time in airports, lounges, hotels and airplanes, and being constantly connected through the Internet and their mobile phones (Castree, Kitchin, and Rogers 2013). This elite often use different routes in airports, access separate lounges and faster safety control queues (Salter 2008).

In the new hybrid environment, boundaries and borders in space are regulated by software. Wood and Graham relate the establishment of boundaries to the implementation of surveillance: "within the city (or indeed any area) boundaries, their permeability (what is allowed to pass through any boundary and how), and the nature of the spaces separated by the boundary, are based on prior categorical work . . . enforced through surveillance" (Wood and Graham 2006:181). From this perspective, surveillance can be intended as the "determination of particular spaces and relationships to those spaces" and being "about defining the relationship of all sorts of actants in relation to boundaries" (Wood and Graham 2006:181). More and more surveillance systems are automated and operated by scripts that control both the boundaries, and the permeability of various flows through them. Such automated surveillance systems operate by following pre-determined categories of people and profiles of individuals that are based on a number of categorising characteristics. These include biometric data, historical and personal data, financial information and information sourced from a variety of connected databases (e.g. tax and revenue, medical databases, crime records, etc.) as pre-sets. To these, surveillance systems add real-time observations of the individual, including behaviour at the airport, posture and walking and ways of articulating sentences at control points. These categorisations are continuously applied to individuals to discern them into groups in order to assess their level of threat (Wood and Graham 2006:178) or prevent any issue that may endanger the continuous flow of people and information in the public space. "This is leading to an increasingly coded or software-sorted society and 'splintered' urban landscape characterized by highly differentiated mobilities: corridors of high mobility and easy access for some, and slow travel and difficult, expensive and blocked access for the majority" (Wood and Graham 2006:178).

There is another important aspect to be considered while observing the boundaries that define objects in the new environment. As we discussed in the previous section, objects are never utterly physical, nor completely digital. As such, to define with certainty the boundaries that delimit an object, defining it in spatial terms, is challenging. We will try to explore this point using two lemmas.

Lemma 1. The discrete logic would impose to have a set of clear and fixed coordinates that identify the position of the object and, with it, the exact extent of the edges that confine the object. The digital logic would assign a series of discrete values to the object, whereby an edge would be defined by points that are either in one unique position in a global system of reference (e.g. GPS coordinates, a Cartesian system, etc.) or not. Through its binary logic, software would assign a unique position to objects in a global system, whether this is a node on the Web, or a building in a city. If the position of the object is univocally identified, with the exact points of the edges corresponding to the identification of that object, and the points immediately outside the edges being identified as non-object (or belonging to another object), the boundaries and borders that confine and define that object are fixed. If boundaries are static, they do not allow for any degree of flexibility in their definition, nor do they allow any permeability between objects.

Lemma 2. Another way of reading the notion that objects are never utterly physical nor digital is to consider their continuous and dynamic extensions that span from the physical to the digital realms. If we assume this, it is also true that objects are equally digital and physical at the same time. The boundaries that identify them are therefore dynamic, as they change according to the extension of the object itself. Not only do these boundaries allow for a continuous permeation of their limits, but they also allow the penetration of objects into other objects. What makes these boundaries continuously moveable is the continuous updating of definition for each object that software imposes on the new environment. The determining element in the new environment is the information layer that continuously updates the information about each object in the environment, thereby computing new datasets. By doing this, software changes the definition of objects, considering new data and revisiting the existing ones. By modifying the object's definition, it also changes its boundaries, making them open and highly permeable.

We argue that the two lemmas are true at the same time. The key factor in this discussion is the notion of time. As discussed in Chapter 2, software operates at a speed that is not human, whereby machines operate continuous changes in the environment based on the output of the most recent computational loop. Objects, and the discrete points that constitute their position, are univocally defined by software in space, but their definition is in continuous evolution as the software progresses in its calculations. At any given time (in the order of fractions of seconds), software identifies the world as a fixed, univocal and discrete geography of objects in space. This configuration changes at any time as the computation evolves in its script. If a spatial configuration is observed in a precise given point in time, it would appear fixed and discretely defined. Conversely, if it is observed through time, for example using an interval of a series of seconds, the spatial configuration will appear in a dynamic evolution, where objects change their position, interacting with each other, and their boundaries are mutually permeable.

Separation of space and body

In 2000 Paul Virilio observed that we are becoming increasingly detached from our physical environment as the result of the extensive offer of remote and distant communications, whereby we are becoming "closer to what is far away than to what is just beside us, we are progressively becoming detached from ourselves" (Virilio 2000:83). This detachment is something assimilable to the physical/digital extent of objects in the new environment. Whereas objects expand their extents from the physical to the digital realm, individuals project part of their private and public life into the digital dimension. This fact poses a few questions about the determination of physical and digital aspects of people's spatial practices.

The first is the idea of context. People changed their consideration of context from the one described merely through the physical characteristics to the one that is defined by a broader set of qualities. The new idea of context encompasses digital aspects, including an updated understanding of spatial geography, whereby places can be located in the global dimension of cyberspace. The context of human actions is today not only the tangible urban space of the place in which an individual lives and works (most likely the city, the neighbourhood, the area, etc.), but rather the global extent of the new digital/physical environment.

The second aspect that emerges from the expansion of human activities into the digital realm is related to the idea of mobility. As previously discussed, data and software are in a state of continuous evolution in terms of their configuration, pervading and transcending the physical space. Individuals connected to the ubiquitous and invisible information layer are part of this configuration. They contribute to the making of the environment and its dynamic spatial configuration by moving into it. Individuals need to move in the physical and digital spaces in order to perform their daily actions. Some authors suggested that the omnipresent layer of information might have a negative impact on people's mobility: "the instant availability of all kinds of information at any time or place means that there will be no need for physical motion" (Cooper et al. 2002:300). Some others advocate that movement of data are related to and have an influence on the mobility of individuals (Mackenzie 2006:144) and that "mobilities do not always simply move, but function as images that channel further action" (Mackenzie 2006:150). As discussed in Chapter 2, the information layer operates in two main ways with regard to individuals in the environment. The first one is the constant logging and computing of people's physical and digital traces that we leave behind as we perform our daily lives. The second is the interaction that software has with individuals any time they connect to the Internet (or the Internet of Things). People move in the physical and digital space while accessing information. More specifically, they interact with the information layer as they move in the environment. This process is relatively new for the majority of people as Castells pointed out recently: "moving physically while keeping the networking connection to everything we do is a new realm of the human adventure, one about which we know little" (Castells 2005:54). MacKenzie (2006) suggested that the synchronisation of the movement of individuals with that of data in the environment is influencing people's habits and behaviour in space, including their mobility (MacKenzie 2006:149).

In 2005 Mark Andrejevic (2005:105) discussed the example of DotComGuy (Copeland 2001) as an experiment of an individual who, in the year 2000, decided to live for a period of his life in the confined space of an unfurnished house and was relying only on online services to conduct his life. From his house, he bought everything he needed from groceries to clothing and various other necessities. During this experiment, DotComGuy maintained a website through which he conducted his public life, interacting with other people, exchanging information and presenting himself to the world (he today holds the online title of "Internet personality"). He epitomises what Andrejevic calls the websurfer who is "physically immobile yet roaming virtual worlds" (Andrejevic 2005:105). The telecommuter, Andrejevic explains, "is no longer limited to the local streetscape, or even to existing physical reality" he is rather enhanced by the idea that "virtual worlds unfettered by physical laws promise to realise the fantasy of pure objectlessness" (Andrejevic 2005:105). The example provided by DotComGuy is perhaps extreme, as the individual decided to remain in his physical location, whilst acting globally through the digital environment. However, it is helpful to visualise the extent to which the physical and virtual dimensions can be combined to various degrees, yet never completely dissociated.

The space of data

Data are the constitutive elements of the information layer that pervades the physical environment. In Chapter 2 we discussed the extent to which data are related to physical space, occupying atoms to exist. Although it is quite challenging to calculate the exact number of data we currently have in the world, we can provide an approximate value for the benefit of this discussion. If we take the equivalence of 1 million atoms to 1 bit (Gibney 2017), we can assume that at the time of writing there are 80.5 zettabytes of data in the world. This rough estimate is based on the fact that every day 2.5 quintillion bytes of data are generated globally (Humbetov 2012; Wu et al. 2014). This datum refers to 2012 as a barometer year. To this, we should add that the volume of data produced every year is rapidly growing, with a compound annual growth rate (CAGR) of 57% calculated from 2006 to 2010 (Humbetov 2012). In these four years we passed from 161 exabytes to 988 exabytes. The International Data Corporation (IDC) forecasts that the total production of data in 2025 will be around 163 zettabytes (a trillion gigabytes): ten times more than the 16.1ZB of data generated in 2016 (Reinsel, Gantz, and Rydning 2017). If we estimate that we currently have 80.5 zettabytes (that is 1,180,591,620,717,411,303,424 bytes), with 1 byte occupying 8,000,000 atoms, we should grossly have 9,444,732,965,739,290,427,392,000,000 atoms of data (in the order of n^{90}). With one atom roughly the size of 100 picometres, we should have around 944,473,296,573,929,042 metres of data.

There are a number of caveats in this to be considered. All the dimensions used in this estimate are not universally accurate. For example, the size of an atom can vary depending on its status, energy, type of atom, etc. We used the size of an atom as 10^{-8} centimetres, whereby 100,000,000 atoms would be equivalent to 1 centimetre. Secondly, we used the CAGR indicated in Humbetov (2012), but this can significantly vary according to the use of the Internet at the global scale. Lastly, we considered the equivalence of 1 bit of information = 1,000,000 atoms but, as seen in Chapter 2, there are promising experiments that might result in a significant reduction of this ration, up to the order of 1:12. As approximate as this estimate is, it is helpful here to visualise the physical space related to the data we have globally. From our estimate, we assume that we have around 944,473,296,573,929 km of data at the moment.

There are two other ways in which we can visualise the physical space occupied by data. The first one is achieved by converting the data into data types and seeing what the space is that results from their application to a new medium. For example, text data can be converted into the number of pages that can be written and printed with their content. A megabyte's worth of data can be turned into circa 873 pages of plain text (Computerhope 2018). Each A4 size page occupies 0.06237m^2 of surface. Therefore, 1MB of data converted in plain text is equivalent to 54,449m^2 of surface. To put this surface in context, roughly 55m^2 is close to the gross internal area (GIA) of a relatively small two-bedroom flat in London (Wilson 2010:6).

This conversion can be applied to a variety of file formats. For example, a gigabyte of data can be translated into: 894,784 pages of plain text (1,200 characters), 4,473 books (200 pages or 240,000 characters), 640 web pages (with 1.6MB average file size), 341 digital pictures (with 3MB average file size), 256 MP3 audio files (with 4MB average file size) or 1, 650-MB CD[1] (Computerhope 2018).

Table 5.1 List of units of information used for data (in binary system)

Unit name	Symbol	Equivalence	Equivalence in bytes
bit	b	0 or 1	
byte	B	8 bits	
kilobyte	KB	1,024 bytes	1,024 (2^{10}) bytes
Megabyte	MB	1,024 kilobytes	1,048,576 (2^{20}) bytes
Gigabyte	GB	1,024 megabytes	1,073,741,824 (2^{30}) bytes
Terabyte	TB	1,024 gigabytes	1,099,511,627,776 (2^{40}) bytes
Petabyte	PB	1,024 terabytes	1,125,899,906,842,624 (2^{50}) bytes
Exabyte	EB	1,024 petabytes	1,152,921,504,606,846,976 (2^{60}) bytes
Zettabyte	ZB	1,024 exabytes	1,180,591,620,717,411,303,424 (2^{70}) bytes
Yottabyte	YB	1,024 zettabytes	1,208,925,819,614,629,174,706,176 (2^{80}) bytes

Figure 5.1 Satellite image of the NSA Utah Data Center, USA
Source: Google Maps

The second way to convert the data space into something more tangible would be to concentrate on the physical places where data are currently stored. Data centres are increasingly scattered around the world and condense the majority of data stored globally into a small number of selected locations.

The Bumblehive, the Utah Data Center built in Bluffdale, Utah, USA by the United States Intelligence Community in 2014, is a large-scale compound designed to store data related to national intelligence and cybersecurity. The total storage size of this centre is classified for national security reasons, but it is esti-mated to be potentially in the order of yottabytes (Domestic Surveillance Directo-rate 2018). The physical footprint of the centre is around 9300m² for the buildings that house the data storage with other 83,600m² for related facilities (Domestic Surveillance Directorate 2018). The size of the data storage areas has been com-pared to a Wal-Mart superstore. (Hill 2013). Within the centre, it is estimated that around 10,000 racks of servers can be housed; this assuming that each rack would occupy 0.9m^2 and contain 1.2 petabytes of data (Hill 2013). To put this in perspective, we can consider that about 200 racks (one fiftieth of the whole space capacity) would be sufficient to store all the recordings of phone calls made in the United States in one year, namely around 272 petabytes (Hill 2013).

By looking at this example, we can roughly infer that the NSA Utah Data Center can house up to 12,000 petabytes (12 exabytes) in roughly 93,000m^2 (considering all the accessory areas of the compound). This gives us a measure of the surface that data can occupy with the current technologies and resources today.

Liminal spaces

The idea of liminal space has been applied to the public space and the human sphere by scholars in different disciplines, from anthropology (e.g. Ashley 1990; Jackson 1990), to geography (e.g. Moran and McGhee 1998), and from urban studies (e.g. Shields 1989) to cultural studies (e.g. Pritchard and Morgan 2006). One of the most relevant works for this research is Victor Turner's observation of liminality, of which the seminal essay *Betwixt and between: The liminal period in rites of passage* (1987), is an epitome. According to Thomassen (2009), the term liminality was introduced in anthropology studies by Arnold van Gennep in 1909 as Rites of Passage (2009:6). Turner (1977, 1983, 1987) observed that liminality is a social construct that varies with industrialisation. In pre-industrial societies, liminality is experienced as religious passage and a transitional moment between social phases. In post-industrial societies the religious component ceases to have importance and gives way to individualism and rationalism and liminoid activities taking the form of leisure, play and divertissement.

With emphasis on the importance of limits, intended as boundaries that identify an in-between spatiality, Klapcsik (2012) examined liminality as an "undecidable oscillation" between oppositions and within post-structuralist and postmodern approaches. In particular, he investigated the urban-social connotations, considering liminality in a broad sense: "as a spatial model that . . . coincides with the (hypothetical) erosion of boundaries in our postmodernist mediaphere" (Klapcsik 2012:2). Thomassen (2009:16) explains that the idea of liminality can be applied to subjects (individuals as well as societies), time (moments to epochs) and space at different scales, from thresholds and doorways to large complexes (airports) and areas (national borders).

On the one hand, Turner and van Gennep presented an idea of liminality as a passage across defined boundaries (social, individual, or referred to activities), while, on the other hand, Klapcsik formulated the idea that social and individual boundaries are dynamic or fading one into the other. Liminality is a passage between moving limits that makes the experience of threshold continuously shift (or oscillate in Klapcsik's terms). The liminal space is not a defined place, where positional conditions may apply (e.g. being in or out of it).

Within this perception, it is easy to consider the work of Tschumi on De-, Dis-, Ex- (1996) as useful in understanding the extent to which the liminal condition can be applied to the built environment, from building and public spaces, to the scale of the city and territorial boundaries, in line with Thomassen's broad categorisation.

Tschumi explained that "today cities have no visible limits, rules that make distinction between inside and outside have disappeared" (1996:2016–217), and that architecture cannot claim today a "permanence of meaning" (1996:218). The overall message that emerges from Tchumi's analysis of the contemporary city in the 1990s is that it is no longer possible to identify clear definitions, boundaries and permanent constraints for the built environment.

The scenario that Tschumi described in the mid-1990s can be traced forward to the observations that Carpo (2014) made two decades later about the changes in the design process brought about by the use of big data. One of the consequences (or shifts in Carpo's words) of the involvement of large datasets in architecture is the freedom from the constraints determined by the use of a certain scale. Carpo explained that a "script contains all the points we would ever need to draw or produce [a] line at all possible scales" (2014:172), and that "designers use 'big data' to notate reality as it appears at any chosen scale, without having to convert it into simplified and scalable mathematical notations or laws" (2014:172).

Liminal spaces emerge as consequence of the use of a large dataset in a given process. At the same time, the limits of such spaces are not statically definable, for they are generated by a computational system that allows for a virtually infinite iteration and, therefore, contains any possible scale. In this sense, the liminal space can be regarded as a construct made possible by machines and which can only be defined once a set of numeric values has been determined. Without a definite set of values, the liminal space remains incremental and virtually regressive (becoming smaller at each iteration).

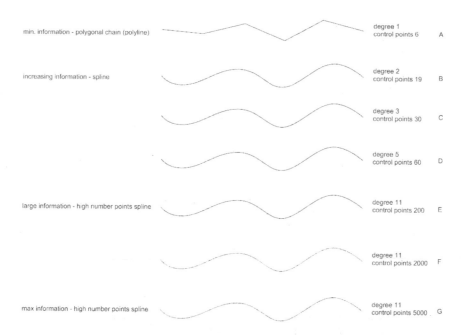

Figure 5.2 Preliminary iterations with control variable number of control points

On a basic level, the emergence of the liminal space can be observed by increasing the amount of information used to describe a curve. Rhino's "rebuild" tool can be used to directly explore the change of behaviour of a curve, as the number of points to describe it varies. Figure 5.3 shows a series of iterations where the same curve is rebuilt with increasing values of control points, from 6 to 5,000. Apparently, the difference in sinuosity of case B (19 points) and G (5,000 points) is minimal. However, if B and G are overlapped, an in-between area can be appreciated. Figure 5.3 illustrates the liminal space obtained when the Boolean subtraction G-B is operated. Figure 5.4 shows the liminal space in its basic form, where the lines obtained with minimum and maximum values are combined (G-A).

Figure 5.6 shows how curves B and G differentiate overall (upper part), and in greater detail (middle section). At the bottom, it shows the liminal space resulting from the two curves.

This principle has been applied to the scale of a generic room, to observe this phenomenon in the human dimension. Figure 5.5 illustrates an example where a series of points with increasing value has been tested. The liminal space emerging in this case is a constellation of small areas and blocks spread all around the containing space of the room.

In order to make sense of such emerging space, a series of experiments have been conducted at the urban scale, to observe the impact of the liminal space for cities and their public spaces.

The data used for this experiment have been provided by Traffic for London (TfL) under version 2.0 of the Open Government Licence.[2] TfL provides a

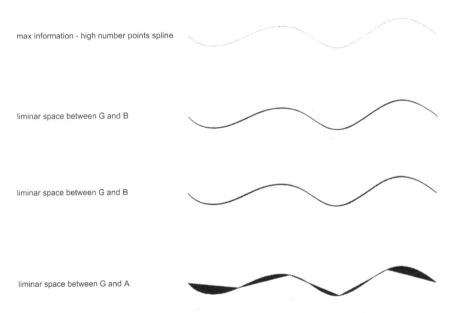

Figure 5.3 Liminal space emerging as difference between curves G and B and as a comparison between different resolutions (G – B and G – A)

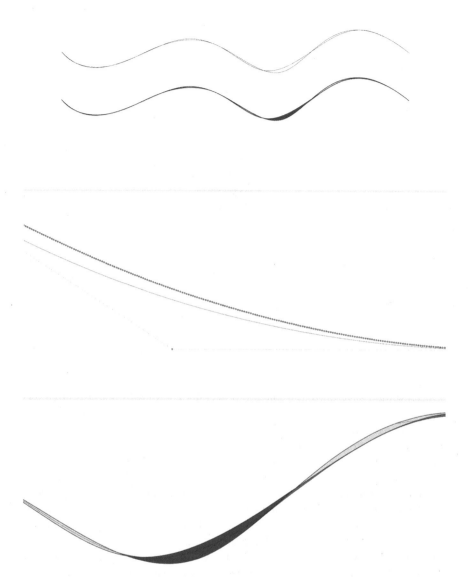

Figure 5.4 A closer look at the liminal space produced with curves

series of open data collected within Greater London, including air quality, tube usage, travels with the Oyster Card and network statistics. The dataset selected for this project contained information about 226,057 trips made between 5 and 12 October 2016 with the Santander Cycles rental bike service.[3] The dataset includes details about the id and address of rental stations (start and end of trip), and date, time and duration of each trip.[4] Data have been rationalised to obtain

Figure 5.5 Liminal space applied to a generic room

740 geo-referenced points representing the stations in London. The coordinates of each station have been translated into WGS84 coordinates (earth-centred terrestrial reference system and geodetic datum), and a shape file has been created that contains all points/stations. In order to generate the paths that represent the journeys between stations, Routino, a route planner for OpenStreetMap (OSM) data,[5] has been used. Routino is a "routing algorithm that takes OSM format data as its input and calculates either the shortest or quickest route between two points" (wiki.openstreetmap.org 2017). A virtual machine (running with Python) has been created on a Linux 64-bit environment to be able to run Routino for this experiment. A Python script has been created to join the coordinates on the map, including start and end station, time and duration of travel, etc. Routino computed the initial data of 226,057 routes, optimising the value to 218,212 routes. The loss of around 3.5% (equal to 7,845 routes) reflects series' double values and null geometries, indicating cases where the start and end stations coincided (e.g. when a person decided to rent a bike, started the renting, but then, eventually, decided to return the bike before starting the trip). The script had the database as input and gave a gpx file (a format to store coordinates) data as output. The points in the gpx file have been connected with curves, following the rule that for each two points (start and end stations) a unique curve is drawn.

These sets of curves connecting all stations in the original data sample represent the large dataset, containing the most accurate and comprehensive information available for this experiment. The same process applied to the curves in Figures 5.3–5.6 has been utilised to generate a second set of curves that represents

Figure 5.6 Curves applied to the urban scale of London

a significantly simplified version of the bike trips. Once a low- and high-resolution curve set had been generated, an in-between surface was created to visualise the emergence of the liminal spaces related to the cycling traffic observed. The high-resolution curve set has been rebuilt with a simplified version, with fewer points used to define it. Subsequently, a "ruled surface" component has been used in Rhino Grasshopper to automate and control the process of generating surfaces between the two curve sets.

The surfaces between the two curve sets have been plotted to a series of urban scenarios, including busy roundabouts, junctions and gyratories in central London (see Figure 5.10 and 5.11). However, while Figure 5.10 shows a series of

Figure 5.7 Surfaces generated as liminal spaces

Figure 5.8 Close-up to the liminal spaces

irregular shapes as a result of the liminal surfaces generation, Figure 5.11 presents a smoother outcome. The nature of the resulting surfaces is the same in both cases and reflects the characteristics of "disconnected, broken, fragmentary, rickety, patchy, and aggregatory" that Carpo pointed out in discussing big data-driven projects (2014:173). However, the emergence of irregularity in the generated shapes depends on the scale of observation. Surfaces in Figure 5.11 are still characterised by a fragmentary logic, but the irregularity would be appreciated only at a closer observation. As considered in Section 1, the emergence of liminal spaces is deeply related to the resolution with which a certain phenomenon is observed.

Figure 5.9 Eye-level view of the liminal spaces

Figure 5.10 Frank Gehry, Public Sculpture, Barcelona 1992
Source: Image provided by Gehry Partners, LLP

The surfaces obtained as output for this process can be considered as a construct generated by a closer observation of a real phenomenon through a highly accurate digital lens. Liminal spaces in the urban environment are not visible to the human eye, but they exist in a computer environment. A "machine eye" can see them as

Figure 5.11 MVRDV datascape

a result of the differential between datasets with different resolutions. Similarly to what we obtained in a theoretical case (Figure 5.7), to the fluid and continuous space that is the urban environment that can be physically experienced, another spatiality can be added as a parallel dimension. This spatiality is characterised by irregular, yet related bits of spaces that emerge as a system of granules (this is strongly visible in Figure 5.7).

The results of this study shed light on three main aspects of this question. Firstly, they demonstrate the existence of liminal spaces as the consequence of increments in data while observing a given phenomenon. Secondly, the increase in the quantity of data in the set is directly proportional to the quality of the liminal space. The larger the dataset, the smaller and more streamlined this space appears to be. Thirdly, the shapes that such spaces assume provide important insights into the characteristics of liminal spaces and, by extension, human activities. More data in the process, in fact, allow for a more fine-grained observation of people's daily activities and behaviour in the urban environment.

Looking at the liminal space pictured in Figure 5.11, the orange surfaces represent the difference between the use of urban space and related people's behaviour, suggested by the sample-based model and individualised behaviour, obtained by looking more closely at the data available, and using the information relative to each individual, without sampling the activities observed. Rather than the real use of space, the liminal space represented in this experiment illustrates the discrepancy between the model-based consideration of human activities and individual, more accurate behaviour in the urban environment. Examining closely the spatial characteristics of the liminal spaces obtained as a result of this experiment, one will notice that the differential (between sample and large dataset) has a non-linear pace. The two curve sets (low and high data resolution) almost coincide at some point and significantly diverge in others. This phenomenon is related to the impact that the built environment has on individuals, as factored by the algorithms used by Routino. This includes factors like the proximity of a building block to a certain route, the morphology of the built environment and the presence of other routes in the same location at the same time.

At a macro scale, the difference between the shape of human activities in the public realm produced with a small dataset (statistic sample) and the fine-grained set (with larger datasets) is not significant. However, the emergence of liminal spaces shows that there are aspects of human life that are not depicted by statistics, and, by and large, by models. This is particularly interesting if considered along with the fact that the majority of urban design approaches and design of public spaces are based on design rules that consider the public as a generic and homogeneous entity. The public (in its generic sense) lives in a sample-based urban environment, where everything, from the width of the sidewalks to the height of benches in parks, is standardised. Observing the characteristics of liminal spaces, we find that, albeit people can be considered to behave similarly at a macro scale, using streets, squares, parks, etc. in a common manner, this is true to a certain extent. The emergence of liminal space shows that there are minor variations in people's behaviour from the commonly accepted standard view.

The use of more data implies information about more people in the sample used for a certain observation. Larger datasets mean considering more facets of standardised common urban behaviour. The more data are considered, the more the uniform picture of the people's common behaviour becomes blurred and small variations and diversions start to emerge. These separations from the main (expected) route of the standardised view are imputable to the emergence of individuals over the crowd, with their peculiarities and nuances reflecting individual choices. The liminal space is directly connected to the consideration of individuals, as opposed to a generic group in the observation of a given phenomenon. The liminal space is the physical representation of what Sennett (2012) considers the "the shifts, uncertainties, and mess which are real life" that characterise our cities.

This class of spaces underpins an idea of freedom of individuals over a suggested or imposed use of space and behaviour within the public realm. Stevens (Karen and Stevens 2013:89) examines the interaction with space at the individual level to explore the negotiation of space and the emergence of liminality in the freedom of space to play in and with the urban elements of the built environment. In *Loose Space* (Karen and Stevens 2013), he examined liminal spaces in urban and architectural terms, focusing on physical elements such as colonnades, stairs, doorways and streets. Stevens' liminal (urban) spaces tackle the post-industrial stream of Turner's liminality, dedicated to leisure, play and the social life of individuals. Liminal spaces are presented as liberating presences in the city:

> at building thresholds which mediate between different behavioural settings, between public and private realms and between indoor and outdoor space, people experience release from the limitations and order of spaces where they have defined roles and commit their attention to specific tasks.
>
> (Karen and Stevens 2013:74)

Similarly, De Certeau (1984) described the urban stroll of individuals as spatial practice, where each person is able to make conscious choices in experiencing the urban environment. He explained that: "a space treated in this way [applying synecdoche and asyndeton as *'walking rhetorics'* and shaped by practices] is transformed into enlarged singularities and separate islands" (1984:101).

Although the liminal space does not represent accurately the real behaviour of individuals in the city, it shows the need to move away from the idea of the city based on an imposed standardisation that is model- and sample-based. Liminal spaces are a dynamic and in-evolution presence in the city that are only visible through complex data crunching operated by computers. From a qualitative aspect, they represent the emergence of the individual and her/his idiosyncrasies over the sampled notion underpinned by the idea of people as a general category. Ultimately, liminal spaces represent the freedom of choice that characterise the individual's behaviour in the urban environment, highlighting the active role that she/he has in producing the public space with everyday activities (Lefebvre 1991:68).

The unfolding of architectural public space

There is a shift from the notion of built environment intended as a fluid container, where everything can happen with a certain degree of indeterminacy (Sennett 2012) and freedom (Mitchell 2004) characterised by space (physical space, distance, etc.) and time (sense of history: present, past, etc.), to the utterly controlled reality where machines are ubiquitous, data are everywhere, connecting everything (Greenfield 2010) and, potentially, anytime and any possible scenarios in history. The public space is inhabited by individuals who are considered single and unique units by computers. Each individual represents a hyperlink of a deluge of data concerning that person. The data can be retrieved at any time at will by computers and distributed networks scattered around the globe. Individuals move in the public space, producing and receiving data actively (for example, through their mobile and tracking devices as seen in Chapter 4), passively (simply being tracked by CCTV, sensors or automatic recognition systems) and indirectly by algorithms that interpret behavioural patterns inferred from various data (bank transactions, spending patterns, etc.), as seen in Chapter 3. This built environment is completely different from the one studied by authors and architects like

Hertzberger (2005) or Gehl (2011), where people use public space while reacting to the physical elements of the built environment. Individuals still utilise low walls as benches, look for the shadowed areas on hot days and use shortcuts in pathways where possible. However, the continuity of such interpretation of the public space is broken by the awareness of ubiquitous data. Today's public space can only be considered in conjunction with the huge and growing amount of data that are produced every day by every individual. This new type of public space can only be managed and controlled through machine-like logics, due to the complexity of information to be interpreted. To factor huge sets of information, computers need to adopt computational models which are modular, rendering the public space as a complex system of discrete elements. This results in a significant consequence: the public space changes from static to dynamic. In Hertzberger and Gehl's public space, the built environment (constituted by columns, walls, balconies, etc.) is considered immutable, and people live around it, in the space left available (think of the white portions of the Nolli map). The big data public space is discretised in nature, but invisible to the naked eye. Moreover, its references and landmarks are constituted by access points, servers, routers, Wi-Fi connections and Internet nodes. In Hertzberger and Gehl's space, people are considered indistinctively, and, thus, sampled, for they are believed to behave in the same way, following a common pattern. In the discretised public space, individuals do not follow patterns, as they all act differently and uniquely. While strolling around the city, commenting on Facebook, or reading an online newspaper, that is described by Pink et al. (2017) as "mundane data", individuals are continuously reconfiguring the shape of these systems while being an essential part of it.

Discretisation in architectural space

This section applies the consideration elaborated in Chapter 1 about the tension between the discrete and the continuum into architecture and the production of the built environment. When architects started using computers in the design process, mathematical logics became part of the architectural design. Particularly, the notion of discreteness as a counterpart to the idea of continuity and continuous space that characterised significant architectural periods, including the Byzantine, Gothic and Baroque (Zevi 1957), has gradually emerged (Carpo 2014). Picon (2010) depicted this contrast, questioning the "gap between fundamentally discontinuous nature of digital procedures and the way they have been mobilized by architects to convey the intuition of a continuous real" (2010:150). With the exponential growth of the computational capacity of computers, big data and ubiquitous and pervading computing, the idea of discreteness has become increasingly more relevant, as it has characterised the architectural spaces we see today. The growing presence of discrete logics in architectural design processes is here identified with the idea that architects are responding to the new capabilities of computing by incorporating mechanisms, algorithms and digital processes that are based on granularity, finite divisions of parts and scalability.

The spatial characteristics resulting from data-driven design and digital design have been extensively studied, along with the impact that they have had on the design processes. Mario Carpo (2012) recently provided a detailed account of the different contributions to this analysis that can be considered a comprehensive summary of the different theories on the subject. However, the introduction of big data in the design process has brought about significant differences in the final outcome of architectural projects (Carpo 2003). Big data-driven architectures have new spatial characteristics that are not noticeable in the data-driven projects realised between the 1990s and 2000s. The impact of big data on architecture and urban design has been explored by many (amongst others, Picon 2015 and Carpo 2017), although they primarily focused on the shifts occurring in the design processes, in the design logic and the authorship, rather than the spatial characteristics resulting from the use of big data technologies. In his Smart Cities, Antoine Picon (2015) provided some considerations of the spatial aspects that emerge in those urban contexts where large datasets are employed. For example, Picon describes the emergence of a spatialised intelligence (2015:11), and the growing predominance of event and occurrence-based understanding of cities (2015:51), but he does not concentrate on the physical aspects of these projects. More recently, Carpo published *The Second Digital Turn* (2017) where he analyses how the technologies, methods and logics available to architects evolved since the 1990s, providing designers today with a new powerful toolkit. Carpo explains how big data allow designers today to work beyond the limits and constraints that colleagues faced in the 1990s. Examples are obsolescence of data compression (2017:19), the new relationship between data sorting and searching (p. 23) and form-searching (p. 40). Mario Carpo describes a number of seminal projects that embody the new digital tools available today. However, his interest seems not to lie in the physical and spatial characteristics of those projects, but rather in the mechanisms that underpin them and their design processes.

The use of digital technologies and urban data in architecture is increasingly related to the notion of complex datasets and big data.

Although several definitions of big data have been produced (e.g. Ward and Barker 2013; Gandomi and Murtaza 2015), in the context of this study, the following is considered: "Big data can be defined as data sets that exceed the boundaries and sizes of normal processing capabilities, thus forcing a non-traditional approach to analysing these data sets" (Nordicity 2014:6).

More specifically, big data can have a significant impact on architecture, with growing technologies like tracking, sensing, mapping, etc. Although the use of big data in architecture can be helpful in a speculative sense, in inferring information from surveying a particular case study (building, urban area or behaviour in public space) in great detail, the focus of this section is chiefly on the results of the use of big data in the final shape and spatial characteristics.

The use of data is here presented in two substantially different ways: one that characterises a manageable amount of data, and one that requires alternative solutions to handle extremely more complex systems, where data are considered "big" in their volume, variety, velocity and veracity.[6]

Digital spaces

Since the 1990s, digital design studies have concentrated on experimenting with new tools and processes, resulting in the gradual digitalisation of architectural projects at a fast pace. Whereas these studies and projects have made it possible for digital architecture to advance quickly and pervade practically any aspects of current design practices, to date, there is still little consideration of the physical characteristics of those spatialities created by machine-generated projects. This absence becomes even more relevant at the point when the entire design process, as well as the configuration of the built environment, is increasingly designed and controlled through ubiquitous computing and big data. The deluge of data factored into each design process results in an array of shapes and configurations that appear new and not experienced before. Such new forms are difficult to cat-egorise within the current paradigms based on geometry, symmetry and quantity. The nature of space is significantly changing as the use of codes increases in any aspect of our life (Kitchin and Dodge 2014:3), resulting in a shift not only in the way we perceive space and the shapes of architecture, but also the way we con-tinuously and actively contribute to its formation (Kitchin and Dodge 2014:68). The notion of transduction of code/space (Kitchin and Dodge 2014), and the idea of spacing (Doel 1999), as seen in Chapter 2, are amongst the most success-ful terms to define the radical shift that big data-generated space is undergoing. The physical space produced by digital design processes has passed from being irregular, fluid, folded, non-linear, non-standard, data-based and virtual, to being characterised by a less-defined and graspable set of qualities: hidden, uncommon, amorphous, discrete, continuously evolving and ubiquitous.

Irregular geometries (analogue to digital)

A possible cornerstone can be identified in the work of Frank Gehry. As explained by Gershenfeld (2005), Gehry is amongst those responsible for transporting the fluidity and irregular geometries generated by hand, or physical modelling, from the drawing board to the computer. In 1989, when Gehry was asked to realise his sculpture for Barcelona's Olympic Village, people like UCLA researcher Bill Mitchell played a crucial role in the implementation of projects of such complex-ity by introducing computer modelling tools from the automotive and aerospace industry into the architect's office (Gershenfeld 2005:106). From the early 1990s on, Gehry's design process became a crucial reference in the avant-garde of digi-tal design. It is important to note that the design process developed by people like Jim Glymph at Gehry's was not utterly digital. The freedom and creativity allowed by working with models was an imperative for Frank Gehry, and the software and processes developed in the office were meant to deduct information in digital format from the analogue (physical) models in order to engineer, and thus build, the desired forms. Bruce Lindsey (2001) explained that the model of the Barcelona Fish was digitised by Rick Smith with CATIA, where the numerical control system of the software allowed the designers to assign a precise spatial location for each point of the surface of the giant canopy. Once the fluid surface was translated into its digital clone, and all its points were mutually referenced, the canopy was no longer described only by its shape, but also from its set of data. Contrary to further developments, such as the form-finding process, the digitalisation was only regarded as a tool at the service of the hand-based creative gesture. Data were only inferred from the design process, and although they began to play a crucial role in the structural and building processes, they still had a limited importance in the creative phase.

Datascapes

Gradually data have become significantly more present in the architect's toolbox. Jane and Mark Burry (2010) analysed the notion of datascape as that place where

> events and phenomena in the physical or virtual world are first translated into digital digestible numerical data, which is processed to generate accessible visual and /or visceral representations through a second translation, which itself recreates events and phenomena, either in the virtual worlds or enacted in a choreographed space in the physical world.
>
> (Burry 2010:210)

The driving purpose, Burry explains, is to utilise the power of algorithms (and the computational capacity offered by today's machines) in order to unveil, collect and manage information "to which we can apply our own innate pattern-finding and spatial intelligence" (Burry 2010:210). A previous experiential unveiling of the use of data in the design of the built environment has been realised by Winy Maas in 2005. The KM3 study (MVRDV 2005) is the design of a hypothetical city for one million inhabitants. MVRDV sought to solve the problem of current cities in terms of increasing density (of functions, needs, programmes and interactions). With the idea of turning from a bi-dimensional configuration of the programme in the city to a "stacked urbanity", the result is a 3D city, where the cube is considered the basic geometrical module to measure and host urban functions, instead of the polygon typical of the more traditional zoning-based approaches. Maas explored further the idea of the 3D city with the students of the Berlage Institute in 2001, grounding the study on the analysis of Dutch statistics sorted by agriculture, air, distribution, energy, forest, industry, leisure, shopping, water and waste (Maas 2001). Each category has been studied separately, providing a partial input for the overall project. Data coming from the Dutch government have been translated into urban spaces (blocks), in order to understand the individual requirements for each inhabitant in the city. The resulting volumes are combined (stacked) together, providing an unplanned (and undrawn) series of massive buildings. This approach, consisting of translating statistics into volumes (originating from a previous MVRDV's study: FARMAX 1998), is known as "datascaping".

Data structures

If reality (an event, a phenomenon or a qualitative aspect of an object) is converted into numeric values, providing the raw matter for computers to elaborate and represent a world where our spatial intelligence can interact, the structure of the raw material, namely data, becomes of crucial importance in the process. Galli and Mühlhoff (2000) described the importance of data hierarchies as sequential patterns; moving through successive groups (Galli and Mühlhoff 2000:14). They indicate in the (2D or 3D) model the means of organising and managing data in the architectural project. All the information and the elements of the building are combined by connections, following a series of principles (structural, compositional, constructive, etc.). This way a load-bearing beam will sit on columns, which will be vertically connected to foundations. Data in the 3D model are sorted into categories (e.g. load-bearing structures), or data sets. Each of these contains a series of subcategories (e.g. vertical load-bearing structures) and the simplest component is represented by the single element (e.g. a column). This organisation allows for the individual elements to be related to other elements in another data set. Basic geometrical functions (equation of a curve) are used to generate basic shapes (a circle), which are associated with "modifiers" (e.g. Boolean operations and extrusions) in order to obtain a column. The column then becomes an object (as the cylinder associated with it) and is stored in a specific data set. The columns are then combined in a bigger category of load-bearing structures, along with beams, foundations and walls. This macro-category is defined as a family, or class, of objects. The crucial importance of such organisation of data sets lies in the fact that the entire design is characterised by a chain of relationships, where the modification of one single function (primitive curve describing the circumference of the column) resonates throughout the entire model.

Nonlinear

The digitalisation of reality and its translation into spatially intelligent bits quickly generated new avenues for designers. A large category can be identified with Nonlinear and Non-standard Architecture. Jencks (1997a) associated the mathematical notion on non-linearity, where the relationship between input and output of a function is not represented by a straight line (Carpo 2012:80), to a certain contemporary architecture production, including Eisenman, Neil Denari and Zaha Hadid's work. The nonlinear space is characterised by "a complexity of shapes and continuous variations" (Carpo 2012:80). The nonlinear space is significantly different from the one conceived by Gehry in the early 1990s. The latter was, in fact, the digitalised version (chiefly for constructive reasons) of a hand-generated gesture, associated with a visual image conceived in the architect's mind. The reduction to data of the analogue model was subservient to the original design. The nonlinear space is not generated by a visual image in the designer's mind, nor is it replicating a physical model or drawing. After the reality is converted into digital data, the relationships between them are so complicated that they have to be organised and managed by (mathematical) logics, such as algorithms and scripts. Jencks pointed out the imperative of using computers in the generation of nonlinear architecture, due to the complexity of computing required by the process (Jencks 1997b).

Folding

The manipulation of data to generate a new spatiality is visible, perhaps more than in other approaches, in the Folding approach. In the early 1990s, Greg Lynn proposed architecture characterised by smooth and continuously curving shapes. Lynn utilised the notion of Architectural Curvilinearity (Lynn 1993) to indicate those projects with "smooth transformation involving the intensive integration of differences within a continuous yet heterogeneous system" (Carpo 2012:30). Lynn's rounded shapes can be considered as the tail of Deconstructivism, in light of the fact that a building is considered the aggregation of different independent elements (column, truss or wall), as opposed to integral parts of the same compositional principle. "Smooth mixtures are made up of disparate elements, which maintain their integrity while being blended within a continuous field of other free elements" (Carpo 2012:30). Curvilinear architectures, or Blobs as they were lately indicated, are a direct expression of the computation of data made by a machine. In his introduction to Lynn's seminal text about Curvilinearity, Carpo (2012:28) explains that the notion of the (digital) fold in architecture did not originate strictly from the computational power of a machine, but, conversely, it has its roots in the discourse about Deconstructivism, and hence in the field of the theory of architecture, involving the Deleuzian notion of *Pli* and *continuous variation* as one of the main references. However, Lynn related the deformation and transformation of surfaces (onto which the folding operation is possible) not merely to a geometrical manipulation (like Gehry would have conceived through his models), but as "the expression of the mathematics of the topological medium" (Lynn 1999:18). Lynn refers to the computer as a powerful "conceptual and organisational tool" (Lynn 1999:19), where the design process hinges on three main properties: topology, time and parameters. The geometries and the formal deformation and transformation in the digital architecture are governed by the manipulation of the three facts. Computers interpret topology, time and parameters as data, input by the architect. A possible "new spatiality" in the digital folding architecture can be found in what Lynn defines as "fitness landscape". Drawing from an array of different notions that originate from biology (Conrad Waddington), physics (Stuart Kauffman) and mathematics (Rene Thom), Lynn elaborated a digitalised version of reality through the metaphor of landscape. "A landscape is a system where a point change is distributed smoothly across a surface, so that its influence cannot be localized at any discrete point. Splines are constituent elements of topological landscape" (Lynn 1999:29). The *fitted landscape* is characterised by oriented surfaces (Virilio and Parent 1996), folds, peaks and valleys which contain potential movements. The geometry of the landscape, in fact, embeds qualities such as direction, elasticity, density and friction. The topological landscape contains and suggests movements by staying still. It is possible configurations are embedded in its facets. The spatiality generated by Lynn's landscape is virtual, limited and dictated (and predictable) by its geometry.

Cyberspace

In the mid-1990s, John Frazer was among the first to theorise the potential of cyberspace. In "The architectural relevance of cyberspace" (Frazer 1995b), he foresees, in the virtual space generated by the growing use of the Internet, an alternative direction for architecture characterised by the possibility of "making the invisible visible" (Frazer 1995b). Architecture is considered an "organ of interaction" between users displaced in different parts of the world and their common environment. Frazer pointed out the significant shift of interest in design, from objects and forms to the existing relationships between forms, forms and environment and forms and users. In the age of cyberspace, the natural arena of architecture shifts from the notion of the architectural object and its context, to the idea of relationship and topology. The potentialities of cyberspace offered to the user are depicted by De Kerckhove (2001) as "the third modality of human perception, after the collective discourse of the oral community and the private mind of the literate person" (De Kerckhove 2001:33). The notion of cyberspace is directly related to a perceptual capacity, namely "cyberspation", a term coined by Roy Ascott in *The architecture of cyberception* (1994). The augmentation of perception is key to Ascott's new account of the virtual world:

> To inhabit both the real and virtual worlds at one and the same time, and to be both here and potentially everywhere else at the same time is giving us a new sense of self, new ways of thinking and perceiving which extend what we have believed to be our natural, genetic capabilities.
>
> (Ascott 1994:para. 1)

In 1995, John Frazer explored the idea of an "Evolutionary Architecture" (1995a). By observing the symbiotic behaviour and the metabolic balance that are characteristic of the natural environment, a series of generative codes have been elaborated to generate architectural projects. In projects like the Reptile Structural System (Frazer 1995a:69), scripts, including possible conflictive evolutional criteria based on the observation of natural selection in the built environment and labelled "genetic algorithms", have been run against an initial architectural shape in order to determine its natural evolution. The development of the architectural object is virtually "naturalised" by means of computation: "The computer can be used not as an aid to design in the usual sense, but as an evolutionary accelerator and generative force" (Frazer 1995b). Carpo depicted cyberspace as a "revolutionary alternative to the Western canon of mimetic, perspectival images" (Carpo 2012:48).

Figure 5.12 John Frazer, The "Evolutionary Architecture" Project by Miles Dobson for tutors John and Julia Frazer 1991

Source: Frazer (1995a:27)

Non-standard

Oxman and Oxman (2014) described the non-standardisation as the natural evolution of the digital generation of the Folding (Oxman and Oxman 2014:3). Following the tenet that formation precedes form, the non-standard logic seems to be the theoretical hinge between the notions of parametric design, topology and biology on the one hand, and the new technological progresses in digital fabrication and production (Oxman and Oxman 2014:2) on the other. The non-standard approach is deeply related to the algorithmic culture in design, and the idea of singularity in the process. This is intended as the "bifurcation along the progression of an algorithm [which] opened the way to a full description of the physical world, to the full discretisation of reality" (Migayrou 2014:19). The non-standard acquired

Figure 5.13 Non-Standard exhibition

a clear identity with the Non-Standard Architectures exhibition in 2003 at the Centre Pompidou in Paris. The aim of the exhibition was to "make the whole architectural process visible from conceptual elements through to experimental objects and prototypes" (Archis 2004:97). The exhibition included work from Asymptote, dECOi Architects, Greg Lynn FORM, NOX, ONL, R&Sie and UN studio amongst others. The layout of the display reflected an algorithmic conception of space, where the work was exhibited in a "non-standard, mathematical space – a moiré pattern created by two grids". The areas were "defined by differential curves, printed on the floor like a mathematical map of spatial distribution" (Archis 2004:97).

Data-driven design

In summary, the data-driven projects developed between the 1990s and 2010s can be described by the following schematic characteristics (see Table 5.2).

The use of big data in the process

The passage from "manageable data" to big data is characterised by two aspects: (a) the increment of computational capacity, and (b) the transition from sampling to determination.

Table 5.2 Data-driven design

Data-driven design (1990–2010)	Characterised by
Irregular geometry	Digitalisation intended as a tool at the service of the hand-based creative gesture
Fluidity and folding (continuous, seamless)	Smooth and continuously curving shapes (splines)
Datascape, data-based and data-structured	Relationship between numeric values and facts, and computer-generated shapes and volumes
Non-linear	Relationship between input and output [that is] not represented by a straight line
Virtual (cyberspace)	Inhabitation of both the real and virtual worlds at one
Non-standard	Search for the singular form

(a) The passage from the use of data to large sets of data has been gradual and never clearly planned. The way the computational capacity has increased over the last decades (and is still growing today) results in a gradual and continuous increase of information involved in every computational process. The definition of big data is an expanding one. Manovich (2011) holds that the term is used when supercomputers are necessary to process the amount of data. Snijders, Matzat, and Reips (2012) describe them as "a data set so large and complex that they become awkward to work with using standard statistical software". Al Nuaimi et al. (2015) hold that big data are: a "large set of data that is very unstructured and disorganized", and "a form of data that exceeds the processing capabilities of traditional database infrastructure or engines" (Al Nuaimi et al. 2015). Batty proposes a very simple definition: "any data that cannot fit into an Excel Spreadsheet" (Batty 2013:274). In the general acceptance of the term, when data sets become so large that standard computers or software are unable to process them, the data become big. Boyd and Crawford (2012) observed that big data are more about the computational capacity (to search, aggregate and cross-reference) and less about the size of data sets per se.

(b) Another distinctive aspect of big data is the capacity to work with the unknown. Castells (2009) explained that one of the main characteristics of the information age is to cope with the uncertainties of a fast-changing economical, institutional and technological environment (Castells 2009:163). One of the main differences between the use of data and big data is described by Hilbert (2013) and lies in the idea that, while every decision is regulated by a certain degree of an "uncertain probabilistic gamble based on some kind of prior information" (Hilbert 2013:3), in the big data environment, the base for prior information is significantly increased, reducing the level of uncertainty. In big data, the high volume of information provides very detailed "models and estimates that inform all sort of decisions" (Hilbert 2013:3). This point is expanded by Mayer-Schönberger and Cukier (2013:26), where the concept of sampling is superseded by the fact of being able to obtain "all" possible data. With the concept of N = all (with N representing all cases used in an observation), Mayer-Schönberger and Cukier hold that it is possible to use big data to significantly increase the degree of detail of each observation.

In order for N = all to happen, the world has to be considered under a digital machine-like logic. All aspects need to be turned into data, or datafied. "To datafy a phenomenon is to put it into quantified format so it can be tabulated and analysed" (Mayer-Schönberger and Cukier 2013:78). Isolated, determined and independent elements appear easier to fit within a tabulating logic. Shapes have to be regarded as a series of finite elements, such as points, lines and surfaces, described by numbers and values. In order to be tabulated, geometries are translated into discrete systems.

This translation has a significant impact on the way the architectural projects are not only conceived, but also composed and materialised.

The eight projects that follow are examined in order to distillate the spatial characteristics that are emerging as a consequence of the datafication of space through (and because of) the use of big data-driven processes. The projects fall under three categories: (a) large-scale, urban projects and public realm, (b) building-scale projects and (c) product design applications.

Case studies

Large-scale urban projects

1. DublinDashboard

The DublinDashboard[7] project epitomises the prototype of the online and open access system that gathers large numbers of urban data, visualising them in real time.[8] The project provides an analytical tool that encompasses transport, environmental, health and crime data, along with industry, employment, labour market and housing indicators. The image of Dublin that results from the dashboard is characterised by a continuous evolution, as the data are continuously changing over time and updated. Subsections like "How's Dublin?"[9] offer a description of the city that is unique and novel at the same time. The visualisations in the Dashboard "Unsurprisingly . . . have been a key means of analysing and interpreting indicator and benchmarking data, used to reveal the structure, pattern and trends of variables" (Kitchin, Lauriault, and McArdle 2015:10). Kitchin highlighted the heterogeneous nature of algorithms (Kitchin 2016:15) and the relevance of considering them as systems of algorithms, "usually woven together with hundreds of other algorithms" (Kitchin 2016:15). The heterogeneity of these systems is reflected in the discrete nature of the outputs, visible in the visualisations in the dashboards. Dublin Reporting[10] or Dublin RealTime[11] describe Dublin through a series of points, elements, coordinates and, more generally, data. As such, the overall image of the city that emerges from the Dashboard is characterised by discontinuity and heterogeneity. The new map of Dublin is furthermore characterised by the ubiquity of the data sources (Kitchin 2014a). Finally, the city described is unveiled in its new and continuously evolving characteristics. The real-time data show the hidden structures of the city (Kitchin 2014b).

2. SmartSantander

With the SmartSantander project, Luis Muñoz et al. (2013) demonstrated that the notion of a smart city is characterised by a continuous evolution, ubiquitousness and discretisation. Using the high-level architecture of the Internet of Things (IoT) and the notion of Future Internet (FI) and Internet of Services (IoS), this project is an attempt to transform the city of Santander into a "world city-scale experimental research facility in support of typical applications and services for a smart city" (Muñoz et al. 2013:1). This project proposes the reconsideration of the physical elements of the city, with the addition of an extra layer of digital technology. SmartSantander demonstrates how a city can operate at a high level of service integration, where the urban form evolves following the precepts governing the IoT. The digital layer is amorphous and invisible, and transcends the physical elements and boundaries of the historic city of Santander, yet it evolves continuously following Internet protocols, middlewares and applications.

3. Regional delineation

In the "Digital Approach to Regional Delineation", Sobolevsky (2014) describes the use of big data to measure human interaction created by human activity. This work examines the physical boundaries of human activity based on telephone calls in the United States, Portugal, France, Saudi Arabia, Ivory Coast, Italy, Belgium and the United Kingdom. The study shows that, under this lens, human interaction transcends physical space, yet it is deeply integrated with it, in a discrete manner. By ignoring geographical and administrative boundaries in the first place, this study shows the actual "structures and communities embedded in the [communication] network" (Sobolevsky 2014:182). A community detection algorithm (Sobolevsky 2014:185) has been used to unveil the activity of communities, identifying them at the same time. By using Newman's modularity technique (Newman 2006), this study shows a new matrix-based map of countries divided in clusters. The description of the regions that emerges is based on networks, as opposed to predetermined delineations. As such, the configuration of the new map of communities is continuously evolving as a consequence of day-to-day human interaction.

Building-scale projects

4. Elytra Filament Pavilion

The Elytra Filament Pavilion designed by ICD/ITKE in the Victoria and Albert Museum courtyard in London consists of a series of glass and carbon fibre canopies built through a machine-led process. The architecture is conceived as an installation where sensors under the canopies capture people's movement and transfer the data to the fabrication system that decides where and how to build the next canopy, automatically calculating the configuration and the quantity of material needed to counteract loads and stresses. The configuration of this project is determined by the on-going factors calculated by the computational system. As such, the project does not have a predetermined shape, neither does it have an overall composition drawn by the architects. The shape of the Elytra Filament Pavilion is in continuous evolution which is related to the data received by sensors.

5. Digital Water Pavilion

Carlo Ratti's Digital Water Pavilion[12] in Zaragoza, Spain, presents an amorphous structure whose water-jet walls are configured in real time, based on an algorithm that factors people's movement and reactions. The overall shape of the pavilion changes over time and its configuration is unpredictable, although it ranged amongst a series of pre-set parameters. As a consequence of the use of algorithm to determine the dynamic configuration of this project, the pavilion has no fixed shape. With this project, Ratti provided concrete evidence of a bottom-up approach "leveraging the sociability of cities to change patterns of activity" (Ratti 2011:46), where the extensive and ubiquitous use of sensors, tracking devices and algorithm-based systems can help redefine the participation of widened collectives in public life (Ratti 2011:45–48).

6. Arup's Future of Stations

The (pre)vision that Arup gives of the future rail system globally is characterised by the integration of different transport means:

> Increases in computer power and the ability to handle the processing of large amounts of data in real time, will lead to more effective use of big data. Big data and the Internet of Things will allow transportation modes to communicate with each other and with the wider environment, paving the way for truly integrated and inter-modal transport solutions.
>
> (Arup 2014:20)

The extensive implementation of integrated systems (Arup 2014:24) results in the reconfiguration of train stations, where their shape and spaces are deeply interconnected with the plethora of services and activities in and around the main building. The station's functions and activities are ramified in the territory, and its reach is within the physical (of the tracks, main buildings, tunnels, passageways, etc.) and the digital (real-time information systems, virtual shopping walls, electronic tagging, etc.). The space of the station is not definable in a fixed manner, nor can its configuration be predetermined. In contrast, the space of the train station of 2050 envisaged by Arup is a hybrid between virtual and physical, highly automated, dynamic and amorphous. Data and algorithm-based systems will govern its extents and adapt its shape over time, accommodating passengers' and freight's smart circulation.

Human-scale applications

7. Audi R18 Ultra Chair

The Audi R18 Ultra Chair designed by Clemens Weisshaar and Reed Kram[13] provides a concrete example of amorphous design, which is strongly based on data. The chair shape and structure are calculated by a simulation software that factors large sets of data, gathered during a public event, and optimises the final shape, incorporating data about materials and loads. The final geometry, size and overall configuration of the chair are determined by software generated specifically

Figure 5.14 Philip Morel's Computational Chair

for this project. The chair is the direct result of data calculation,[14] and, as such, the evolution of its shape is altered gradually, following discrete variances of the same core structure.

8. Computational Chair Design

The Computational Chair Design project by EZCT Architecture & Design Research demonstrates that the rigorous application of a genetic algorithm results in a high level of optimisation in the design process. The Computational Chair is a non-standard product developed by using "an artificial population of individuals by modifying their characteristics randomly of one onto another one, and by selecting those who answer best the composed question" (EZCT 2004:3).

The design is based on the use of voxels and Voronoi diagrams (EZCT 2004: 5–6), and its discreteness is reflected both in the configuration of the cubic elements that are swapped according to load calculation, and in the final shape, which is irregular and bumpy. The form of this chair is determined by the forces factored by the algorithmic system; therefore, its configuration is potentially, continuously evolving, as the forces involved change.

Spatiality of big data architectures

Hidden (unveiling)

Big data-driven projects appear to be characterised by the incomplete manifestation of their physical space. Since the employed data increase the information about the project and its context significantly, the number of elements at stake in each design is increasingly vast. As such, the physical and visual representation of the design is twofold. On the one hand, what is seen as the physical space generated by the design does not include every existing aspect of its configuration. Morel's computational chair (2.4) assumes just one configuration at a time, hiding the other multitude of options that precedes it in the simulation process. On the other hand, the design unveils aspects of its context that were otherwise invisible. Sobolevsky's regional delineation illustrates how the use of large datasets enables the materialisation of new shapes (identified by their boundaries in that case) in the territory, based on actual use of networks of communication.

Uncommon

The extensive use of datasets in the process allows designers to operate in uncharted territories of design, challenging common practices, standards and well-tested techniques. The final results of the design are governed by the algorithmic logic and the process used. Their outcomes are often unexpected and unusual. Morel's Computational Chair is the machine's result of a calculation strategy, based on multiple loading scenarios, where the chair is "always stable, whatever way the seat is positioned" (Carpo 2012:200). With a set of behavioural rules as the main drive for the final configuration of the chair, it is likely that the final result will not align with the canons of shapes and materials one may expect from a traditional chair.

Continuously evolving (not changing: going forward)

Big data-driven projects seem not to have a definitive configuration at the end of the design process. In contrast, their shape is related to the data that are factored in their creation and varies accordingly. Since data are often continuously updated, the final shape evolves along with them. In this respect, one may note that the shape is not changing, but evolving. This is determined by the fact that the final configuration depends on the trail of operations performed by the algorithms used. The modifications of shape are subsequent to each other in an evolutionary sequence.[15]

Amorphous

The big data-driven designs are characterised by a continuous evolution. As such, their shape is not static, but dependent on the live stream of data factored in the process. The shape that can be observed is not the final one, but a still of the progression of their evolution. These projects have not a determined form per se; they can rather be described and visualised by a certain phase in their evolution. Elaborating on the notion of transduction, Kitchin and Dodge (2014) explained that: "space is always in the process of becoming, . . . in the process of taking place. . . . Space is a practice, a doing, an event, a becoming – a material and social reality forever (re)created in the moment" (Kitchin and Dodge 2014:68).

Ubiquitous (network)

Big data projects are highly dependent on data and networks of information. With the progress of Information and Communications Technology (ICT), the data that flow into the design processes are increasingly connected to networks and Internet based. The notions of pervasive computing (Kitchin 2014b:84) and ubiquitous computing (Kitchin 2014b:84) characterise big data projects by conferring them a global scale, and a "continuous context and location awareness" (Kitchin 2014b:84). Projects like SmartSantander highly rely on the IoT and IoS for their development and success. The thesis of *everyware* (Greenfield 2006) as "ubiquitous information technology [that] will appear in many different contexts and take a wide variety of forms [that] will affect almost every one of us, whether we're aware of it or not" (Greenfield 2006:9) is always more concrete and realistic.

Discrete

Big data projects are based on the extensive use of data. Algorithm-based digital processes determine the configuration and appearance of the physical space of these projects. Configurations are the outturn of the systematic use of the digital logic, where the notion of discreteness is embedded in the very basic nature of the dichotomy O-I. All the projects observed present the common aspect of being discrete and are characterised by discontinuity. At the urban and territorial scale, DublinDashboard is composed by bits of information gathered by several means. The overall picture of the city is characterised by a heterogeneous series of dots that represent a specific behaviour or activity. The city of Dublin is represented by a system of points where a selected trend takes place, as opposed to a continuous and analogue system. Similarly, SmartSantander depicts the city of Santander as a connected system of various networks that operate synchronically to optimise the city's resources and accommodate citizens' needs in a smarter way. The regions described by Sobolevsky Senseable City Lab's Regional Delineation project are described with a discrete system of points in a communication network, where any communication link between two persons represents a thread in the fabric that constitutes the new map of the region. The new delineation provided is based on points and lines, leaving the gaps between these elements unconsidered (and not represented in the new regional chart). The Elytra Filament Pavilion is built bit by bit, by robots that translate the information received by sensors and processed by algorithm into shapes. The digital nature of the generative process is reflected in the geometry of the canopies, where the surfaces are constituted by lines (filaments) and nodes (where filaments join) developed in three dimensions. Similarly, the geometries of Ratti's Digital Water Pavilion materialise the syncopated nature which underpins the digital logic, where bits of information (in the form of I/O) correspond to the presence or absence of the water jets that create the walls of the pavilion. Arup's future train stations are characterised by a systematic combination of parts whose functions are governed by different streams of information. The overall configuration of the stations reflects the continuous flowing of information, services and people into sectors which are physically separated, yet functionally interrelated. The R18 Ultra Chair is characterised by sharp edges and a clear-cut geometry, as a result of the digital process applied whereby a large dataset has been used in the calculation of the shape. Finally, the configuration of Morel's Computational Chair Design is based on voxels, resulting in large scale cubes, where gaps and grooves are clearly visible. The composite nature of this chair reflects the digital logic used to determine its shape.

The data-driven projects described above were characterised by the irregularity of geometry, fluid and seamless movements; their structure was based on data. They were non-linear and non-standard, and some of their parts were hosted in a virtual environment. On the other hand, big data-driven projects appear to feature continuous evolution, to be amorphous and uncommon. Part of them is hidden and part of the design process is meant to unveil or reveal some of their aspects. Unlike the data-driven group, these projects are not only structured following a digital logic, but are utterly digital in their nature, process and appearance. If the first group includes projects that are adapted to incorporate a digital logic (e.g. a building conceived through the use of spline), the latter are "digital native", as they are the result of processes entirely governed by algorithms.

Table 5.3 Spatial characteristics of big data projects

Project	Spatial characteristics					
	H	*U*	*CE*	*A*	*U*	*D*
Large-scale, urban projects and public realm						
1 DublinDashboard Rob Kitchin	✓		✓	✓	✓	✓
2 SmartSantander Luis Muñoz	✓		✓	✓	✓	✓
3 Regional Delineation – Sobolevsky (Senseable City Lab)	✓		✓	✓	✓	✓
Building-scale projects						
4 Elytra Filament Pavilion		✓	✓	✓		✓
5 Digital Water Pavilion Carlo Ratti		✓	✓	✓		✓
6 Future of Stations ARUP	✓		✓	✓	✓	✓
Product design applications						
7 Audi Chair R18 Ultra Chair		✓	✓	✓		✓
8 Computational Chair		✓	✓	✓		✓

Source: Notes: H – Hidden, U – Uncommon, CE – Continuously evolving, A – Amorphous, U – Ubiquitous (network), D – Discrete

Their shape is the formalisation of a series of strings of code. Finally, big data-driven projects are characterised by a non-fluidity of their geometry that is reflected in gaps, lumps and steps. Whilst the systems and processes that underpin these projects are seamless in their logic, they are discrete in their structure, where points, dots, lines and knots are the recurring elements.

The characteristics of the data-driven group can be clustered in two main strands: (a) data (including: datascape and virtual/cyberspace) and (b) geometry (including: irregularity, fluidity/Folding, non-linear and non-standard). The big data-driven projects can be grouped in: (a) data (including: hidden and ubiquitous/network) and (b) geometry (including: continuously evolving, uncommon, amorphous and discrete). Table 5.4 summarises the evolution of these two groups in the transition from data to big data projects. The use of datum-based structures in the design process (e.g. MVRDV's Datascape) hinged on the translation of datasets into physical shapes, mostly cubes and extruded volumes. These data originated from a single off-line datasheet, which contained all the information factored in the design process in isolation. With the advent of big data and the increase of computational capacity of machines, data have become more elaborated and, most relevantly, shared amongst different networks that work together. Extruded datasets have evolved into ubiquitous information that governs the functioning of buildings.

The irregular geometries of data-driven projects, where continuity, fluidity and non-standard shapes were sought, have naturally evolved into the amorphous and uncommon shapes of the big data projects. The elegant and streamlined forms that characterised the 1990s and 2000s digital architectures (ONL's 2006 A2 Cockpit) have been substituted by formless and continuously evolving territorial boundaries (Sobolevsky's Regional Delineation) and unwieldy shapes (Morel's Computational Chair). The more data are employed in the design process, the more the digital logic becomes pervasive in the final shapes of the design. The quantity and

Table 5.4 Comparison of characteristics

Data-driven design (1990–2010)	Big data-driven design (2010–)
Irregular geometry	Hidden
Fluidity and folding (continuous, seamless)	Uncommon
Datascape, data-based and data-structured	Continuously evolving
Non-linear	Amorphous
Virtual (cyberspace)	Ubiquitous (network)
Non-standard	Discrete

Table 5.5 Evolution of characteristics

Data-driven design (1990–2010)		Big data-driven design (2010–)
Datascape, data-based and data-structured + virtual (cyberspace)	→	Hidden + ubiquitous (network)
		↓
Irregular geometry + fluidity and Folding (continuous, seamless) + non-linear + non-standard	→	Continuously evolving + uncommon + amorphous + discrete

volume of data involved in the process seem to have a qualitative impact on the project. Shapes and structures have changed as a consequence of volume, velocity and variety that are characteristics of big data (Kitchin 2016).

Since 2011, big data have become a growing topic in scientific and layperson discussions about data, processes, computing and privacy. The possibility of acquiring and storing a great number of details about individuals has raised a number of concerns, especially from the social sciences and geography camps. For example, Wang (2013) reflects on the supremacy of the quantitative dimension in big data analyses that can be unrelated to the quality or the nature of insight in the data observed. Hargittai (2015) speculates on the biases that can lie behind some of the methods currently used in big data analyses. Miller (2015) examined the potential of employing big data in geography and spatial modelling, offering a series of cautionary notes regarding the potential pitfalls represented by superfluous data and patterns. Boyd and Crawford (2012) raised a very clear set of relevant points that challenges the use of big data, including a shift in the definition and nature of knowledge, validity and objectivity of data collected, quality of data, the importance of context, questions about ethics and privacy and, finally, the issue of data access, which might present a social divide in the future.

Although such cautionary notes and concerns in the utilisation of big data in design processes are important and necessary for a better understanding of this phenomenon, the nature of space generated by big data-driven approaches is naturally evolving. This section has pointed out a series of spatial characteristics that define big data spatiality which grows from the digital space. Six main characteristics have been discussed in an attempt to define the new spatiality: hidden, uncommon, continuously evolving, amorphous, ubiquitous (network) and discrete.

The spatial characteristics of the new environment

In this chapter, we have discussed several spatial aspects that characterise the new hybrid digital/physical space. These can be summarised in the following five points. Firstly, space is not fixed, but rather in a state of continuous evolution. The continuous becoming of space is informed and determined by the constant influence of computers that actively interact with the environment. As seen in Chapter 2, this mechanism is elegantly theorised by Kitchin and Dodge in their definition of transduction of space/code (Kitchin and Dodge 2011). The time of this continuous transduction is related to the computing power of machines operating in the environment and it is not appreciable through human senses. We can observe a spatial configuration only in a given time in the past (or in the future through a simulation), but not in the present, for space is evolving at the same time as it is becoming (Doel 1999). We used the term amorphous to describe the impossibility of crystallising space in a determined configuration in the process of its continuous becoming. This means that we cannot attribute a characterising form to this space, other than its distributed and dynamic configuration.

Secondly, space is never only physical or digital. We referred to this space as partially hidden to describe the dual physical/digital extent that objects have. As seen in this chapter, objects are never completely physical, nor utterly digital. This implies the impossibility of describing (or observing) an object purely based on its characteristics in the physical or digital dimensions. Every object should be considered for its dual and hybrid nature. We saw, for instance in this chapter, that it is impossible to directly map the digital space (for example, that of the Wi-Fi network) onto the physical space. We observed phenomena of disarray between the two (for example, with the idea of excess and overflow of digital information flows over the physical space) (Mackenzie 2006). We discussed how the hybrid conceptualisation of digital/physical space results in the disconnection of the individual (intended as body and physical presence) from her/his physical context. With the example of DotComGuy, we noted how physical presence and the context in which individuals exist become mutually independent. Moreover, we discussed the extent to which a physical object has a digital extension and, conversely, how data have a physical dimension and are translated into physical space. This dual relationship confirms the necessary hybrid nature of the space in the new environment.

Thirdly, space is everywhere, ubiquitous and pervasive. This means that space is not comparable to a solid state that can be understood as distance between objects or extension of the objects themselves. Space is rather a fluid element that percolates into any dimension of the environment: the physical and the digital. Building on Lefebvre's definition of social space, space in the new environment is relational. However, the relations that govern its spatiality are characterised by the information layer. Space is pervasive because computing's reach is virtually everywhere. As the information layer flows in the physical and digital space at the same time, these spaces are configured by information. The pervasiveness of computing results in the boundaries of objects in space to be permeable to each other. In a sort of Einsteinian space-time, objects can penetrate each other through the blurred boundaries of the transducting space, with the information layer governing the mechanisms of the permeation.

Fourthly, space is dependent on resolution. The more data are utilised to describe a spatiality, to exchange information, to analyse a specific situation, to understand a given context, the more resolution the resulting space will have. As seen in the analysis of the liminal spaces, those spatialities emerge as the consequence of the change in the number of data used in the computation.

Fifthly, space is discrete. As discussed in Chapters 1 and 2, space in the digital/physical environment is informed, influenced and formed by the computer's digital logic. As such, its very nature is digital, whereby the discrete prevails on the continuum. Not only is this space discrete in its nature, as it is conceived by machines as complex and articulated systems of digits (the only information that machines, at their very low level can understand), but it is also perceived as such by people. As seen in the example of the grey Wi-Fi areas in Chapter 4, individuals experience the new environment in a hybridised manner, whereby the information gathered through the senses is mediated by the informational layer that surrounds them ubiquitously.

Notes

1 www.computerhope.com/issues/chspace.htm.
2 https://tfl.gov.uk/corporate/terms-and-conditions/transport-data-service. Last accessed 4 June 2017.
3 https://tfl.gov.uk/modes/cycling/santander-cycles?intcmp=2295. Last accessed 4 June 2017.
4 Complete dataset can be found at: http://cycling.data.tfl.gov.uk/. Last accessed 2 April 2017.
5 www.routino.org/uk/. Last accessed 4 June 2017.
6 IBM, The Four V's of Big Data www.ibmbigdatahub.com/infographic/four-vs-big-data. Last accessed 19 May 2017.
7 http://progcity.maynoothuniversity.ie/dublin-dashboard/. Last accessed 1 September 2016.
8 www.dublindashboard.ie/pages/index. Last accessed 1 September 2016.
9 www.dublindashboard.ie/pages/DublinDoing. Last accessed 1 September 2016.
10 www.dublindashboard.ie/pages/DublinReport. Last accessed 2 August 2016.
11 www.dublindashboard.ie/pages/DublinRealtime. Last accessed 2 August 2016.
12 www.carloratti.com/project/digital-water-pavilion/. Last accessed 2 August 2016.
13 www.kramweisshaar.com/projects/r18-ultra-chair. Last accessed 2 August 2016.
14 http://r18ultrachair.com/beta_videos/2012-04-17. Last accessed 2 August 2016.
15 Being big data projects entirely governed by a software-based logic, their nature is characterised by what Kitchin and Dodge (2014) defined as an ontogenetic conceptualisation in opposition to a stable ontology (p. 246). The projects are always in the "process of becoming" (ibidem), and never statically designed.

References

2004. "Non-Standard Architecture." *Archis*.
2017. Routino. Last accessed April 13, 2019. https://www.routino.org/uk/.
Al Nuaimi, Eiman, Hind Al Neyadi, Nader Mohamed, and Jameela Al-Jaroodi. 2015. "Applications of Big Data to Smart Cities." *Journal of Internet Services and Applications* 6 (1): 1–15. doi:10.1186/s13174-015-0041-5.

Andrejevic, Mark. 2005. "Nothing Comes between Me and My CPU: Smart Clothes and 'Ubiquitous' Computing." *Theory, Culture & Society* 22 (3): 101–19.

Ascott, Roy. 1994. "The Architecture of Cyberception." *Leonardo Electronic Almanac* 2 (8).

Ashley, Kathleen M. 1990. *Victor Turner and the Construction of Cultural Criticism: between Literature and Anthropology*, Vol. 594. Indianapolis, IN: Indiana University Press.

Batty, Michael. 2013. "Big Data, Smart Cities and City Planning." *Dialogues in Human Geography* 3 (3): 274–79. doi:10.1177/2043820613513390.

Boyd, Danah, and Kate Crawford. 2012. "Critical Questions for Big Data: Provocations for a Cultural, Technological, and Scholarly Phenomenon." *Information, Communication & Society* 15 (5): 662–79.

Burry, Jane, and Mark Burry. 2010. *The New Mathematics of Architecture*. London: Thames and Hudson.

Callon, M, Barry, A and Slater, D. 2002. "Technology, Politics and The Market: An Interview with Michel Callon." *Economy and Society* 31 (2): 285–306.

Carpo, Mario. 2003. "Drawing with Numbers: Geometry and Numeracy in Early Modern Architectural Design." *Journal of the Society of Architectural Historians* 62 (4): 448–469.

Carpo, Mario. 2012. *The Digital Turn in Architecture 1992–2012*. London: John Wiley & Sons.

Carpo, Mario. 2014. "Breaking the Curve: Big Data and Design." *ArtForum International* 52 (6): 168–73.

Carpo, Mario. 2017. The second digital turn: design beyond intelligence. MIT Press.

Castells, Manuel. 2005. "Space of Flows. Space of Places." In *Comparative Planning Cultures*, edited by Bishwapriya Sanyal. New York: Routledge.

Castells, Manuel, et al. 2009. *Mobile Communication and Society: A Global Perspective*. MIT Press.

Castree, Noel, Rob Kitchin, and Alisdair Rogers. 2013. "Kinetic Elite." *A Dictionary of Human Geography*. Oxford University Press. Last accessed May 1, 2018. http://www.oxfordreference.com/view/10.1093/acref/9780199599868.001.0001/acref-9780199599868-e-1005.

Cooper, Geoff, Nicola Green, Ged M. Murtagh, and Richard Harper. 2002. "Mobile Society? Technology, Distance." *Virtual Society? Technology, Cyberbole, Reality*: 286.

Copeland, Libby. 2001. "For DotComGuy, the End of the Online Line." *The Washington Post*: C2.

De Kerckhove, Derrick. 2001. *The Architecture of Intelligence*. Basel, Switzerland: Birkhäuser.

Directorate, Domestic Surveillance. 2018. "Utah Data Center." https://nsa.gov1.info/utah-data-center/.

Doel, M. A. 1999. *Poststructuralist Geographies: The Diabolical Art of Spatial Science*. Lanham, MD: Rowman & Littlefield.

EZCT with Hatem Hamda, and Marc Schoenauer. 2004. *Studies on Optimization. Computational Chair Design Using Genetic Algorithms*. Last accessed May 1, 2018. https://www.academia.edu/8171471/Computational_Chair_Design_using_Genetic_Algorithms_by_EZCT_Architecture_and_Design_Research.

Forlano, Laura. 2009. "WiFi Geographies: When Code Meets Place." *The Information Society* 25 (5): 344–52.

Franck, Karen, and Quentin Stevens. 2013. *Loose Space: Possibility and Diversity in Urban Life*. Abingdon, Oxon: Routledge.

Frazer, John H. 1995a. *An Evolutionary Architecture*. London: Architectural Association.

Frazer, John H. 1995b. "Architectural Experiments." In *Architects in Cyberspace*, edited by Martin Pearce and Neil Spiller, 78–80. London: John Wiley & Sons.

Frazer, John H. 1995c. "The Architectural Relevance of Cyberspace+ Architectural Experiments and the Interactivator-Model." *Architectural Design* (118): 76–81.

Galli, Mirko, and Claudia Mühlhoff. 2000. *Virtual Terragni: CAAD in Historical and Critical Research*. Basel: Birkhäuser.

Gandomi, Amir, and Murtaza Haider. 2015. "Beyond the Hype: Big Data Concepts, Methods, and Analytics." *International Journal of Information Management* 35 (2): 137–44.

Gehl, Jan. 2011. Life between buildings: using public space. Island press.

Gershenfeld, Neil. 2005. *Fab: The Coming Revolution on Your Desktop – From Personal Computers to Personal Fabrication*. New York: Basic Books.

Gibney, Elizabeth. "Magnetic Hard Drives Go Atomic." *Nature*. March 2017. Retrieved from https://www.nature.com/news/magnetic-hard-drives-go-atomic-1.21599

Graham, Stephen. 2004. "Beyond the 'Dazzling Light': From Dreams of Transcendence to the 'Remediation' of Urban Life: A Research Manifesto." *New Media & Society* 6 (1): 16–25.

Greenfield, Adam. 2006. *Everyware: The Dawning Age of Ubiquitous Computing*. Berkeley, CA: New Riders.

Greenfield, Adam. 2010. *Everyware: The Dawning Age of Ubiquitous Computing*. New Riders.

Gutiérrez, Verónica, Galache, José Antonio, Sotres, Pablo, Santana, Juan Ramón, Casanueva, Javier, Muñoz, Luis. 2013. "SmartSantander: Experimentation and Service Provision in the Smart City." *2013 16th International Symposium on Wireless Personal Multimedia Communications (WPMC)*. IEEE.

Hargittai, Eszter. 2015. "Is Bigger Always Better? Potential Biases of Big Data Derived from Social Network Sites." *The ANNALS of the American Academy of Political and Social Science* 659 (1): 63–76.

Hertzberger, Herman. 2005. Lessons for students in architecture. Vol. 1. 010 Publishers.

Hilbert, Martin. 2013. "Big Data for Development: From Information-to Knowledge Societies." SSRN 2205145.

Hill, Kashmir. 2013. "Blueprints of NSA's Ridiculously Expensive Data Center in Utah Suggest It Holds Less Info Than Thought." *Forbes*.

Hope, Computer. 2018. "How Much is 1 Byte, Kilobyte, Megabyte, Gigabyte, etc.?". www.computerhope.com/issues/chspace.htm.

Humbetov, Shamil. 2012. "Data-intensive Computing with Map-reduce and Hadoop." *6th International Conference on Application of Information and Communication Technologies (AICT)* 2012. New Jersey: IEEE.

Jackson, Jean E. 1990. "'DEJA ENTENDU' the Liminal Qualities of Anthropological Fieldnotes." *Journal of Contemporary Ethnography* 19 (1): 8–43.

Jencks, Charles. 1997a. "Landform Architecture Emergent in the Nineties (The Complexity Paradigm in Architecture)." *Architectural Design* (129): 14–31.

Jencks, Charles. 1997b. "Nonlinear Architecture: New Science= New Architecture?" *Architectural Design* 129: 6–7.

Kitchin, Rob. 2014a. *The Data Revolution: Big Data, Open Data, Data Infrastructures & their Consequences*. London: Sage.

Kitchin, Rob. 2014b. "The Real-time City? Big Data and Smart Urbanism." *GeoJournal* 79 (1): 1–14.

Kitchin, Rob. 2016c. "Thinking Critically about and Researching Algorithms." *Information, Communication & Society*: 1–16.

Kitchin, Rob, and Martin Dodge. 2011. *Code/Space: Software and Everyday Life*. Cambridge, MA: MIT Press.

Kitchin, Rob, and Martin Dodge. 2014. *Code/Space: Software and Everyday Life, Software Studies*. Cambridge, MA: MIT Press.

Kitchin, Rob, Tracey P. Lauriault, and Gavin McArdle. 2015. "Knowing and Governing Cities through Urban Indicators, City Benchmarking and Real-time Dashboards." *Regional Studies, Regional Science* 2 (1): 6–28.

Klapcsik, Sandor. 2012. *Liminality in Fantastic Fiction: A Poststructuralist Approach*. Jefferson, NC: McFarland.

Lefebvre, Henri, and Donald Nicholson-Smith. 1991. *The Production of Space*, Vol. 142. Oxford: Blackwell.

Lindsey, Bruce, and Frank O. Gehry. 2001. *Digital Gehry. Englische Ausgabe: Material Resistance Digital Construction*. Basel, Switzerland: Birkhäuser.

Lynn, Greg. 1993. "Architectural Curvilinearity, the Folded, the Pliant and the Supple." *Architectural Design* (102): 8–15.

Lynn, Greg, and Therese Kelly. 1999. *Animate Form*, Vol. 1. New York: Princeton Architectural Press.

Maas, Winy. 2001. "3DCity. An Introduction." In *Hunch 3. The Berlage Institute Report*, edited by J. Sigler, 96–131. Rotterdam: Berlage Institute.

Mackenzie, Adrian. 2006. "From Café to Park Bench: Wi-Fi and Technological Overflows in the City." In *Mobile Technologies of the City*, edited by Mimi Sheller and John Urry, 137–51. Oxon: Routledge.

Manovich, Lev. 2011. "Trending: The Promises and the Challenges of Big Social Data." *Debates in the Digital Humanities* 2: 460–475.

Mayer-Schönberger, Viktor, and Kenneth Cukier. 2013. *Big Data: A Revolution that will Transform How We Live, Work, and Think*. London: Houghton Mifflin Harcourt.

McArthur, John A. 2016. *Digital Proxemics: How Technology Shapes the Ways We Move*. Bern: Peter Lang International Academic Publishers.

Migayrou, Frédéric. 2014. "The Order of the Non-standard: Towards a Critical Structualism." In *Theories of the Digital in Architecture*, edited by Rivka Oxman and Robert Oxman, 17–34. London: Routledge.

Miller, Harvey J., and Michael F. Goodchild. 2015. "Data-driven Geography." *GeoJournal* 80 (4): 449–61.

Mitchell, William J. 2004. *Me++: The Cyborg Self and the Networked City*. MIT Press.

Moran, Leslie J., and Derek McGhee. 1998. "Perverting London: The Cartographic Practices of Law." *Law and Critique* 9 (2): 207–24.

MVRDV. 2005. *KM3: Excursions on Capacity*. Barcelona: Actar.

Newman, Mark E. J. 2006. "Modularity and Community Structure in Networks." *Proceedings of the National Academy of Sciences* 103 (23): 8577–82.

Nicholas, Negroponte. 1995. *Being Digital*. New York: Vintage Books.

Nordicity. 2014. "Big Data for Public Good: A Primer." *Global Pulse*. Last accessed May 1, 2018. http://www.unglobalpulse.org/sites/default/files/Primer%202013_FINAL%20 FOR%20PRINT.pdf.

Oxman, Rivka, and Robert Oxman. 2014. *Theories of the Digital in Architecture*. London: Routledge.

Parent, Claude, Paul Virilio, and Mohsen Mostafavi. 1996. *The Function of the Oblique: The Architecture of Claude Parent and Paul Virilio 1963–1969*. Architectural Association.

Picon, Antoine. 2015. *Smart Cities: A Spatialised Intelligence*. John Wiley & Sons.

Pink, Sarah, Sumartojo, Shanti, Lupton, Deborah, Heyes La Bond, Christine. 2017. "Mundane data: The routines, contingencies and accomplishments of digital living." Big Data & Society 4.1: 2053951717700924.

Poldma, Tiiu. 2011. "Transforming Interior Spaces: Enriching Subjective Experiences through Design Research." *Journal of Research Practice* 6 (2): 13.

Pritchard, Annette, and Nigel Morgan. 2006. "Hotel Babylon? Exploring Hotels as Liminal Sites of Transition and Transgression." *Tourism Management* 27 (5): 762–72.

Ratti, Carlo, and Anthony Townsend. 2011. "The Social Nexus." *Scientific American* 305 (3): 42–48.

Reinsel, David, John Gantz, and Johnl Rydning. 2017. "Data Age 2025: The Evolution of Data to Life-critical Don't Focus on Big Data; Focus on Data that's Big." *IDC*. Seagate. https://www.seagate.com/files/www-content/our-story/trends/files/idc-seagate-dataage-whitepaper.pdf.

Salter, Mark B. 2008. *Politics at the Airport*. Minneapolis, MN: University of Minnesota Press.

Sennett, Richard. 2012. "No One Likes a City that's Too Smart." *The Guardian*.

Shields, Rob. 1989. "Social Spatialization and the Built Environment: The West Edmonton Mall." *Environment and Planning D: Society and Space* 7 (2): 147–64.

Sloterdijk, Peter. 1988. *Critique of Cynical Reason*. London: Verso.

Snijders, Chris, Uwe Matzat, and Ulf-Dietrich Reips. 2012. "'Big Data': Big Gaps of Knowledge in the Field of Internet Science." *International Journal of Internet Science* 7 (1): 1–5.

Sobolevsky, Stanislav. 2014. "Digital Approach to Regional Delineation." In *Decoding the City: Urbanism in the Age of Big Data*, edited by Dietmar Offenhuber and Carlo Ratti, 180–90. Germany: Birkhäuser.

Soja, Edward W. 1989. *Postmodern Geographies: The Reassertion of Space in Critical Social Theory*. Verso.

Stewart, Colin, Chris Luebkeman, Marcus Morrell, and Lynne Goulding. "Future of Rail 2050." *Arup, Technical Report* (2014).

Thomassen, Bjørn. 2009. "The Uses and Meanings of Liminality." *International Political Anthropology* 2 (1): 5–27.

Tschumi, Bernard. 1996. *Architecture and Disjunction*. Cambridge, MA: MIT Press.

Turner, Victor. 1977. "Process, System, and Symbol: A New Anthropological Synthesis." *Daedalus*: 61–80.

Turner, Victor. 1983. "Liminal to Liminoid, in Play, Flow, and Ritual: An Essay in Comparative Symbology." In *Play, Games and Sports in Cultural Contexts,* edited by Janet C. Harris and Roberta J. Park, 123–64. Champaign, IL: Human Kinetics Publishers.

Turner, Victor. 1987. "Betwixt and Between: The Liminal Period in Rites of Passage." In *In the Forest of Symbols: Aspects of Ndembu Ritual*, 3–19. Ithaca, NY: Cornell University Press.

Virilio, Paul. 2000. *Polar Inertia*. London: Sage.

Wang, Tricia. 2013. "Big Data Needs Thick Data." *Ethnography Matters* 13.

Ward, Jonathan Stuart, and Adam Barker. 2013. "Undefined by Data: A Survey of Big Data Definitions." *arXiv preprint arXiv:1309.5821*.

Wilson, Scott. 2010. "Dwelling Size Survey." *Housing Standards: Evidence and Research, CABE*. UCL Press. Last accessed May 1, 2018. https://webarchive.nationalarchives.gov.uk/20110118111541/http://www.cabe.org.uk/files/space-standards-the-benefits.pdf.

Wood, David, and Stephen Graham. 2006. "Permeable Boundaries in the Software-sorted Society: Surveillance and the Differentiation of Mobility." *Mobile Technologies of the City*: 177–91.

Wu, X., X. Zhu, G. Q. Wu, and W. Ding. 2014. "Data Mining with Big Data." *IEEE Transactions on Knowledge and Data Engineering* 26. doi:10.1109/tkde.2013.109.

Zevi, Bruno, Milton Gendel, and Joseph A. Barry. 1957. "Architecture as Space. How to look at Architecture."

6 Built environment, big data and the new public life

A new role for individuals

As discussed in Chapter 4, the three main actors in the configuration of the new environment are: individuals, software and the built environment. Individuals play a substantially different role in the making of the public space. The new role of individuals in the public life is underpinned by a number of aspects that characterise it.

Firstly, individuals are not sampled but considered unique. Although they use sample-based models in their algorithms (see Chapter 3), machines compute the geography of the environment by assigning unique IDs to any entity, including objects, places and individuals. From this perspective, people are not a generic category whose members are sampled and treated as if they have common characteristic. People as a general group do not exist in the software representation of the world. Rather, there are individual units who are unique in their existence, location, behaviour, characteristics and data. All individuals in the world are qualified by their data.

Mayer-Schönberger and Cukier (2013) argue that the idea of sampling loses its raison d'être in the age of big data (2013:26), wherein a large dataset can be gathered about practically everybody. They use the formula n = all to indicate the possibility to consider a large number of samples in statistical approaches, extremely close to the real number of elements (2013:26). Comprehensiveness becomes one of the distinctive features of possible definitions of big data. Kitchin describes big data as characterised, amongst other things, by being "exhaustive in scope, striving to capture entire populations or systems" (Kitchin 2014a:1). The fact of having precise information about any fact or any person eliminates any level of approximation in the observation and analysis of phenomena, thereby avoiding the "risk of blurriness", as described by Mayer-Schönberger and Cukier (2013:30).

This idea has been challenged by a series of authors (Davies, Frow, and Leonelli 2013; Leonelli 2014), including Harford (2014), who claims that N = all, although a seductive idea, is practically unrealistic. In his article, Hartford recalls a series of authors who are, to some degree, sceptical about the success of big data as a completely comprehensive approach to statistics, including Wolfe (2013),

Fung (Walker and Fung 2013) and Crawford and Schultz. (2014). Contra, Hildebrandt (2013) offers a more impartial view of big data as a vehicle for reaching all information about virtually every individual, where both potentials and pitfalls are discussed together. Hildebrandt evaluates two camps: on the one hand, there are Mayer-Schönberger and Cukier who advocate for an increase of quantity (of data) leading to a supremacy of data in the creation of information and knowledge (Hildebrandt 2013:5–6); opposed to this, Hildebrandt places Boyd and Crawford (2012), who claim that greater quantity of data does not necessarily increase their quality (2012:668).

However, several examples can be helpful here to clarify the impact of big data in processing complex systems where large datasets are involved, showing the extent to which individuality in the new environment emerges as one of the main characteristics.

Katharine Miller (2012) pointed out the potential of large datasets in biomedicine. For example, within the genomics area, each person generates about 4 terabytes of (raw) data (Miller 2012), with "typically tens to hundreds of patients but millions or at least tens of thousands of variables" (Miller 2012). A possible way to deal with such a large dataset is provided in the example in Miller (2012) of Colin Hill's "reverse engineering and forward simulation" (REFS): "we break the dataset into trillions of little pieces, evaluating little relationships", where "after scoring all of the possible pair-wise and three-way relationships, REFS grabs the most likely network fragments and assembles them into an ensemble of possible networks that are robust and consistent with the data". Albeit such techniques are still to be explored and made available to a larger public, they represent a "real possibility of personalised medicine; the ability to treat individuals on a case by case basis, tailored to their specific genomic blueprint" (O'Driscoll, Daugelaite, and Sleator 2013:780).

In explaining the advantages of using big data processes in cybersecurity and fraud-prevention activities, Eaton et al. (2012) said that, usually, only about 20% of the available customer information is processed for reasons of cost-effectiveness, including: data storage; computing power; and processing time. This fraction is used as a segment of the total information available (Eaton et al. 2012:22). *Ad hoc* big data-based processes are able to analyse the remaining 80% of data and discern the valuable from the useless data (Eaton et al. 2012:23). Through handling accurate information about each individual part of the system (e.g. bank card transaction, personal details, etc.), big data-based processes enable "fraud detection models [to be in place] as the transaction is happening", and to reduce the latency time between the transaction and the fraud detection from weeks to a couple of hours (Eaton et al. 2012:22–23). Big data allow for in-depth knowledge of every transaction within the system observed.

Perhaps Mayer-Schönberger and Cukier's standpoint of N = all is true today only in theory, and this would partially justify critics of this theory; however, the fast-pace growth of computing technologies undoubtedly promises a good chance of success. It is not unrealistic to imagine that, in a quite near future, the amount of data that will be globally available, and computable by complex networked systems, will reach a quantity near to the totality, eliminating what Mayer-Schönberger and Cukier defined as the blurriness of information generated by sampling. In this scenario, individuals will be considered separately and discretely, as single and unique units in a giant computational system governed by principles similar to Wolfram's cellular automata (Chapter 1). Manovich (2011) provides a clear account of the difference between using samples and having exact information about, for instance, individuals. He uses the example of a digital image, in which the rescaling of the resolution (in pixels) does not provide any extra information about the picture, but only "larger pixels" (2011:462). A number of experiments mentioned by Manovich, including Eagle and Pentland (2003, 2006) and Eagle, Pentland, and Lazer (2009) epitomise the use of individual data (not sampled) to describe, investigate and predict social activities and behaviours.

Summarising, individuals have unique identities and are uniquely identifiable in the new environment. In the digital realm, these identities take the form of an IP (Internet Protocol) address, an avatar or a Twitter (or similar) account with which individuals can express their own opinion on any fact or phenomenon, from a comment on the food served in a restaurant to the latest public announcement by a political candidate in general elections. Those comments and opinions are not sampled and generalised as in a statistical approach; on the contrary, they are exclusive to those individuals and contribute in a granular manner to what will then become the general opinion. Within this perspective, it is plausible to reconsider the validity of such broad definitions as people's opinion, general public, common interest, etc. In the big data scenario, every individual has a unique voice; therefore, the people's opinion would be better described through a quantitative account. Although an exact datum for each individual is in practice difficult to collect with the current technologies, Bizer et al. (2012) explain that "more challenging . . . elements that describe aspects . . . at different level of abstraction" are available, such as "physiology, social network membership, salary, education" for each individual. Projects carried out to observe the mobility of individuals, like Nokia's Mobile Data Challenge (Laurila et al. 2012) and others (De Montjoye et al. 2013; Yue et al. 2014) provide an example of how unique tracking of individuals results in accurate information about a plethora of social aspects, including behaviour and current and future locations of individuals while using smart mobile devices.

If individuals are considered discrete and unique elements of a global system, the nature of information that each of them produces and receives is to be considered unique. Each person has her or his own informational idiosyncrasy, whereby a personal identity distinguishes them from everybody else in the word. Some of these data have already existed for a long time, including personal identity documents, passports, bank details, national insurance number, vehicle registration plates, etc. However, these data are often stored and managed in separate networks and systems whose lack of interconnectivity results in individuals having different bank accounts, personal documents or VAT numbers in different countries. Such data are inflexible (Kitchin 2014b:2), while the idea of truly ubiquitous computing promises to globalise all these, using large databases that combine all sorts of data for each individual, both in space (transcending national borders) and time (being able to retrieve data from each point in history).

The second aspect that characterises the unique role of individuals in the new environment is underpinned by their agency in the system. A global system made of unique individuals requires reconsidering the notions of agency and authorship of actions, decisions and opinions. Melissa Gregg (Boellstorff Maurer, Bell, and Gregg 2015:59–60) explains that, in a data-driven society, a significant amount of work is done on the backend by computers that follow scripts and coded instructions. In order to automate humans' labour, algorithms have been written so they can take decisions on our behalf within certain limits. In this category fall programmes whose objective is to match a set of information to produce a legible outcome (e.g. profiles in a dating website), with "data forming social relationships on our behalf" (Boellstorff et al. 2015:59). Automated data gathering and processing is having an impact on the way urban areas are administered. In providing a comprehensive account of enablers and source of data, Kitchin (2014c) explains that a rescaling and re-ordering of socio-technical systems is in process as the consequences of implementing smart cities principles with data from various sources collected into a single hub (2014b:99). As seen in Chapter 3, in Automatic Number Plate Recognition (APNR), for example, algorithms use optical character recognition technologies to store plate numbers and compare them with other data. Such technology can be combined with others (e.g. speed cameras) in order to monitor automobile drivers' behaviour on motorways. Algorithms can automatically decide whether a car is under or above the speed limit, and proceed with a fine in the second case. In this example, the road is regulated in a scripted way; in other words, an algorithm follows accurately a series of predetermined instructions governed by an "if-else" logic, with no human behind the camera.

Other authors have emphasised the changing nature of authorship in the digital age, with particular attention to architecture and urban spaces. Mario Carpo (2011) examined the shift in social participation from a consensus-sought approach, to the broadened open-ended perspective offered by the Wiki-based platforms (2011:114). In these, "interactive digital versioning posits a never-ending accrual of independent, diverse, and individual edits and changes, where consensus is never sought after nor ever achievable" (2011:114). Carlo Ratti (Ratti and Claudel 2015) implemented this notion in an interesting experiment, producing a proposal for an Open Source Architecture. The project "is an emerging paradigm that advocates new procedures in imagination and formation of virtual and real spaces within a universal infrastructure".[1] While the idea of shared authorship and collective endeavours is not new (think of the authors of religious texts, or the architects of centuries-long building projects such as medieval cathedrals), digital technologies and big data enable these projects to share a digital infrastructure (made of software, algorithms, codes, tools, techniques and expertise), being in continuous evolution, using an "open canvas".[2] In the open source, and within this reconsidered notion of agency, individuals still contribute to global projects in a unique manner from their unique locations, yet choose to be part of a larger entity, namely a collective agent.

Public life from bottom up

The digitalisation of the world through the pervasive action of software is having a significant impact on the way individuals perceive, use and contribute to the public space in urban contexts and the making of the public life. This production is happening in two opposite directions.

On the one hand, software operates as an over-imposing entity on the city with a top-down approach. For instance, there is no negotiation in the way CCTV or ANPR systems operate. These machine-based systems apply their logic on the urban environment while observing, representing and managing it. Airports probably epitomise an extreme application of the control exercised by software in public spaces. Interestingly, the computer presence not only superseded the human action but became the only agent that makes flows of people and information move (Dodge and Kitchin 2004). Graham (1998) and Marvin (Graham and Marvin 2002a) demonstrated the extent to which, if software fails in an airport, everything stops working with it, including flights, the movement of goods and people and any other function that would normally happen.

On the other hand, individuals with their daily activities play an active part in the production of the public space. Space is increasingly influenced by people who are active in the practice of place-making and the co-production of public space (Hou 2010). This happens in the making of the public life, as each individual has an active life in both the physical and the digital environment. Individuals leave traces of their online activities with any message they send or website they visit. Any action performed through a computer is logged and stored for future reference, and forms digital evidence (Casey 2011). This occurs at the level of a local machine and at the level of online activity. Servers, in particular, record any visit to sites, access to platforms and portals, data downloaded or uploaded. The logging also happens at the level of mobile phones, where the movement of telephones through the cell towers is recorded by the telecommunication providers (Sohn et al. 2006). People also leave traces while moving through the built environment. Their actions are perceived both by other people through interactions, encounters, personal contacts, etc. and by computers using cameras, CCTV systems and sensors.

By this perspective, the nature of the production of space is increasingly dual. It cannot be described as utterly imposed by software, nor as emerging spontaneously from individuals. Public space is rather produced as the combination of the two approaches triggered and regulated by the relations that are entangled among individuals, software and the built environment.

As seen in Chapter 2, the extensive and growing application of big data technologies to the design and management of urban infrastructures is conferring new capabilities on individuals through the ubiquitous application of the discrete logic that characterises the functioning of machines. The amount of data available to each person is growing exponentially every day. Each action people perform in the public realm, like driving on a motorway or entering a public building, is recorded and stored. All this information is correlated to the individual in a unique manner, so that, at any point in time, any datum can be retrieved from the growing stack of personal details. Where the discrete logics allow a group of people to be considered as individual entities with the same characteristics and behaviour in the public space, big data processes endow each entity with its own identity. In a big data scenario, individuals are to be considered as unique elements in societies and communities. This contrasts with the pre-big data models that are based on the idea of sampling and average. In the pre-big data age, societal trends were studied by means of statistical methods, on the assumption that a relevant number of individuals would represent the trend of the totality. In the new environment, machines factor in every single individual, who has a unique self. In this, society is a multitude of single, distinct and unique entities, as opposed to a generic group whose characteristics are inferred from a number of members taken as a sample.

In *Breaking the Curve*, Carpo (2014) examined the passage from continuous splines (intended as mathematical functions) to their discrete evolution in big data digital design. This study is crucial to understand how computers are changing not only the shape and appearance of projects and architectural spaces, but also their intimate nature. Today, we are witnessing the encounter of a series of epochal events that are unrelated *per se*, but inevitably correlated. On the one hand, computer scientists are continuously developing new tools (software and hardware) to increase the performance of the digital environment, cloud and ubiquitous computing, artificial intelligence, learning algorithms, automation systems and granular computing being just a few examples. On the other hand, people are increasingly interested in digital technologies and digital social infrastructures, including social media, quantified-self and various off/online activities (e.g. virtual/augmented reality). In the design camp, due to technological and computational advancements, architects and designers in general are increasingly using big data, open data, shared infrastructures (BIM) and robots to shape and build products, buildings and cities (see Chapter 3). People involved in each of these streams are either solely focused on their own field, or perhaps aware of the developments in other camps. The common denominator is the extensive use of computer-based logic, and big data provide the technological infrastructure that makes all this possible.

The urban space results from the daily encounter of developments in: computer science (think of Google and its spatial ramifications like Google Earth, Google Maps, Google Maps Timeline, etc.); evolving people's social behaviour (think of social media); and digital-driven urban design and management (e.g. smart cities). This is a continuously changing entity, made of finite and quantifiable elements, wherein individuals are discovering a new and central role, whose idiosyncrasies, reflected in the data they generate, seem to be the most important part.

Digital discrimination

In its way of operating, software proceeds by sorting elements in a given system (see Chapter 3), assigning attributes, grouping objects in categories, and routinely separating and aggregating items in lists. This method can be regarded as a way of discriminating objects, namely elements in the built environment and individuals, in a system. The ultimate aim of surveillance software is to classify the items in the environment in order to rationalise its complexity in an automated manner (Lyon 2003:13). In this section, we try to use the term discrimination in a neutral way, whereby we look back at the etymology of the word: from the Latin verb *discriminare* (*discrimino, discriminare, discriminavi, discriminates*), meaning differentiate, distinguish, separate, divide, distribute, or sift. By using the term objectively and without the various negative social connotations that it gradually assumed in the social sphere (as social divide, mistreatment, differentiation of groups by ethnicity, social status, country of origin, etc.), we want to analyse how software discerns entities in a system and what consequences this might entail for the public life.

There are several facets to this question to consider. Firstly, in the last 50 years we witnessed the transition of social data from a state of scattered, unorganised and unlinked series of information to an organised, interconnected and global system of databases where we now have what David Lyon calls *data doubles*. These are intended as: "various concatenations of personal data that, like it or not, represent 'you' within the bureaucracy of network" (Lyon 2003:22). Data doubles are subject to variation and approximation as information is exchanged amongst the nodes of the various networks, converted in different file format, stored and retrieved in and from multiple databases managed by different organisations (Lyon 2003:22).

Secondly, data might incorporate biases, prejudice and judgments of various sorts whereby "values, opinions and rhetoric are frozen into code" (Bowker and Leigh Star 1999:35). The measurement and assignment of values through data influence many aspects of social life (Lupton 2016:56). This may sound paradoxical, for data are neutral by definition. In their own intimate nature, they are strings of numbers and instructions made by machines, or by individuals using machine-based languages for machines. At a higher level, data are values that express facts, quantities and attributes that are used to generate, in the case of surveillance for example, descriptions of urban areas, people's behaviour and functioning of flows (of people, information, goods, etc.). However, in the context of surveillance, one of the software's main goals is to use the available data (gathered directly and interpolated with a series of databases) to classify people and objects. Oscar Gandy's notion of *panoptic sort* (Gandy 1993c) is helpful to describe the extent to which technology carries an intrinsic discriminatory function. This can be defined as: "a discriminatory process that sorts individuals on the basis of their estimated value or worth [and] reaches into every aspect of individual life today" (Gandy 1993c). Therefore, software's role in this case is to scan the environment in search of objects to sort into categories, following a set of parameters already embedded in the programme (or retrieved by an updateable database) in order to produce an assessment and judgement (Lyon 2013:20).

We can easily see that the part of the process where potential biases in judgements can be contained is represented by the sorting factors used in the programme. The software is objective by nature, but the parameters embedded in it and used for the sorting are subject to human interpretation and steering. The negative discriminatory action of software can easily be manipulated and controlled at this stage. The programme should be considered here as a blind machine that processes whatever data it is fed. Depending on the sorting parameters with which we ask the programme to work, the output can be significantly different. Stepanek et al. provide the example of bank customers who are treated differently, that is attended by differently trained staff, wait in short or long queues to be able to talk to some employee, or simply considered differently depending on an A to C rating system that identifies the individual's worth. This rating is calculated by an algorithm that computes as factors several social and financial aspects (Stepanek 2000). We can see here how these factors in a sort of *digital redlining* (Jupp and Perri 2001) may have an influence on the way individuals are attended in the bank and, conversely, also on the way people perceive their experience in the bank. Considered under this light, software can then affect individuals' lives in ways that are "frequently opaque to the public and which easily evade conventional democratic scrutiny" (Widmer and Klauser 2017:218).

This point has been discussed by Shannon Mattern while observing the informational ecologies of the contemporary city. For her, software's remit exceeds the mere computing of urban data: "urban information is made, commodified, accessed, secreted, politicized, and operational" (Mattern 2017). Both Mattern and Boyd and Crawford (2012) concur that the inclusion of the appropriate context is crucial in the interpretation of data around an individual. They hold that data automatically imply more than the numeric values that constitute them, for data are not generic (Boyd and Crawford 2012:671). However, in their analysis they refer to data as considered at the other end of the process, when data gathered and processed by machines are read and interpreted by other individuals, or other machines instructed with some sort of bias.

Possible biases can also be considered along with an idea of positional displacement. Discrimination that happens as the consequence of a specific programme in some part of the world and is thus related to the local social, political and cultural balances can be embedded into the code that runs the programme and be used as a rule to classify objects in another part of the world, whereby the programme is employed to "rank or prioritize rights, mobilities and access to a huge range of goods, services or entitlements on the other" (Graham 2004:24).

Concluding, the statement with which we started this section should be rephrased: data do not incorporate biases, prejudice and judgment *per se*; databases (namely the rationale used to aggregate datasets) and parameters might do. Digital systems can be considered as a combination of writing and reading, whereby writing is any type of manipulation of data in a system and reading "implies nothing about understanding (or even recognition) but only differentiation by type and position" (Haugeland 1989:53).

Thirdly, access to data and data exchange (through the Internet) may determine spatial segregation. As we saw in Chapter 5, the presence or absence of open networks can result in certain urban areas being preferred by individuals for their work, leisure and socially related activities. Expanding this notion, we can observe those phenomena that Stephen Graham indicated as *information black holes* or *electronic ghettos*, where "the poor remain confined to the traditional marginalised life of the physically confined, and there are intense concentrations of infrastructure in city centres and élite suburbs supporting the corporate classes and transnational corporations" (Graham and Marvin 2002b:380)

Fourthly, data and software might discriminate in the access to information and data based on practical knowledge. In this case a portion of the population in a city would know how to access the Internet and therefore can take advantage of all the relations it makes available to them, whereas other people will simply not have access to the flow of information and be "relegated" to the use only of physical space. One way of studying this type of divide would be to consider the knowledge about the Internet and its functioning mechanisms that characterises that group of people called digital natives. Interestingly, in her work on the social lives of networked teens, Danah Boyd holds that digital nativeness is not a characteristic that is automatically related to age. In this case, 1982, the date she provides as an example of watershed between those who were "born digital" and those who were not, would not be sufficient (if not utterly wrong) to qualify that shared common culture and experience that allows people to interact proficiently with technology (Boyd 2014:196). A comparable example is provided by Mark Andrejevic in his study about the big data divide, whereby a number of people have been interviewed about their relations with online marketing campaigns and their perception. What emerged is that the perception of ownership and control over communication resources to which they have been exposed in this study is characterised by a certain level of vagueness. There are details that simply are not clear enough in the information exchange.

> This vagueness, then, is not necessarily an artifact of laziness or ignorance due to users' failure to educate themselves about the technologies they use (or to read legalistic, vague privacy policies) but may be a defining characteristic of the data collection strategies to which they are subjected.
>
> (Andrejevic 2014:1685)

This can be explained by considering the degree of complexity that regulates online resources such as browsers, APIs or trackers of various sorts. As seen in Chapter 3, what the user sees in the frontend of an online tool is significantly different from and user-friendly than the backend, namely the algorithmic mechanisms that collect data and process them to generate information as an output that can be useful for third parties. The lack or presence of knowledge of how data are mined and processed by computers significantly impacts the ways in which users approach technology, and in particular the Internet.

Concluding, discrimination is neither a detrimental nor improving practice. It is simply the way computers work, and the mechanism by which machines are able to gain an understanding of the complexities of the real world. Digital discrimination should thus be considered for what it is: a digital sorting mechanism through which computers can analyse the new environment.

Surveillance

As one of the elements of the tripartite new environment, software, by its nature, interacts with the other two entities: the individuals and the built environment. It does so by observing them. This happens by the employment of what we named in Chapter 3 "the machine's eye", namely the assemblage of all those devices that allow machines to scan the world, including sensors, microphones and cameras. Surveillance is, then, the mechanism by which computers understand the public spaces, including physical spaces, the individuals and the entanglement of relationships among them. The continuous observation and logging of software of the environment focuses on the relational aspects of the urban life: "surveillance is not about individual people, but about defining the relationship of all sorts of actants in relation to boundaries: it is a technocratic form of territoriality and the (attempted) control of mobilities and flows" (Wood and Graham 2006:181). After the phase of identification of each entity in the environment and the assignation of a unique ID number in the global system of the Internet of Things, software focuses on the extent to which all the entities interact with each other and their ambient. Relations that occur among actants are fundamental for computers to be able to learn (Chapter 3) and predict the most probable action of each of them in the future.

The actual implementation of this mechanism at the global scale is defined by the notion of geosurveillance (Dodge, Batty, and Kitchin 2004; Dodge 2004). This can be considered as surveillance improved by geotagging at the global scale. Each actant in the new environment can be accurately located in almost real time through a plethora of "networked digital devices, systems and infrastructures [that] mediate movement, work, consumption, communication, and play" (Kitchin 2015).

In the new environment, the Internet of Things connects all actants (more relevantly the objects of the built environment) together in a virtual global system. Once connected, objects become an extension of the ubiquitous computing, capturing and sensing data about the environment in an automated way. This phenomenon has been defined as sousveillance (Mann, Nolan, and Wellman 2003) and elaborated by Dodge and Kitchin (2007). Sousveillance is the mechanism by which "interior capta [selected data that constitute a continuous record of the past of an individual]" are generated by smart objects and automatically captured "through life-logs" in an auto-produced story of the self (Dodge and Kitchin 2007:434). The surveillance, intended as a top-down capture of data operated by computers in the environment, and sousveillance, namely a bottom-up automated feeding of individual data to computers, are combined through the pervasive presence of the Internet of Things. The result can be defined as: the "socio-spatial archives that document every action, every event, every conversation, and every material expression of an individual's life" (Dodge and Kitchin 2005:1).

Public realms in the new environment

In this study, we explored the notion of the new environment, namely the combination of individuals, software and built environment to describe the ecology in which we all live today. In this theory, the three elements are considered actants, thus actively involved in the dynamics that underpin the environment. In Chapter 5, we discussed the extent to which individuals have a new role, where they actively produce and modify the environment as they act into it. In Chapters 3 and 4, we saw how software plays an active part in structuring and shaping the environment, applying the digital logic by which computers function. The built environment is increasingly expanding its physical dimension to incorporate elements of the digital realm (Chapter 5), blurring the boundaries between physical borders and edges of objects, and combining the physical characteristics of its elements with the dispersed and global extent of the digital realm.

The public dimension of this new environment is characterised by a high degree of information exchange. Data are exchanged between individuals through software. They move from computer to computer through individuals, and every generation and movement of data is determined by software. In this scenario, Lefebvre's definition of public realm should be reconsidered in light of the new tripartite configuration. Space is the product of human activities and their relations with the environment, but these interactions are orchestrated by software. Similarly, Castells' notion of space of flows needs to be considered along with the idea that software imposes its rigid logic structure, which is discrete and does not admit continuity at the very intimate scale of the objects (Chapter 1). The new environment is dominated by flows (of information, goods, people, etc.), yet these are structured by code. In this sense, Kitchin and Dodge's notion of space/code perfectly represents the relationship that underpins the production of space and the action of software in the new environment.

In this perspective, public realms are shaped by software, where the individuals' action is underpinned by the discrete spatial structure provided by computers, and the built environment is digitally expanded (its boundaries are permeable and extend from physical to digital and vice versa). Two examples can help here to visualise a discrete public realm.

The first one is the study that Hampton, Livio, and Sessions Goulet (2010) carried out in the observation of wireless Internet users in various public spaces in New York City, Toronto, Philadelphia and San Francisco. In this study, they employed person-centred and place-centred behavioural mapping approaches, whereby they tracked the location and the use of space of each individual producing various observation maps (Hampton et al. 2010:707). In their study, they found that the most successful public realms were those characterised by a good urban design and a history of public use of the same space. Such spaces are more likely to attract Wi-Fi use (Hampton et al. 2010:717). This study shows that the number of users that were co-located (physically present at the same time in the same place) was very low; contra, people who were co-present (digitally connected through the Internet at the same time in different places) were large in number (Hampton et al. 2010:715). Hampton et al. concluded that the presence of a Wi-Fi network by itself is not a sufficient condition to populate urban spaces. Other factors influence the popularity of a certain area, including the quality of the architecture and urban design and the activities already happening in the area.

Bryant Park in New York would be popular despite the availability of Wi-Fi networks. However, this represents a strong incentive for people to use that public space to communicate with others via the Internet from a pleasant and convenient physical space. If an open Wi-Fi network is available within the perimeter of the park, people are more likely to be inside rather than outside when they want to use that time to be co-present with acquaintances. The reach of the Wi-Fi radio signal becomes the factor that determines where people would stay in the public space, turning the park into a successful public realm at certain times of the day. If we consider the case study of the Wi-Fi mapping in Leicester Square in London (Chapter 5), we can easily recognise some similarities with these findings. Individuals choose a physical location based on various aspects, with Wi-Fi availability being one of the major decision factors. This happens purely on the basis of the activities or shop (e.g. a certain coffee shop) and the presence of a Wi-Fi signal. Even within the stretch of the same street, if the factors are not present at the same time – if, for example, there is a coffee shop with no Internet, or an establishment that has free Internet access but is unpleasant or unpopular – people will not be likely to use that particular space.

The second example is the use of happn, a dating app for mobile phones that allows users to see the public profile of other users in their proximity. Happn is a location-based application that not only enables users to visualise some public information like profile picture, age, name and interests of other users within the same spatial range but, more significantly, indicates how many times users cross paths to maximise the chances of a physical encounter. The app sends notifications to the user every time the selected other users pass through the user's same path. Put simply, happn tracks and logs each user's routes via GPS and date-stamps the logs. It then compares the logs with other selected users to output compatibility and informs the individual users. Interestingly, this app helps individuals to acquire information about a person they encountered in the physical space (a tube carriage, in a coffee shop, or in the street). This helps users to acquire information about another person without exposing themselves to a physical social encounter. In a sense, the app differs from a social encounter by avoiding to a certain level the uncertainties that come with a physical meeting with no previous information other than what can be deduced by simple observation. Outside the context of dating apps, this is a general possible benefit represented by the global implementation of ubiquitous computing, whereby social exchanges can be triggered and facilitated through common shared interests and experiences that can result in online communities (Kang and Cuff 2005:131). To the spatial and geo-located referencing, happn adds the temporal dimension to social encounter (Xiao, Sun, and Naaman 2017:41). In this case, we see software in full action, taking full control of the physical space by using its tools (GPS, tracking, algorithmic interpolation for match profiles and overlapping cross paths, etc.) and deploying its discrete interpretation of the world. The app generates a hybrid practice of place-making (Xiao, Sun, and Naaman 2017:47), where the digital and physical spheres interact mutually. The physical experience of walking along a street is tracked and represented in the digital realm. In the digital dimension, the tracked paths are gathered and computed along with other data (profiles, preferences, habits, etc.). These digital outputs are then re-inputted in the physical dimension through the individuals' behaviour in space (e.g. when they decide to use that particular path at that time to meet a specific person whose information is already known through the app). The work of David Beer and Roger Burrows on digital archives and the social life of data (2013) is helpful here to expand on how digital output that originates from the physical dimension is reversed again into the physical through people's actions and presumption practices. The user profile created in happn relies on the ramification to other profiles that the user might already have, including Facebook, Twitter, Instagram and Spotify as examples. This expands the extent of the public profile that a user may build over time. At the start, the app accesses information from Facebook, using this information only as part of the computation when assessing possible matches. In principle, the information from other platforms is not shared with other users, as it is not visible. However, Di Luzio, Mei, and Stefa (2018) clearly demonstrated how users with malicious intentions (or simply data brokers) can easily retrieve private information through the app. This includes details about friends, work colleagues, family and information about place of work, residence, routines, buying patterns and preferred activities and destinations for leisure, all with an accurately pinpointed location in almost real time (Di Luzio, Mei, and Stefa 2018:839). The public realm that results as the consequence of the use of apps like happn describes a physical space that is continuously influenced by digital activities, whereby the built environment and its digital parallel (e.g. the overlapping crossing paths of happn users) are increasingly blurred and combined, and dominated by space/code.

Notes

1 Definition from the official Open Source Architecture wiki page: https://en.wikipedia. org/wiki/Open-source_architecture. Last accessed 21 May 2017.
2 Cf. http://senseable.mit.edu/osarc/. Last accessed 22 May 2017.

References

Andrejevic, Mark. 2005. "Nothing Comes between Me and My CPU: Smart Clothes and 'Ubiquitous' Computing." *Theory, Culture & Society* 22 (3): 101–119.

Beer, David, and Roger Burrows. 2013. "Popular Culture, Digital Archives and the New Social Life of Data." *Theory Culture, and Society* 30 (4): 47–71.

Bizer, Christian, Peter Boncz, Michael L. Brodie, and Orri Erling. 2012. "The Meaningful Use of Big Data: Four Perspectives – Four Challenges." *ACM SIGMOD Record* 40 (4): 56–60.

Boellstorff, Tom, Bill Maurer, Genevieve Bell, and Melissa Gregg. 2015. *Data, Now Bigger and Better!* Chicago, IL: Prickly Paradigm Press.

Bowker, Geoffrey, and Susan Leigh. 1999. *Sorting Things Out: Classification and Its Consequences.* Cambridge, MA: MIT Press.

Boyd, Danah. 2014. *It's Complicated: The Social Lives of Networked Teens.* New Haven, CT: Yale University Press.

Boyd, Danah, and Kate Crawford. 2012. "Critical Questions for Big Data: Provocations for a Cultural, Technological, and Scholarly Phenomenon." *Journal of Information, Communication & Society* 15 (5): 662–79.

Carpo, Mario. 2011. *The Alphabet and the Algorithm*. Cambridge, MA: MIT Press.

Carpo, Mario. 2014. "Breaking the Curve: Big Data and Design." *ArtForum International* 52 (6): 168–73.

Casey, Eoghan. 2011. *Digital Evidence and Computer Crime: Forensic Science, Computers, and the Internet*. Waltham, MA: Academic Press.

Crawford, Kate, and Jason Schultz. 2014. "Big Data and Due Process: Toward a Framework to Redress Predictive Privacy Harms." *Boston College Law Review* 9355 (1). Boston, MA. http://lawdigitalcommons.bc.edu/bclr/vol55/iss1/4.

Davies, Gail, Emma Frow, and Sabina Leonelli. 2013. "Bigger, Faster, Better? Rhetorics and Practices of Large-scale Research in Contemporary Bioscience." *BioSocieties* 8 (4): 386.

De Montjoye, Yves-Alexandre, César A. Hidalgo, Michel Verleysen, and Vincent D. Blondel. 2013. "Unique in the Crowd: The Privacy Bounds of Human Mobility." *Scientific Reports* 3: 1376.

Di Luzio, Adriano, Alessandro Mei, and Julinda Stefa. 2018. "Uncovering Hidden Social Relationships through Location-based Services: The Happn Case Study." *IEEE INFOCOM 2018-IEEE Conference on Computer Communications Workshops (INFOCOM WKSHPS)*. New Jersey: IEEE.

Dodge, Martin. 2004. "Lost in the Crowd No Longer? Mobile Phones and the Prospects of Continuous Geosurveillance." Visualisation and Multimedia: Wireless GIS and Location Based Services. Presentation at UCL. Last accessed February 1, 2019. https://personalpages.manchester.ac.uk/staff/m.dodge/cv_files/bristol_geosurveillance.pdf.

Dodge, Martin, Michael Batty, and Rob Kitchin. 2004. "No Longer Lost in the Crowd: Prospects of Continuous Geosurveillance." *Association of American Geographers Annual Conference*. Presentation at UCL. Last accessed February 1, 2019. http://www.casa.ucl.ac.uk/martin/aag_geosurveillance.pdf. Philadelphia, March.

Dodge, Martin, and Rob Kitchin. 2004. "Flying through Code/Space: The Real Virtuality of Air Travel." *Journal of Environment and Planning A* 36 (2): 195–211.

Dodge, Martin, and Rob Kitchin. 2005. "The Ethics of Forgetting in an Age of Pervasive Computing." (CASA Working Papers 92). London: Centre for Advanced Spatial Analysis (UCL).

Dodge, Martin, and Rob Kitchin. 2007. "'Outlines of a World Coming into Existence': Pervasive Computing and the Ethics of Forgetting." *Journal Environment and Planning B: Planning and Design* 34 (3): 431–45.

Eagle, Nathan, and Alex Sandy Pentland. 2003. "Social Network Computing." In *UbiComp 2003: Ubiquitous Computing. 5th International on Ubiquitous Computing*. edited by Anind K. Dey, Albrecht Schmidt, and Joseph F. McCarthy Seattle, WA. Proceedings. Seattle, WA: Springer, October 12–15.

Eagle, Nathan, and Alex Sandy Pentland. 2006. "Reality Mining: Sensing Complex Social Systems." *Personal and Ubiquitous Computing* 10 (4): 255–68.

Gandy Jr, Oscar H. 1993. *The Panoptic Sort: A Political Economy of Personal Information (Critical Studies in Communication and in the Cultural Industries)*. Boulder, CO: Westview. Graham, Stephen. 1998. "Spaces of Surveillant Simulation: New Technologies, Digital Representations, and Material Geographies." *Journal Environment and Planning D: Society and Space* 16 (4): 483–504.

Graham, Stephen. 2004. "Beyond the 'Dazzling Light': From Dreams of Transcendence to the 'Remediation' of Urban Life: A Research Manifesto." *Journal of New Media, and Society* 6 (1): 16–25.

Graham, Steve, and Simon Marvin. 2002a. *Splintering Urbanism: Networked Infrastructures, Technological Mobilities and the Urban Condition.* Routledge.

Graham, Steve, and Simon Marvin. 2002b. *Telecommunications and the City: Electronic Spaces, Urban Places.* London: Routledge.

Hampton, Keith N., Oren Livio, Craig Trachtenberg, and Rhonda McEwen. 2010. "The Social Life of Wireless Urban Spaces." *Journal of Contexts* 9 (4): 52–57.

Harford, Tim. 2014. "Big Data: A Big Mistake?" *Significance* 11 (5): 14–19.

Haugeland, John. 1989. *Artificial Intelligence: The Very Idea.* MIT press.

Hildebrandt, Mireille. 2013. "Slaves to Big Data. Or Are We?" *IDP. Revista De Internet, Derecho Y Política* 17, 7–44 http://doi.org/10.7238/idp.v0i17.1977.

Hou, Jeffrey. 2010. *Insurgent Public Space: Guerrilla Urbanism and the Remaking of Contemporary Cities.* Abingdon, Oxon: Routledge.

Jupp, Ben, and Perri. 2001 The 'digital divide' and the implication of the new meritocracy Six. "Divided by Information." Demos. London.

Kang, Jerry, and Dana Cuff. 2005. "Pervasive Computing: Embedding the Public Sphere." *Washington and Lee Law Review* 62: 93.

Kitchin, Rob. 2014a. "Big Data, New Epistemologies and Paradigm Shifts." *Big Data & Society* 1 (1).

Kitchin, Rob. 2014b. *The Data Revolution: Big Data, Open Data, Data Infrastructures and their Consequences.* London: Sage.

Kitchin, Rob. 2014c. "The Real-time City? Big Data and Smart Urbanism." *GeoJournal (2014) 79: 1. https://doi.org/10.1007/s10708-013-9516-8*

Kitchin, Rob. 2015. "Continuous Geosurveillance in the 'Smart City'." *Dis Magazine* 15. Last accessed May 1, 2018. http://dismagazine.com/dystopia/73066/rob-kitchin-spatial-big-data-and-geosurveillance/.

Laurila, Juha K., Daniel Gatica-Perez, Imad Aad, Olivier Bornet, Trinh-Minh-Tri Do, Olivier Dousse, Julien Eberle, and Markus Miettinen. 2012. "The Mobile Data Challenge: Big Data for Mobile Computing Research.". Proceedings of the Mobile Data Challenge Workshop (MDC) in conjunction with *Pervasive Computing*. Newcastle. Last accessed May 1, 2018. https://pdfs.semanticscholar.org/8dae/ecc84fcaf42172cba7ef58e5068fae7bbcbc.pdf.

Leonelli, Sabina. 2014. "What Difference Does Quantity Make? On the Epistemology of Big Data in Biology." *Big Data & Society* 1 (1).

Lupton, Deborah. 2016. *The Quantified Self.* Cambridge, UK: Polity.

Lyon, David. 2003. *Surveillance as Social Sorting: Privacy, Risk, and Digital Discrimination.* London: Routledge.

Ma, Xiao, Emily Sun, and Mor Naaman. 2017. "What Happens in Happn: The Warranting Powers of Location History in Online Dating." Proceedings of the 2017 ACM Conference on Computer Supported Cooperative Work and Social Computing (CSCW). Portland, OR: ACM.

Mann, Steve, Jason Nolan, and Barry Wellman. 2003. "Sousveillance: Inventing and Using Wearable Computing Devices for Data Collection in Surveillance Environments." *Journal of Surveillance and Society* 1 (3): 331–55.

Manovich, Lev. 2011. "Trending: The Promises and the Challenges of Big Social Data." *Debates in the Digital Humanities* 2: 460–75.

Mattern, Shannon. 2017. "A City is not a Computer." *Places Journal.* Last accessed May 1, 2018. https://placesjournal.org/article/a-city-is-not-a-computer/.

Mayer-Schönberger, Viktor, and Kenneth Cukier. 2013. *Big Data: A Revolution that will Transform How We Live, Work, and Think.* Houghton Mifflin London: Harcourt.

Miller, Katharine. 2012. "Big Data Analytics in Biomedical Research." *Biomedical Computation Review* 2: 14–21.

O'Driscoll, Aisling, Jurate Daugelaite, and Roy D. Sleator. 2013. " 'Big Data', Hadoop and Cloud Computing in Genomics." *Journal of Biomedical Informatics* 46 (5): 774–81.

Ratti, Carlo, and Matthew Claudel. 2015. *Open Source Architecture.* London: Thames & Hudson.

Sohn, Timothy, Alex Varshavsky, Anthony LaMarca, Mike Y. Chen, Tanzeem Choudhury, Ian Smith, Sunny Consolvo, Jeffrey Hightower, William G. Griswold, and Eyal De Lara. 2006. "Mobility Detection Using Everyday GSM Traces." International Conference on Ubiquitous Computing. Heidelberg: ACM.

Stepanek, Marcia. 2000. "Weblining: Companies Are Using Your Personal Data to Limit Your Choices—and Force You to Pay More for Products." *Bloomberg Business Week* 2. Retrieved from https://www.bloomberg.com/news/articles/2000-04-02/weblining

Widmer, Sarah, and Francisco Klauser. 2017. "Surveillance and Control." In *Understanding Spatial Media*, edited by Kitchin, Rob, Tracey P. Lauriault, and Matthew W. Wilson, 216–224. London: Sage.

Wolfe, Patrick J. 2013. "Making Sense of Big Data." *Proceedings of the National Academy of Sciences* 110 (45): 18031–32.

Wood, David, and Stephen Graham. 2006. "Permeable Boundaries in the Software-sorted Society: Surveillance and the Differentiation of Mobility." *Mobile Technologies of the City*: 177–91.

Yue, Yang, Tian Lan, Anthony G. O. Yeh, and Qing-Quan Li. 2014. "Zooming into Individuals to Understand the Collective: A Review of Trajectory-based Travel Behaviour Studies." *Travel Behaviour and Society* 1 (2): 69–78.

Zikopoulos, Paul, and Chris Eaton. 2011. *Understanding Big Data: Analytics for Enterprise Class Hadoop and Streaming Data.* McGraw-Hill Osborne Media.

Index

Note: Page numbers in *italics* indicate figures and page numbers in **bold** indicate tables on the corresponding pages.